Bound Only Once

BOUND ONLY ONCE

THE FAILURE *of* OPEN THEISM

EDITED BY

DOUGLAS WILSON

CANON PRESS
MOSCOW, IDAHO

Douglas Wilson et al, *Bound Only Once: The Failure of Open Theism*
Published by Canon Press, P.O. BOX 8729, Moscow, ID 83843
www.canonpress.org
(800) 488–2034

06 05 04 03 02 01   9 8 7 6 5 4 3 2 1

Cover design by Paige Atwood Design, Moscow, ID
Formatted by Ruptured Disc Studios, Moscow, in 11 on 13 Adobe Jenson

Library of Congress Cataloging–in–Publication Data

Bound only once : the failure of open theism / edited by Douglas Wilson.
    p. cm.
    Includes bibliographical references and index.
    ISBN 1–885767–84–6 (pbk.)
    1. God—Omniscience. 2. Free will and determinism—Religious aspects—Christianity. I. Wilson, Douglas, 1953–
    BT131 .B67 2001
    231–DC21   2001001707

CONTENTS

GOODNESS

Contributors

Thomas K. Ascol, Ph.D, is the editor of *The Founders Journal* and pastor of Grace Baptist Church, Cape Coral, Florida.

John M. Frame is a Professor of Systematic Theology and Philosophy at Reformed Theological Seminary, Orlando.

R.C. Sproul, Jr. is editor of *TableTalk*, a pastor of Saint Peter Presbyterian Church, and the director of Highlands Study Center.

Phillip R. Johnson is the executive director of Grace to You and an elder at Grace Community Church, Sun Valley, California.

Douglas M. Jones is a fellow of philosophy at New St. Andrews College, Moscow, Idaho and a senior editor of *Credenda/Agenda* magazine.

Peter J. Leithart, Ph.D., is a fellow of theology and literature at New St. Andrews College, Moscow, Idaho and an ordained minister in the Presbyterian Church in America.

John MacArthur, Jr. is president of Master's Seminary and College, Santa Clarita, California, featured teacher of Grace To You, and pastor of Grace Community Church, Sun Valley, California.

Ben R. Merkle is a lecturer in theology at New St. Andrews College, and a contributing editor of *Credenda/Agenda* magazine.

Joost F. Nixon is pastor of Christ Church, Spokane, Washington and a contributing editor of *Credenda/Agenda* magazine.

Steve M. Schlissel is pastor of Messiah's Congregation, Brooklyn, New York.

Douglas J. Wilson is pastor of Christ Church, Moscow, Idaho, editor of *Credenda/Agenda* magazine, and a fellow of theology and philosophy at New St. Andrews College.

Foreword

John H. Armstrong

To the surprise of no thoughtful evangelical Christian, attacks upon the classical view of God have come from mainstream liberal theology for well over a century. What is quite surprising, in the past ten years or so, is that these same attacks now come from deep within the evangelical camp. As noted by the evangelical flagship publication *Christianity Today*, as far back as 1990, a so-called "megashift" has taken place within evangelical Christian schools and ministries. This change not only alters the worldview of classical theism but also eviscerates orthodox evangelical theology of both its power and pastoral appeal. This shift affects a number of related doctrinal truths that have stabilized the witness and prayer life of the Church for centuries. It particularly impacts how we understand divine sovereignty, omniscience, and providence. This shift not only changes how we talk about God but also goes to the very heart of the doctrine of God, the most basic truth of our Christian faith. One result of this megashift is that the word "evangelical" has begun to lose both meaning and usefulness for many of us. A theological megalovirus, which has a host of serious consequences, has attacked the very immune system of the Christian faith. This deadly virus will wipe out a whole generation of Christian teachers and ministers if the cure is not disseminated quickly and accurately.

It is important that the reader of this present volume understands at the outset that this present fuss is not about the long-standing debate between Calvinists and Arminians, as some Open theists insist.[1] Greg Boyd, professor at Bethel College, a respected evangelical

---

[1] Cf. Greg Boyd, *The God of the Possible* (Grand Rapids: Baker, 2000), 15–17, 114–18.

institution, insists that he believes in the omniscience of God but defines this as "God knowing all that is possible to know." The point Boyd and Open theist allies make is that God simply doesn't *know* the future actions of "free" persons. (This is most definitely *not* Arminianism of any historical type.) The reader of this present volume will quickly discern that the contributors are robustly Augustinian in their perspective. This should not cloud the *major* issue at stake. To be robustly Augustinian is no vice. It has historically, in almost every serious theological conflict, been a virtue. The approach, in itself, is also sound in the present debate, so long as it is rigorously submitted to the Holy Scriptures afresh. "To the law and to the testimony! If they do not speak according to this word, they have no light of dawn" (Is. 8:20).

The arguments of Open theists are generally rooted in the notion that the classical view of God presents him as a despot or a domineering sovereign. They insist that God has knowledge, *but not all knowledge.* He does not know the future acts of free beings or these acts could not be the actions of truly free creatures. Since God does not know what will happen in your life tomorrow, he is not a detached and distant divinity but an involved and personal god. The god of Open theism is ready to enter into new experiences and to become deeply involved in helping us cope as we, with him, face things we simply did not know would happen. Clark Pinnock, a theologian who favors Open theism, states that omnipotence should be understood as the power of God to deal with any *new* situation. David Basinger, another Open theist, even suggests that "God voluntarily forfeits control over earthly affairs."[2] In the most basic sense these theologians deny "simple foreknowledge" in God since they believe human freedom demands such a conclusion.

The reader who comes to this subject for the very first time needs to understand that Open theists make considerable appeal to Scripture itself. Some, such as exegete Greg Boyd, do this with greater concern than others. This being the case they all ultimately make such appeals in ways that often appear disingenuous. Truth here is truly stranger than fiction. Though these writers consistently appeal to the text of Scripture (e.g., "God repenting" and similar texts), the reader

[2] Cf. Clark Pinnock, et al, *The Openness of God* (Downers Grove: Illinois: Inter-Varsity, 1994), 159.

of this present volume will quickly discover that Open theists make such an appeal with a very selective use of *some* texts. They also employ a hermeneutic that is bereft of both clarity and consistency.

For all of their denial that Open theism is not process theology, one strains to see any essential difference between the older process thought and this modern "evangelical" heresy, except that the Open theists insist that God created the world and is, therefore, separate from it. Process theology sought to construct a picture of reality based upon Newtonian physics that saw God as participating in the same categories of reality as human beings. In this older view, God, with respect to actuality, is contingent, dependent, temporal, relative, and constantly changing. So much for singing, and meaning, "Immortal, invisible, God only wise . . ."

But what does Open theism owe to this earlier liberal thought? Greg Boyd, one of the more biblically nuanced proponents of Open theism, freely admits that "the fundamental vision of the process worldview, especially as espoused by Charles Hartshorne, is correct."[3] What this means is simple: Open theism shares with process theology a "dipolar theism." Theologian Millard Erickson is correct when he notes that "It conceives of God as both absolute and relative, necessary and contingent, eternal and temporal, changeless and changing."[4]

Classical conceptions of God are not always perfectly stated. They do need to be fine-tuned by continual exegetical work in the text of Holy Scripture. We are indebted to both the fathers and the reformers of the Church in this regard. But we must admit that at times philosophical and cultural ideas have too frequently influenced the work of serious biblical theology and our understanding of God. I personally believe Open theists object to several wrong conceptions of God that have surfaced in the history of Christian theology. For this we should be grateful. The great tragedy is that in the process of rejecting the idea of God as "unrestrained power . . . they too readily divorce the biblical concept of power from coercion."[5] This is not a *minor* shift. It really is a megashift of immense proportions.

---

[3] Cf. Gregory A. Boyd, *Trinity and Process: A Critical Evaluation and Reconstruction of Hartshorne's Di-polar Theism Towards a Trinitarian Metaphysics* (New York: Peter Lang, 1992), preface.

[4] Millard J. Erickson, *The Evangelical Left: Countering Postconservative Evangelical Theology* (Grand Rapids: Baker, 1997), 91.

[5] Donald G. Bloesch, *God the Almighty* (Downers Grove: InterVarsity, 1995), 258.

Recently, a number of useful articles and books have been published that deal directly with the rise of Open theism. *Bound Only Once*
is such a book. It is a useful, original, and helpful entry into this growing debate. It reflects a healthy variety of approaches to the issue, since
it is a multiple-author work. It includes philosophical, biblical, and
theological critique. One does not have to agree with every word here
to profit by the workout and the general approach taken by the writers. It will make some readers a bit squeamish to wrestle with this
book since many evangelicals are not used to dealing with theology
seriously in our time. But this is a needed critique. It is also one that
I hope will have a wide readership. I commend it to those who are taking their first look at Open theism as well as those who are already
deeply immersed in this profoundly important debate. Sadly, I have to
agree with Douglas Wilson's concluding observation that "if this 'new
model' theology is not heresy, then there is no such thing as heresy."

John H. Armstrong
President, Reformation & Revival Ministries
Carol Stream, Illinois

Bound only once, the Lamb of God was slain,
The hyssop red, the guilty cleansed and white.
Before the world was made the Lamb took in
The sacrifice, and never more to die.
But minds of men this richness still disdain
So they must bind and taunt our lesser lords,
Our gravid words which bear incarnate light,
The metaphors which speak the greater truth.
And so they grind their syllogistic grain
To make their hollow bread, their loaves of air;
And so they tread their small Euclidian grapes
To make and drink their thin and tepid wine.
But men will make ethereal worlds in vain,
Bound only once, the *Word* of God will reign.

BEAUTY

I

The Loveliness of Orthodoxy

Douglas J. Wilson

INTRODUCTION

Bishop Warburton once said that orthodoxy "is my doxy; heterodoxy is another man's doxy." The quip tends to delight us because it appeals to our very modern notion that, at bottom, all questions of truth or error are subjective and matters of personal taste. Two ministers from different denominations talk, and one says to the other, "Of course, we both serve the same God—you in your way, and I in His." And so, modernity, with a wave of the hand, and a knowing, urbane chuckle, seeks to dismiss the very idea of orthodoxy.

But, of course, it is not as easy as all that. The concept of orthodoxy is actually inescapable, and so no man can operate outside its constraints. The Greek word *orthos* means straight, or correct, and *doxy* is descended from the verb *dokein*, which means to think. The word *doxa*, the immediate ancestor of *doxy*, means opinion. And thus, *orthodoxy* means straight belief or correct opinion. Who could be against this, one wonders. As it turns out, no one is against it—every man affirms that what *he* maintains is the truth. Every person in the world, all day long, every day, thinks he's right. Even those hapless relativists and nihilists think they *understand* that there is no truth. And good for them, as far as they go, which isn't very far. They don't get out much.

No one has ever rebuked an orthodoxy except in the name of another orthodoxy. Those many who avow allegiance to "no orthodoxy" are evidence, not that this foregoing observation is incorrect, but rather that woolly thinking is well on the way to becoming a national virtue. In actual fact, we have only established orthodoxies and *aspiring* orthodoxies acting (for the time being) like heresies. So every position is an orthodoxy. The only question is, whose? The issue for

Christians concerns how the straight line is to be drawn. Do we define that which is true and right according to the words of men? Or not? Do we appeal to the Word of God? Or not?

The antithesis of straight is crooked or twisted. So on the question of orthodoxy, we have only two options. Either men will say that God's word is crooked, or God will say that the word of man is crooked. One will pronounce judgment on the other, and necessarily, in that judgment, the judge assumes himself to be the arbiter of all that is true, good, and lovely. And so the question comes down to an unavoidable point—whose claim, God's or man's, is correct?

The apostle Peter speaks, and not very highly, of those who mangle the truth of God. "And account that the longsuffering of our Lord is salvation; even as our beloved brother Paul also according to the wisdom given unto him hath written unto you; as also in all his epistles, speaking in them of these things; in which are some things hard to be understood, which they that are unlearned and unstable wrest, as they do also the other scriptures, unto their own destruction" (2 Pet. 3:15–16). The word translated as *wrest* here is *streblao*, which refers to putting something on the rack and twisting it out of all recognition. Of course, those who are occupied in this activity do not *themselves* describe it this way. They do not advertise their seminars as being taught by ignorant and unstable people. Peter's statement here is perhaps a little biased and hidebound. Their impression on their most helpful activity is that they are actually making things straight. But are they right?

When we turn to God's Word as the standard, as we must do, we discover that more is expected than simple propositional assent. When we are operating within biblical categories, we see that orthodoxy involves far more than mere head-nodding, mere intellectual going-along. Orthodoxy requires all our faculties, our reason, our imagination, our bodily habits, our *affections*. Straight thinking is inconsistent with crooked lives. Faith without works is dead; stories without dragons are boring; worship is a matter of sound doctrine *and* well-cooked meat on the grill; and a god chained to earth, however noble the portrayal, is some kind of Prometheus and not the God of Abraham. The fact that, to many, the foregoing seems to be a chain of *non sequiturs* helps to demonstrate our problem. We fail to see that orthodoxy is actually a bodily habit that, naturally, has to include the mind. And this is why true orthodoxy is lovely and involves the whole man.

And so we should expand our earlier observation. Either men will claim that the Word of God is ugly, or God will say that the word of man is. Either men will claim that the sweet is bitter, like so many dwarves in a stable, or God will claim that men have forsaken Him, the fountain of living water. So the way of salvation can be found not in affirming the truths of orthodoxy with a long face, but rather by coming to see and know that the words of God are life itself. They are refined gold, they are honey to the lips, they are aged wine, they summon us to a banquet in the kingdom that beggars description.

Our Lord Himself has set the table with crisp, white linens, and the silverware is lined up perfectly straight, in the orthodox manner. The crystal is glorious, and every glass is filled with red wine, the deep red wine of the everlasting covenant. Next to every place setting is a white stone serving for a name card, with a name written on it, written out by hand, before time began. The mystery is glorious—if there is no *time*, then how can we have temporal referents like *before?*—and the food is even better.

But as we look forward to this feast, and as we long for it, there are some unstable men who want to distract us. They have an alternative conception for the feast, one more in keeping with our contemporary, on-the-go, 24–7 lifestyle. Life is open, and dinner is not prepared because we have to help prepare it and *we* were too busy. Life is a process, they say, and so truth can be found at a convenience store near you. They want some help in getting the shrink-wrap off a package of Ho-Ho's, and if we collect enough of the coupons, we might eventually solve the problem of evil.

THE OPENNESS OF GOD

C.S. Lewis once commented that whatever is not eternal is eternally out of date. But this is an unacceptable sentiment to contemporary Americans. We believe in irresistible progress, and we want "new and improved" emblazoned on everything, including our theology. One cover blurb on a recent Openness book says, "This book is an important act of courage that invites readers to *new*, courageous thinking."[1] But in order to have this kind of improvement, everything we hold has to be "improvable" in principle, which keeps us from any kind of

---

[1] John Sanders, *The God Who Risks* (Downers Grove: InterVarsity Press, 1998), (back cover). Emphasis mine.

settled dogmatism. Consider this example: "The trinitarian model seems superior to process theism in this matter of the divine openness."[2] He thundered.

Of course, a number of things should make us suspicious from the outset. I think it was Charles Hodge who said that if it is true it is not new, and if it is new it is not true. When folks, even learned folks, actually, especially learned folks, start discovering that what the Bible has been saying all along is really what we here in our own day have only just recently discovered, they are just half a step away from saying that it does not matter what the Bible has been saying all along. This is because the whole project is rationalistic from the start, and wants the locus of authority to reside *within man* and not with God.

One of my children once asked me what God was standing on when He made the world. This kind of mistake is understandable in a child, and even endearing, but when Openness theologians make the same mistake over and over, it ceases to be quite as cute. The mistake works this way: One biblical statement about God is taken at face value while all the other statements are ignored. The *direction* of all statements is also ignored, and the one selected statement is interpreted in human terms. Then the question is asked. God made the world, and when I make things I am standing on the world. And since God must stand on something as I do, and the world wasn't made yet, what was He standing on?

Note the method. "God repeatedly sent Elijah to call King Ahab to repent, but the king refused to do so. Was God playing a cat-and-mouse game with Ahab? If God foreknows from the moment he gives the invitation that it will be pointless, then God is being deceitful in holding out a false hope."[3] In other words, if *I* did something like that, then I would be guilty of deception. When I make things, *I* have to be standing on the world. And of course if I destroyed cities with earthquakes, I would be guilty of genocide.

All this is not to say that every classical theist is innocent of this same problem. It does happen, and too often. But when it occurs, it happens because the exegete or theologian inconsistently allows creaturely and rationalistic concerns to dictate to the text what it should

[2] Clark Pinnock, ed., *The Openness of God* (Downers Grove: InterVarsity Press, 1994), 108.

[3] John Sanders, *The God Who Risks* (Downers Grove: InterVarsity Press, 1998), 74.

be saying. But this is exactly the same problem we find with Openness writers. An example of a classical theist stumbling in this way can be found in Albert Barnes' commentary on the second psalm. His comments are on the phrase, "in his sore displeasure." "Of course, all such words are to be interpreted in accordance with what we know to be the nature of God, and not in accordance with the same passions in men. God is opposed to sin, and will express his opposition *as if* he felt angry, but it will be in the most calm manner, and not as the result of passion."[4] Of course this is appalling, but it is an example of an orthodox exegete adopting the methods we are objecting to in the Openness writers.

The Bible tells us that God's displeasure will be great. The literal expression refers to *heat* or *burning*, as when one is inflamed with anger. The Openness theologian would say that this is an expression of God's anger and then haul it down to interpret it in terms of human anger. But Barnes also hauls it down to the creaturely level in order to interpret it in terms of a pond on a summer day—*calm*. One says that God's anger is like human anger while the other says that God's anger is like human calm. But both ignore the purpose of figures of speech. The expressions in the Bible about God, all of them together, invite us further up and further in. Symbols and figures of speech are *less* than what they represent, not greater. They point to something beyond themselves, and, in the case of God, to someone transcendent. Of course God does not fly off the handle like a sinful human being. His anger is far more *terrible* than that. It *transcends* anger. Of course God is not patient the way a man is patient—His serenity is everlasting and has no bounds. It transcends serenity.

John Sanders speaks more wisely than he knows when he says, "Asserting that it is a nonliteral expression does not solve the problem because it has to mean something. Just what is the anthropomorphic expression an expression of?"[5] It is an expression of something *like* the figure used, and points to something *beyond* the figure used. And when we look beyond a particular figure, we must remember all the Bible teaches us about God and look, by faith, beyond every word He has given to reveal His character and nature.

God reveals Himself in the historical narrative, poetry, and didactic

[4] Albert Barnes, *Barnes' Notes/Psalms* (Grand Rapids: Baker, 1987), 17.
[5] John Sanders, *The God Who Risks* (Downers Grove: InterVarsity Press, 1998), 69.

portions of Scripture. It is not the case that we find nearly all anthropomorphic expressions in the poetry, and a few more in the histories.
Even the didactic portions tell us in a straightforward way that we had
better look in faith past the words.

God "hath saved us, and called us with an holy calling, not according to our works, but according to his own purpose and grace, which
was given us in Christ Jesus before the world began" (2 Tim. 1:9; cf.
Tit. 1:1–3). The phrase rendered here as "before the world began" is
literally "before eternal times." How is this possible? How can we
have a temporal reference before temporality itself? We need to take
this together with everything the Bible teaches elsewhere and just
deal with it. We deal with it rightly when we humble ourselves in worship. This worship does *not* mean that we don't know that we are using finite words to glory in the infinite God. "If I said God is 'outside'
or 'beyond' space-time, I should mean 'as Shakespeare is outside *The
Tempest*'; i.e., its scenes and persons do not exhaust his being."[6] To say
that Shakespeare is outside one of his plays is to use a figure of speech.
We could just as easily say that he was above it, before it, inside it, or
beneath it. And if we are comparing this to God's relationship with
the creation, we would soon be forced to use every preposition we
could think of.

But using the illustration of a play is offensive to us. We say that
Hamlet is a fictional character, whereas *we* are real. It is not a good
comparison, we mutter, but notice where and why we take offense. *We*
are much greater than Hamlet, and zeal for the glory of mankind fills
the room. No one is concerned to say that God is much greater than
Shakespeare. Of course the analogy is limited—just like the scriptural analogy of the Potter and the pots—and it does not completely
cover every aspect of our discussion. But the illustration still *works* because it is pointing by means of a metaphor to something far grander
and more mysterious than a mere play. "Known unto God are all his
works from the beginning of the world" (Acts 15:18).

The Openness view must also be rejected because its advocates do
not really hold to their own methods and assumptions. Because they
want to continue (for the time being) to be considered evangelicals,
they want to place some things off limits. For example, Pinnock says
that God's omniscience of things present is clearly a necessary item.

---

[6] C.S. Lewis, *God in the Dock* (Grand Rapids: Eerdmans, 1970), 184.

"Obviously, God must know all things that can be known and know them truly."[7] But how is this? Does this not fly in the teeth of Bible verses, when handled in the wooden fashion of Openness proponents?

"And the LORD said, Because the cry of Sodom and Gomorrah is great, and because their sin is very grievous; I will go down now, and see whether they have done altogether according to the cry of it, which is come unto me; and if not, I will know" (Gen. 18:20–21). I will go down, the Lord says, and check things out. Not only does He not know what will happen in the future, He doesn't appear to know what is going on *at that moment* in Sodom. Connected to this is the fact that He doesn't know the past—He is going down to investigate what they "have done."

Openness proponents themselves shrink back from the ugliness of their own storytelling methods. This is either because they themselves are hesitant to walk so far toward the abyss or, less charitably, because they have seared consciences and know that the evangelicals whom they are trying to seduce will not be willing to go so far so fast. But give it time. Within a generation, evangelicals have started to worship a god who resembles Thor more than he resembles the God of Abraham, Moses, David, Jesus, and Paul. Thor, as we know, has been known to experience trouble. And this new god "expresses frustration."[8] Where will it all be after one more generation?

"God is not cool and collected but is deeply involved and can be wounded."[9] A god who can be "wounded" is a god who can eventually be killed. The death of god is perennially the hope of sinful man—because it opens up a vacancy to which man aspires—and it is the destination of all forms of theological liberalism. And all forms of Openness theology most certainly are a new strain of theological liberalism. When we finally come to the death of this god, some might pretend to weep at the funeral, but by that time there will be no tears in their hearts. This will not be a noble twilight of the gods surrounded by pagan despair, but rather the final removal of a tiresome god who, despite our best efforts at idolatrous truncation, still reminded us too much of the God of Scripture.

[7] Pinnock, *Openness*, 121.

[8] Clark Pinnock, ed., *The Openness of God* (Downers Grove: InterVarsity Press, 1994), 122.

[9] Ibid., 118.

THE FAILURE OF IMAGINATION

When a biblical vision of the living God is given to us, human imagination staggers, and human reason lies prostrate on the floor. Isaiah is undone, a man of unclean lips, and Moses is hidden in the cleft of the rock so that he will not be dissolved. In the revelation of Himself to us, God describes Himself in *countless* creaturely ways so that we never make the mistake of confusing Him with a creature. He is above, beneath, behind, and before, so that we might know that He is all of these and yet, strictly speaking, none of them. He is a warrior, shepherd, king, builder, and husband, and in these images the sanctified imagination is invited to gather them all together, and then to transcend them all, in order to worship and adore.

Human language is necessarily inadequate whenever men speak about God the Father Almighty, Maker of heaven and earth. But there is creaturely inadequacy, a holy limitation, revealed in virtually every word of Scripture, and then there is an impudent inadequacy. The thing which differentiates the two is not the element of anthropomorphic images (which are ubiquitous and unavoidable), but rather an ethical and aesthetic difference. Certain creaturely images of God are worthy of Him, and others are not. His grace in forgiving our sins can readily be compared to the healing of leprosy, but it cannot be compared to a really good decongestant. His salvation is like living water, and not at all like zippy Diet Dr. Pepper. The inability of those in the Openness of God camp to see how their portrayal of God *clanks*, is, at bottom, a failure of the imagination.

The majesty of biblical poetry always lifts our thoughts *up*. Biblical poetic expression is incarnational, which means that there is a body of "flesh," *but it is a body which reveals the Father*. Idolatrous poetic expression reveals nothing from above, and spends its energy in rearranging matter down here below. Idolatrous images of the divine are consistently bad metaphor because they are so truncated, and they drag our thoughts down to the level of man, giving us ludicrous and twisted images of God. Consider just a few grossly inadequate statements about God, and reflect on how they make one feel that our Open god is soon to appear as a guest on Oprah. "God is the best learner of all."[10] We expect to read in the next line that he plays well with others and

---

[10] Ibid., 124.

does not run with scissors. "Obviously God feels the pain of broken relationships."[11] Oh? Is he seeing his therapist?

Then compare these (and many more like them) with some of the exultation found in Isaiah's glory, his fortieth chapter.

> O Zion, that bringest good tidings, get thee up into the high mountain; O Jerusalem, that bringest good tidings, lift up thy voice with strength; lift it up, be not afraid; say unto the cities of Judah, Behold your God! Behold, the Lord God will come with strong hand, and his arm shall rule for him: behold, his reward is with him, and his work before him. He shall feed his flock like a shepherd: he shall gather the lambs with his arm, and carry them in his bosom, and shall gently lead those that are with young. (Is. 40:9–11)

The images are homely, creaturely, limited, and yet glorious. When Isaiah cries out that we are to behold our God, he does so in a way that does not encourage us to start looking under the furniture. This is not altered in the slightest by his use of an image taken from the created order. Yet even here, each single image, however wonderful, if absolutized in isolation from the others, could lead us away from profound and orthodox oceans and into the backwater shallows of heresy. The Lord certainly is our shepherd, but He isn't only a shepherd. And so the prophet shifts to another image.

> Who hath measured the waters in the hollow of his hand, and meted out heaven with the span, and comprehended the dust of the earth in a measure, and weighed the mountains in scales, and the hills in a balance? (v. 12)

We have here a series of rhetorical questions, and the assumed answer in all of them is that anyone who has a hollow in his hand, or a tape measure, or a set of scales, did not have anything to do with the apportionment of all creation. Hands, spans, and scales mentioned in order to teach us that this thing had nothing to do with hands, spans, and scales. Only God holds the oceans in the palm of His hand, and He is able to do this because He doesn't have any hands.

> Who hath directed the Spirit of the LORD, or being his counselor hath taught him? With whom took he counsel, and who instructed him, and taught him in the path of judgment, and taught him knowledge, and

[11] Ibid., 119.

shewed to him the way of understanding? Behold, the nations are as a drop of a bucket, and are counted as the small dust of the balance: behold, he taketh up the isles as a very little thing. And Lebanon is not sufficient to burn, nor the beasts thereof sufficient for a burnt offering. All nations before him are as nothing; and they are counted to him less than nothing, and vanity. (vv. 13–17)

Who has directed the Spirit of the Lord? Why, do ye not know? Have ye not heard? It's Clark Pinnock. Who has been His counselor in order to teach him in the path of judgment? Why, ye slow of heart, and lunk-headed of soul—it's Greg Boyd. Who has taught him knowledge, and who showed to Him the way of understanding? Well, you know, there is always John Sanders, whose book has lots of footnotes and academic respectability.

Unfair? They don't claim this for themselves. Well, actually, they do, and not for themselves only, but also for all the rest of us puny, little godmakers, whose breath is in our nostrils. In Open theism, the future is currently uncreated and comes into being as the result of a cooperative effort between god and man, in which process god learns lots of keen stuff. He is surprised every day, and he *learns* from what we do. In short, he is not the God of Isaiah.

To whom then will ye liken God? or what likeness will ye compare unto him? The workman melteth a graven image, and the goldsmith spreadeth it over with gold, and casteth silver chains. He that is so impoverished that he hath no oblation chooseth a tree that will not rot; he seeketh unto him a cunning workman to prepare a graven image, that shall not be moved. Have ye not known? have ye not heard? hath it not been told you from the beginning? have ye not understood from the foundations of the earth? It is he that sitteth upon the circle of the earth, and the inhabitants thereof are as grasshoppers; that stretcheth out the heavens as a curtain, and spreadeth them out as a tent to dwell in: That bringeth the princes to nothing; he maketh the judges of the earth as vanity. Yea, they shall not be planted; yea, they shall not be sown: yea, their stock shall not take root in the earth: and he shall also blow upon them, and they shall wither, and the whirlwind shall take them away as stubble. (vv. 18–24)

Only the most profound kind of spiritual blindness can keep a man from seeing what Isaiah is doing here. "To whom then will ye liken God?" Isaiah has been comparing God to all kinds of things throughout this chapter, and therefore the point of every comparison must be to show that *all* of them collapse under the weight of eternal glory. They are holy metaphors that make us look *up* to that which transcends them all. And, as we are glorying in this scriptural language, along come some very pedestrian exegetes, with a poetic ear comparable to about three feet of tin foil, who want us to acknowledge that the text compares God here to a *shepherd,* and every shepherd *they* have ever met didn't know the future.

> To whom then will ye liken me, or shall I be equal? saith the Holy One. Lift up your eyes on high, and behold who hath created these things, that bringeth out their host by number: he calleth them all by names by the greatness of his might, for that he is strong in power; not one faileth. (vv. 25–26)

To what may we liken God? The answer, friends, is nothing. And we show that we may compare Him to nothing by comparing Him to *everything* that is worthy of Him, and, of course, nothing completely is. In Him we live, and move, and have our being. This is not zen Christianity; it is the recognition that the Bible does not give us a tiny schematic version of the attributes of God, carefully drawn to scale. Rather, the Bible points, sings, shouts, eats, alliterates, teaches, glories, compares, and exults. Do you not *see?* Lift up your eyes on *high,* Isaiah says.

> Why sayest thou, O Jacob, and speakest, O Israel, My way is hid from the LORD, and my judgment is passed over from my God? Hast thou not known? hast thou not heard, that the everlasting God, the LORD, the Creator of the ends of the earth, fainteth not, neither is weary? there is no searching of his understanding. He giveth power to the faint; and to them that have no might he increaseth strength. Even the youths shall faint and be weary, and the young men shall utterly fall: But they that wait upon the LORD shall renew their strength; they shall mount up with wings as eagles; they shall run, and not be weary; and they shall walk, and not faint. (vv. 27–31)

Isaiah's conclusion of this wonderful passage is noteworthy. He comes at the end of this glorious exhortation to a statement of God's knowledge. Given what we have just read, why do Jacob and Israel say *that God does not know something?* Don't you know, silly little theologians—sorry, very important cutting-edge theologians—that there is no searching out the understanding of God? He knows the end from

the beginning, and it is precisely this, in Isaiah's mind, that distinguishes Him from those blind idols who cannot in fact tell us what is
to come. He points to this expressly in the next chapter. *They* do not
know the future, not because it does not exist to be known, but because they are no gods at all (Is. 41:23–24). Gods who do not know
the future do not inhabit the highest heaven, as our God does, but
rather are all face down in the ruins of Babylon, presided over by owls
and jackals.

When passages like this are read, and preferably aloud, there is a
temptation to conclude the problem with Open theists is not their
exegesis, but rather their tone deafness. This is a profound failure of
imagination.

CONCLUSION

Samuel Butler once dismissed those who "prove their doctrine orthodox by apostolic blows and knocks." Not quite. Orthodoxy is easy to
mock in a fallen world, but only because our flesh loves what is
crooked. The severity of the Tishbite does not flatter us adequately.
But if we change a few of the words around to show what kind of
thing is actually happening in such theological debates, the jibe
doesn't work as well. "With apostolic zeal and strife he tried to save
his lovely wife." Only a cad wouldn't.

It is the part of humility to remain silent if God has left something
unrevealed. "The secret things belong unto the LORD our God: but
those things which are revealed belong unto us and to our children
forever, that we may do all the words of this law" (Deut. 29:29). But
if God has revealed something plainly, as He has done concerning His
knowledge of the end from the beginning, it is *not* humility to pretend
that He said nothing about it. Nor is it humility to accuse of arrogance
those who have heard and remembered the words of God.

This is not a debate over the nature of time. If someone were to
maintain that God knew nothing about the layout of South Dakota,
our subsequent debate would not be a debate over the nature of geog-
raphy. It would be over whether God is being honored as God or
whether He is being insulted.

The hope of the gospel is really at stake here. Our redemption was
brought about by "the precious blood of Christ, as of a lamb without
blemish and without spot: *Who verily was foreordained before the*

foundation of the world, but was manifest in these last times for you" (1 Pet. 1:19–20; cf. Eph. 1:4). Ideas have consequences, and destinations, and one of the consequences of our trying to read the Scriptures without any poetry in our souls will be the eventual destruction of any possibility of ministering to souls. Just imagine the hymn writer trying to lift up the downcast.

> "I know not what the future holds,
> But I know Who also doesn't know much about it either."

2

Metaphor in Exile

Douglas M. Jones

The Enlightenment project was doomed to fail because it was inherently lame in regard to the aesthetic dimension of life, especially the dimension of metaphor. Without a healthy appreciation for the pervasiveness and power of metaphor and imagination, a story of any sort will never last. Metaphor is not some sideline decoration of language; it involves patterns of association and inference that pull together the most important aspects of knowing. Creation itself, especially human life in the image of God, is woven through with metaphor, and the failure of any view to connect with this deeper reality will always produce unsatisfying stories. The Enlightenment tale was particularly boring, and thus it lasted only a few centuries. Orthodox Christianity, however, growing out of Old Testament realities, has always lived and moved and enjoyed its being within the world of deeper meanings and images, connections that unveil trinitarian truth, goodness, and beauty, resurrecting the cultures they embrace. All this means that we cannot ignore the aesthetic dimension when evaluating views of any sort, let alone theological. Failure in the aesthetic points to a failure in truth and goodness; they are intimately connected in Scripture.

But what is it specifically about Enlightenment/modernist categories that *suffocates* the aesthetic dimension of life? That is the motivating question of this essay. More specifically, the answer given by the advocates of the Openness of God theology is the same as that given by the Enlightenment. That both views end up killing the aesthetic is a key indicator of their falsity. But we need to examine specifics before that charge is well-founded. My strategy, then, will be to begin by examining an intriguing tension that surfaces in the account of

metaphor given by Openness advocate John Sanders. To resolve this
tension, Sanders follows a particular anti-aesthetic path that ends up
determining almost everything else in his defense of Openness theology. That fork in the road is central to his entire project. My conclusion will be that Openness theology is not some new "honest" and
"courageous" treatment of biblical texts, but rather a view that drops
out quite unimaginatively from Enlightenment assumptions that aim
to grind off the aesthetic dimension from scriptural theology.

SANDERS ON METAPHOR

In the opening pages of *The God Who Risks*, the fundamental tension
that should immediately signal to us that something is deeply amiss is
the conflict between Sanders' views of metaphor and logical consistency. He wants both but can't have them. He sees himself as taking
metaphor very seriously, and the Openness project as presenting a
new, iconoclastic metaphor:

> The sensibilities of many people will be shocked by the notion that
> God is a risk taker, for the metaphor goes against the grain of our
> accustomed thinking in regard to divine providence. Theorists on met-
> aphor, however, hold that a good metaphor is supposed to challenge
> conventional ways of looking at things and suggest an alternative
> perspective.... When certain metaphors (for example, God is king)
> reign for so long in theology, we risk being conditioned to overlook
> aspects of God's relationship with us. When this happens, we need new
> "iconoclastic" metaphors that reveal to us something that we over-
> looked. It is my contention that the metaphor of God as risk taker
> opens up new ways for us to understand what is at stake for God in
> divine providence.[1]

The tension in question arises in his explanation of metaphoric/
anthropomorphic language and the constraint of logical consistency.
On the one hand, he correctly recognizes that "Metaphors have the
peculiar quality of saying that something both 'is' and 'is not.'"[2] That
is, he maintains that metaphors and anthropomorphic language
in general communicate via implicit contradictions and category

---

[1] John Sanders, *The God Who Risks: A Theology of Providence* (Downers Grove;
InterVarsity Press, 1998), 11.
[2] Ibid., 15.

mistakes—"is" and "is not." Paul Ricoeur and other expositors of
metaphor note the same feature: "The paradox consists in the fact
that there is no other way to do justice to the notion of metaphorical
truth than to include the critical incision of the (literal) 'is not' within
the ontological vehemence of the (metaphorical) 'is.'"[3] Similarly,
Gemma Fiumara notes that, "the paradox of a metaphor is that it
seems to affirm an identity while also somehow denying it."[4] For
example, when Scripture reveals that "Christ is a lamb," it conveys to
us that Christ both *is* and *is not* a lamb at that same time. In part, a
metaphor leads us to imagine or embrace one thing in terms of some,
but not all, of the characteristics of another (in contrast, literalism
attributes all of the characteristics of the one to the other). We really
have no difficulty grasping this sort of truth. It doesn't "kill" communication at all. It's an exceedingly natural part of our normal discourse.
Most of our language and thought is metaphoric, and we all communicate and interpret the built-in tensions and contradictions of metaphor with very little problem in day to day conversation.

Yet, just a page later, Sanders tells us that all theological models,
including his, must satisfy the demands of "public" and "conceptual
intelligibility." Part of this demand of intelligibility is that "If a concept is contradictory, it fails a key test for public intelligibility, *since
what is contradictory is not meaningful*"[5]:

> In order for the model to make sense, the set of concepts that it entails
> must be unpacked and examined for internal consistency, coherence
> with other beliefs we affirm, comprehensiveness. . . . If concepts inte-
> gral to the model are mutually inconsistent, the coherence of the model
> is called into question. A model with too many internal tensions lacks
> cohesiveness.[6]

The first irony here is that, like most attempts to make the world
safe from metaphor, this statement itself has to employ the implicit
tensions of metaphor. Notice that concepts are things that can be "un-
packed," as if from a suitcase, and are located *inside* a *model* whose

---

[3] Paul Ricoeur; trans. Robert Czerny, *The Rule of Metaphor* (London: Routledge &
Kegan Paul, 1978), 255.
[4] Gemma Corradi Fiumara, *The Metaphoric Process Connections Between Language
and Life* (New York: Routledge, 1995), 11.
[5] Sanders, *Risks,* 17 (emph. mine).
[6] Ibid.

gluey bonds, if too brittle, can lack "cohesiveness" and fall apart. Concepts, for Sanders, are and are not suitcased, and are and are not bound together inside other things. The second and more important irony is that he positively wants to take metaphor seriously, even in its implicitly "is and is not" form, though here he claims that "what is contradictory is not meaningful." On such standards, metaphor, above all things, should be quite meaningless (along with most of Scripture). Yet we understand such metaphors just fine, even though they don't satisfy the demands of strict logical consistency. So one aspect of his approach wants to make room for statements like "Christ is a Lamb" while the other constraint insists that such phrases are not even meaningful. And yet his whole case for interpreting the anthropomorphic language of Scripture hinges on going down one or the other of these paths.

But still, what more specifically is it about an Enlightenment/Openness approach to reason that produces this tension with metaphor? We have to realize that the Enlightenment was but a revival of most aspects of ancient Hellenism, apart from the existence of Platonic-Aristotelian Forms. The two periods still shared the same commitments to the ultimacy of reason and its intellectualism, the view that knowledge was primarily a mental thing. And both Plato and Descartes and all their friends modeled knowledge in terms of mathematical precision, whether in Socratic definitions or Descartes' "clear and distinct ideas." In order for an autonomous mind to fulfill divine functions, every claim to truth had to be lit up clearly so that the individual could have absolute power and control over it. But this meant that everything unclear or not directly intellectual had to be demoted from reality. Thus the Greeks and their Enlightenment grandchildren had to denigrate the body, emotions, imagination, metaphor, etc., since these couldn't be captured by their rather narrow intellectualism.

For Aristotle, metaphor was a deviation from and a mere ornament on the literal. Everything metaphorical can in the end be reduced to the literal. Metaphor can't fit into the propositions of a syllogism because that logic can't process the noncognitive mysteries of metaphor. This ancient opposition to metaphor still shows up in contemporary logic textbooks. Consider the following seemingly innocent move against metaphor in David Kelley's *The Art of Reasoning*:

In the context of reasoning . . . where we are concerned with the logical relationship among propositions, a literal translation is usually necessary. To know how a given proposition is logically related to others, we have to know exactly what the proposition does and doesn't say. If two people are using metaphorical terms in an argument, we won't know whether they are really talking about the same issue until we formulate their positions in literal terms.[7]

Here, as in most of the Hellenistic/Enlightenment tradition, metaphor is a messy obstacle to be conquered so we can get to the "real" literal claims beneath. Note that this is done to satisfy a particular conception of knowledge: "we have to know exactly what the proposition does and doesn't say." Only fully transparent things can count as knowledge. Presumably, metaphor cloaks truth and the literal reveals it. We find an even more heated contrast between logic and metaphor in various Enlightenment thinkers such as Galileo, Montaigne, Descartes, and Leibniz. Thomas Hobbes (1588–1679), sums up the Enlightenment contrast between logic and metaphor in this way:

[It is an abuse of language] when they use words metaphorically; that is, in another sense than that they are ordained for, and thereby deceive others. . . . the light of human minds is perspicuous words, but by exact definitions first snuffed, and purged from ambiguity; reason is the pace; increase of science, the way; and the benefit of mankind, the end. And, on the contrary, metaphors, and senseless and ambiguous words, are like *ignes fatui* [will-o'-the-wisps]; and reasoning upon them is wandering amongst innumerable absurdities; and their end, contention and sedition, or contempt.[8]

Similarly, John Locke (1632–1704) argued:

Since wit and fancy finds easier entertainment in the world, than dry truth and real knowledge, *figurative speeches*, and allusion in language, will hardly be admitted, as an imperfection or abuse of it. . . . But yet, if we would speak of things as they are, we must allow, that all the art of rhetoric, besides order and clearness, all the artificial and figurative application of words, eloquence have invented, are for nothing else

---

[7] Kelley, David, *The Art of Reasoning*, second edition (New York: W.W. Norton, 1994), 72.

[8] Thomas Hobbes, *Leviathan* (Indianapolis: Bobbs-Merrill Educ. Publ., 1982 [1651]) I, IV, 38 and I, V, 50.

but to insinuate wrong *Ideas*, move the passions, and thereby mislead the judgment; and so indeed are a perfect cheat. . . . [T]hey are certainly, in all discourses that pretend to inform or instruct, wholly to be avoided; and where truth and knowledge are concerned, cannot but be thought a great fault, either of the language or person that makes use of them.[9]

Notice again, as is so typical, one can't fight metaphor without using it. Hobbes tells us that words are "ordained" like a pastor; the mind is a "light" which can be "snuffed" and "purged." Locke describes truth as "dry" that can refuse "admittance" to metaphor; words can be "applied" like paint; eloquence—a string of symbols—can "invent" and "cheat" and be a "fault"—a mountainous crevice. Though false, the passages are quite understandable and meaningful. Their use of metaphor doesn't kill communication.

Still, why would these thinkers enter upon such convoluted denials? With the Enlightenment devotion to mathematics as the model for thinking, only clear and quantifiable items could qualify as knowledge. Metaphor calls up many aspects of our being (emotional, moral, aesthetic, imaginative, bodily) that are central to knowledge but don't fit into neat mathematical boxes (see more below). Thus, metaphor and an Enlightenment view of logical consistency cannot fit together; one has to go, and these Enlightenment thinkers were only too happy to dispose of the metaphorical. But Sanders and the Openness advocates want to synthesize the two worlds—the biblical and the Enlightenment—and embrace both metaphor and a narrow view of reason. But something has to give.

How, then, does Sanders (and other Openness advocates) resolve this dilemma of embracing and rejecting metaphorical discourse? He could either embrace the noncognitive depths of metaphor and a richer approach to reasoning within metaphorical/scriptural bounds (see below) or side with the Enlightenment and embrace its narrow conception of rationality, which seeks to reduce all metaphor to tame, logically acceptable claims. He opts for the latter, and this reveals itself in his discussion of anthropomorphism.

---

[9] John Locke, *An Essay Concerning Human Understanding*, ed. Nidditch, Peter (Oxford: Clarendon Press, 1991 [1689]) Bk. III, X, 34, 508.

SANDERS ON ANTHROPOMORPHISM

In moving toward his reductionist account of metaphor, Sanders lays out four key aspects of anthropomorphism that can be summarized as follows:

1. The Bible does indeed teach the hiddenness and incomprehensibility of God, but this is not due to inadequacies of language. Instead it is due to the Creator-creature distinction and the fact that no persons can be fully circumscribed by language.[10]

2. Anthropomorphism is unique and pervasive in the Old Testament in contrast to more abstract understandings; moreover, in the Incarnation, God Himself has human characteristics predicated of Him.[11]

3. The contexts of traditional transcendence passages, especially Isaiah 55:8, do not refer to ontological or epistemological differences between man and God, but only moral differences.[12]

4. In the broader sense of anthropomorphism, all our language about God is human language, i.e., all language inevitably predicates properties of God that are derived from human categories. Anthropomorphism is unavoidable otherwise God is unknowable.[13]

The first two points above are not objectionable in themselves, but that depends upon how they are fleshed out by point four. And in explaining point four, Sanders has to invoke point three, so it can be addressed then. My focus will be on point four's dichotomy between agnosticism and univocal predication (i.e., a reductionist account of metaphor). Here is how the argument for point four above works itself out by premises in Sanders' own words:

4a. "If God speaks to us through Scripture, then God knows how to use human language and concepts in such a way that they are adequate for understanding that which God desires us to know."[14]

4b. "This requires us to presuppose a shared context between God and creation" ("shared context" means "the conditions of our existence, including our language, history, and spatiotemporal world").[15]

---

[10] Sanders, *Risks*, 21.
[11] Ibid.
[12] Ibid., 21–22.
[13] Ibid. 22.
[14] Ibid., 24.
[15] Ibid.

4c. "God enters into that context with us by being in relation to us."[16]

4d. "By being in relation to us, ... God makes use of human ways of knowing and speaking to communicate with us.... We know nothing of a God unrelated to us."[17]

4e. "Related to us" thus means univocal predication (in contrast to mere analogical predication): "There must be some properties that are used of God in the same sense that they are used of things in the created order. Otherwise we will be back in the cave of agnosticism."[18]

The conceptual connections in this argument thus run like this: divine revelation requires a shared context, which requires relatedness, which requires univocal predication. Note how these notions flow together in his closing summary of the argument:

> Anthropomorphic language does not preclude literal predication to God. Of course, the question must be asked, What is it to which the anthropomorphisms refer? If God shares the same context with us by entering into relation with us, as the biblical revelation presupposes, then we have a basis for our language about God. What I mean by the word *literal* is that our language about God is reality depicting (truthful) such that there is a referent, an other, with whom we are in relationship and of whom we have genuine knowledge.[19]

Thus, according to Sanders, our theological model of God must opt either for univocal predication (strong literality) or agnosticism (total unrelatedness). As a disjunctive syllogism, Sanders' argument reduce to: Either we have univocal predication of God or we must be agnostic about Him; but we are not agnostic, given that we have genuine divine revelation. Thus our predication must be univocal.

Nonetheless, Sanders then uses this main argument to answer the objections against his account of anthropomorphism, namely objections coming from concerns of radical transcendence and antinomy (which are raised primarily by the Reformed tradition). His answers to these objections are relevant here because they help elaborate his reductionistic account of metaphor.

Against the first objection—radical transcendence—raised by more speculative theologians, both pagan and Christian, who have

[16] Ibid.
[17] Ibid., 24–25.
[18] Ibid., 25.
[19] Ibid.

posited God as "wholly other," totally beyond human apprehension, infinitely differentiated from us, Sanders argues that it is impossible, invoking forms of premises 4d and 4e above:

> [W]e cannot know what God is like *in se* apart from us because all of our knowledge of God is embedded within the conditions in which God has placed us. God may be different in himself (*in se*) than God is with us (*quoad nos*), but we can have no knowledge of that difference. The Lord our Creator and Redeemer is what God is really like in relation to us. If God is different in himself we cannot say.[20]

His other main answer to the radical transcendence objection also employs an aspect of 4d above:

> How do those who claim that the finite cannot contain the infinite *know* this to be the case? It is logically possible that ultimate reality is beyond human knowing, but how does the person affirming this know that it is? . . . Such people claim both that something is unknowable and that they know something about the unknowable.[21]

The second, and I think, more pressing objection to Sanders' anthropomorphism is an appeal to antinomy or apparent contradiction. Those of us in the Reformed tradition often elucidate the relationship between divine sovereignty and human responsibility in terms of mystery, paradox, or antinomy, much like the similar appeal made for the Trinity and the Incarnation. Where Openness advocates seek a clear and distinct logical explanation of the sovereignty/responsibility relationship, we Reformed will often deny that such things are comprehensible in a rationalistic form. As the Westminster Confession of Faith teaches, God did unchangeably "ordain whatsoever comes to pass: yet so, as thereby neither is God the author of sin, nor is violence offered to the will of creatures" (III, 1)—predestination and genuine freewill side by side. This truth, the Confession declares, is a "high mystery" (III, 8) in the "unsearchable wisdom" of God (IV, 4). Sanders rejects this reply for various reasons, most of which are semantic quibbles with "antinomy," but the most interesting answer is a further elaboration on 4d and 4e above. His answer is so revealing that I will quote it at length:

---

[20] Ibid., 30.
[21] Ibid., 31.

A final point against the antinomy objection is that it seeks to escape the rules surrounding intelligibility. What philosophers call contradiction some theologians refer to euphemistically as antinomy, or logical paradox. But in doing theology, we simply have to "play by the rules" of the game, and one of these rules is that our discourse must make sense. Interestingly, theologians who claim the right to be inconsistent expect us to make sense of what they are saying. My position here does not rule out paradox and mystery (as defined above) or metaphors and riddles. It simply excludes discourse that lies outside the boundaries of consistency and coherence—that is nonsense....

To be rational in the practice of theology is to enter the domain of public criteria of intelligibility. The exclusion of contradictions from theological discourse is not an idiosyncratic one, but a public one imposed by the community. To be intelligible we have to be able to communicate with one another. This means that we must operate within the boundaries in which God created us. We simply have no other choice but to think and speak within these limits. If we lapse into contradiction or incoherence, then we violate some of the conditions of the public criteria by which theology is considered meaningful. This does not mean that logic is the standard to which God is subject, but it is the standard for our meaningful discourse about God. I have no desire to be a rationalist, placing logic above God. There may be realities that are incomprehensible to us, lying completely outside our abilities to understand them. However, if God desires to communicate meaningfully with us, then he will have to do so within the conditions of his own creation. One of these conditions is that intelligibility excludes antinomies.[22]

The two intertwining theses to draw out from this passage are: (a) all discourse that violates the "boundaries" of logical consistency (note the metaphor) is meaningless; (b) all meaningful communication must be reducible to the literal (i.e., must be able to be plugged into a logical syllogism). *This logical reductionism is the key to the whole Openness project.* In short, Openness of God theology is simply what happens when you force all divine descriptions into the categories of the Logical Positivists of the mid-twentieth century. The epistemological assumptions are the same. In the passage above, Sanders says that "logic...is the standard for our meaningful discourse about God" and "if God desires to communicate meaningfully with us, then he will have to do so within the conditions of his own creation."

[22] Ibid., 37.

Anything beyond those logical boundaries is "incomprehensible" and irrelevant. The early Wittgenstein said the same: "the limits of my language means the limits of my world. Logic pervades the world: the limits of the world are also its limits.... The right method of philosophy would be this. To say nothing except what can be said."[23] And that quintessential Logical Positivist A.J. Ayer explained the intelligibility-literality connection as: "it is only if it is literally meaningful ... that a statement can properly be said to be either true or false.... [Otherwise] it would not be capable of being understood in the sense in which either scientific hypotheses or common-sense statements are habitually understood."[24] And so all anthropomorphic and metaphorical language has to be reduced to the literal, the univocal.

Consider three brief examples of Openness argument that reveal this common reductionism:

(a) John Sanders: "if we take our status as creatures seriously, then we shall have to content ourselves with knowing and speaking about God within the conditions of our createdness. In other words, ... the use of metaphors and anthropomorphic language (in the broad sense) when speaking of God is necessary.... The purpose of this book is not to reduce God to the limits of human understanding, but to propose that from within the boundaries of our createdness God can be known and to propose a model of the divine-human relationship that reexplores old vistas for our understanding of God and deepens our appreciation of the freedom, love, wisdom and power of God.... If God decides to disclose himself to us as a personal being who enters into relationship with us, who has purposes, emotions, and desires, and who suffers with us, then we ought to rejoice in this anthropomorphic portrait and accept it as disclosing to us the very nature of God."[25]

Sanders here begins with the language of metaphor and anthropomorphism. But we already know, given Sanders' rationalistic constraints, that such language cannot remain truly figurative. It must be reduced to the literal. And so by the time Sanders gets to citing the issues at hand, namely, genuine purposes, emotions, desires, love, suffering, we can only understand these in a strictly univocal sense.

[23] Wittgenstein, Ludwig, *Tractatus Logic Philosophicus* (London: Routledge and Kegan Paul, 1995 [1922]) 5.6; 5.61; 6.53.
[24] A.J. Ayer, *Language, Truth, and Logic* (New York: Dover Publications, 1952), 14–15.
[25] Sanders, *Risks*, 38.

No other option is available. The literal (Sanders' "anthropomorphic") now discloses univocally "the very nature of God." Metaphorical imagination is closed off. We can no longer say God "is and is not"
emotional or loving in any creative way. It has to fit the constraints of
syllogism. And I thoroughly agree that many classical theologians fall
into the same error in reverse (many of them followed Plato,[26] the
Openness folks prefer Descartes and Locke; no giant difference). But
why go either route? Why not see metaphorical language as truthful
but not mathematical?

(b) Gregory Boyd (in a series of separate but similar challenges):

"When a person is in a genuine relationship with another, willingness to adjust to them is always considered a virtue. Why should this
apply to people but not to God?"

"How can someone sincerely intend to do something they are certain they will never do? And how can they truly change their mind if
their mind is eternally made up?"

"If the classical view is correct, we have to be willing to accept that
God could in one breath say that the Israelites' behavior 'did not enter
my mind,' though their behavior 'was eternally in my mind.' If this is
not a contradiction, what is?"

"Could you genuinely look for a coin in your house that you always
knew was not there?"

"Common sense tells us that we can only regret a decision we made
if the decision resulted in an outcome other than what we expected."[27]

All these sorts of rhetorical questions rest upon metaphoric reductions too. In each case and countless others, Boyd offers some psychological item for consideration: relational adjustments, sincerity,
repentance, acquaintance, searching, and regret. We could conceiv-
ably have two options for interpretation; we could understand these
in a truth-revealing metaphorical sense or immediately reduce them
to syllogism fodder. The metaphorical approach at least would leave
open the question as to whether these passages are speaking purely
univocally or allowing transcendent and genuine versions of each of
these. But given Boyd's Enlightenment approach to metaphor, he can't
allow a particular passage or the whole of Scripture to determine such

[26] See Peter Leithart's essay in this volume.
[27] Gregory Boyd, *God of the Possible: A Biblical Introduction to the Open View of God*
(Grand Rapids: Baker Books, 2000), 78, 77, 62, 63, 56.

questions. Like Sanders, he has to reduce each to the most literalistic level, since that is what "common sense" demands. As Boyd notes, "Striving to have a plausible theology is necessary because, for many of us, the mind must be thoroughly convinced if the heart is to be thoroughly transformed.... [T]he Open view of God and of the future makes more intellectual sense than the classical view.... The Open view is the only option that avoids the impenetrable paradox (or, as many of us would argue, the contradiction) of asserting that self-determining free actions are settled an eternity before free agents make them so."[28] And we can hear Hobbes cheering in the background. Faith, Boyd seems to want to say, is the substance of a thoroughly convinced intellect, the evidence of things deduced.

(c) William Hasker: "The notion of God's being 'in control' is similarly ambiguous. The parents of small children certainly desire to be 'in control' of what happens ... and often manage this to a considerable degree. But they do not, if they are wise, attempt to exercise this control by determining every detail of what their children do and experience.... Should not a similar account be given of God's control over us?"[29]

Here fatherhood or parenthood gets reduced. A healthy approach to metaphor would again at least leave open some poetic mystery as to which ways God is and is not a father. Perhaps He operates in some wonderfully superior manner in which the Father controls all things, like a sculptor or author, but in which we have genuine freedom? But that can't even be a legitimate alternative for Hasker. Metaphor must be exiled. Hasker also plays by Enlightenment rules: "an intelligible doctrine must be expressible in grammatically well-formed sentences. ... We may also require that an intelligible doctrine should not be contradictory or otherwise logically impossible. It would seem, furthermore, that a proposition is not understood unless it is possible to give an account of at least some of the nontrivial inferential relationships that hold between it and other relevant propositions."[30] Genuine metaphor can't play by these rules, and even though metaphors have

---

[28] Ibid., 91.

[29] William Hasker, "A Philosophical Perspective," in Pinnock, Clark, et al, *The Openness of God: A Biblical Challenge to the Traditional Understanding of God* (Downers Grove: InterVarsity Press, 1994), 142.

[30] William Hasker, *God, Time, and Knowledge* (Ithaca: Cornell University Press, 1989), 147.

plenty of inferential relationships, many of which we can show but not tell, these are far too subtle for Enlightenment strictures.

THE PROBLEMS WITH OPENNESS AESTHETIC REDUCTIONISM

My original charge was that Openness theology must be false because it precludes the categories of the aesthetic; specifically, it takes a reductionistic view of metaphor, excluding all meaningfulness that doesn't fit into quantifiable reference and literality. Though I've made passing criticisms along the way, I'll now pull them together:

1. *Metaphor's Violation of the Disjunction:* the central argument upon which all of Sanders' exegesis built was the disjunctive syllogism: either we have univocal predication of God or we must be agnostic about Him. But we are not agnostic, given that we have genuine divine revelation; thus our predication about God must be univocal. In Sanders' words, "There must be some properties that are used of God in the same sense that they are used of things in the created order. Otherwise we will be back in the cave of agnosticism."[31] The first premise fails if we can find only one other option besides univocity and agnosticism. And the other option isn't even just the plain analogical option explained by the medievals. The assumptions of metaphor are actually more subtle than analogical predication, since metaphor invokes rational but noncognitive aspects of our persons (see below). But either one could break the exclusivistic disjunction of Openness theology. And the fact, as cited above, that Openness theologians can communicate arguments in favor of literality by means of nonunivocal metaphors is sufficient proof that univocity and agnosticism are not the only options. If Openness theologians can communicate to other humans outside of the disjunction they require for divine revelation, then perhaps God can speak nonunivocally too.

2. *Meaninglessness of Most Discourse:* even apart from questions of univocity, the demands of logic and communicability are very different. If meaningfulness can only apply to what can be logically consistent, then most of our language and many disciplines will be ruled out by Openness theology. Logic will only tolerate complete indicative statements, and only indicative statements are capable of meeting the Enlightenment/Openness criterion of "logical consistency," since

---

[31] Sanders, *Risks*, 25.

only they have clear and distinct and identifiable referents. Not only will all figurative language have to be excluded but also most questions, imperatives, exclamations, etc. None of these even rise to the height of privileged indicative statements. Not only does the Openness meaning criterion exclude much of our (and biblical) language as meaningful, but, in Logical Positivist fashion, the realms of ethics, aesthetics, emotion, imagination, etc. will have to go silent too, since much of their subject matter can't be pinned down in syllogistic form.

3. *Failure of Meaning as Reference*: the problem just identified stems from a common but simplistic notion of meaning-as-reference that pervades Openness writings. This is the main tie to Enlightenment categories, especially the sorts of Logical Positivist statements noted earlier. Linguistic meaning is obviously a complex affair, and twentieth-century philosophy has largely sought to exclude talk of ideas or the mental when discussing meaning (medieval philosophy was much more sophisticated than to go down this path). But one of the twentieth-century moves was to drop out talk of meaning as mental in favor of meaning as referent in the world (the extensional project). In order for Openness's notion of univocity to work, as well as its desire to receive only statements capturable by logic, it too has to assume that meaning is reference. Note this assumption working in Sanders' discussion of anthropomorphism: "What I mean by the word *literal* is that our language about God is reality depicting (truthful) such that there is a referent, an other, with whom we are in relationship and of whom we have genuine knowledge."[32] It is this sort of tying of meaning to referent that nullifies metaphor, as well as all the sorts of language noted just above. But many thinkers, Christian and not, have shown that meaning is more than referent. So much of our language can't even be tied to a referent in the world ("the," "and," "for," etc.), and yet these are meaningful. But also, such a view starts making mere physical symbols take on quasi-magical properties. Inert symbols all of a sudden gain the ability to "refer" and "point" to objects in the world, like rocks sprouting arrows. Meaning is much more complex, involving not only referents but also social conventions and mental intentions and more. Reducing meaning to referent allows the Openness's univocity to shine and do its damage, but when we see that the project rests on a simplistically false view of meaning, the project

---

[32] Ibid., 25.

pales. In a footnote, Sanders seeks weakly to distance himself from this charge: "affirming univocity does not commit us to the 'picture theory' of meaning according to which one word refers to one empirical referent."[33] But this misunderstands the issue at stake. Sanders is just concerned here to allow for multiple referents, but he does not back off his more basic assumption that meaning is reference, as opposed to a combination of use, intent, etc. And he can't back off that claim without bringing down the whole Openness project.

4. *Irreducibility of Metaphor*: the prior point about reference allows a fleshing out of the Openness hostility to genuine metaphor. For them and other Enlightenment thinkers, every metaphor can and must be reduced down to a literal core before it can count as meaningful and logically presentable. And reducibility means finding the referent. But referents of metaphor are often images (sometimes actual mental images or patterns) that can't be broken down into indicative propositions, or they invoke referents that are cognitively important but which aren't purely intellectual in the Enlightenment sense, namely, emotional frameworks, aesthetic attitudes, subjective connotations, ethical virtues, etc. As several thinkers have noticed, metaphor is much more like music than mathematics. Music is very cognitively powerful and meaningful, though it can't be reduced to simple propositions. Music can go deep and connect with parts of our persons that can never qualify for syllogistic duty, though they are often more determinative in framing our intellectual judgments. Metaphor works the same way. Quite ironically, Sanders sympathetically cites several thinkers (Lakoff, Johnson, Gill)[34] who share a view of metaphor similar to that which I'm defending, but he apparently fails to realize how their conclusions would utterly undermine the entire Openness project. Jerry Gill, for example, summarizes the depth and irreducibility of metaphor in a way that reflects many of my criticisms above:

> Metaphor is helpfully understood as a mediational phenomenon in which certain intangible qualities and aspects among the various dimensions of experienced reality may be expressed by means of the context, use, and configuration of certain tangible qualities and aspects of that reality. What this means, of course, is that the meaning of a deep and rich metaphor cannot be exhausted by any amount of analysis, that

---

[33] Ibid., 286.
[34] Ibid., 15, n. 283.

there are mysteries in our experience that can only be encountered and engaged mediationally. In fact, it may well be that the nature of the metaphoric mode is itself such a mystery, one that can only be approached indirectly.[35]

Openness theology is not only hostile to metaphor and the aesthetic dimension in its reductions of divine metaphor, but it also reveals an almost gnostic intellectualism that feeds its mathematical bent. Though Sanders and others, especially Boyd, aim rightly to berate any Christian captivity to Hellenistic categories, they themselves embrace the primacy of the intellect (a perennial feature of Hellenism and modernism) in a way that would make even Plato blush: "the mind must be thoroughly convinced if the heart is to be thoroughly transformed."[36]

5. *Misapplication of Logic:* Logic, of course, has its place, but Openness theology's rather naive swinging of its bat is a root cause of its confusion. When we see people blindly using pagan categories, it's important to search out the original motivations. What was it, after all, that motivated the discipline of logic? For both Hellenism and the Enlightenment, the goal of logic was to help preserve the objectivity of knowledge against relativistic skepticisms. Mathematics stood out as the model of epistemological objectivity, what with its universal formulae and deductive proofs. In the hope of imitating this objectivity in other areas of knowledge, they aimed to mathematize human thought by finding an intellectual calculus that could churn out objective knowledge. The twentieth century aside, most eras have realized that mathematics can't apply to all areas of life. Not everything is quantifiable; not everything has the sort of edges requisite for calculation. But this truth was especially neglected in regard to logic. Though it had its origins in mimicking mathematics, logic was quickly applied to all aspects of reality too. Thus, the "sovereignty of reason" became a hallmark of the Enlightenment, and soon even the likes of Immanuel Kant were trying to rein in its reach. The origins of logic should give us a clue of its limits. Like mathematics, the world of logic (as noted above) is limited to that which is quantifiable and measurable. For something to be able to be contradictable it has to be

---

[35] Jerry Gill, *Mediated Transcendence: A Postmodern Reflection* (Macon: Mercer Univ. Press, 1989), 142.
[36] Boyd, *Possible*, 90.

pretty simple and negatable. And like math, the physical realm fits this bill rather handily (with minor qualifications). We can easily talk about the physical impossibility of having a ball that is red and not-red or a door that is rectangular and not-rectangular at the same time. Suspicions should arise when we start trying to apply logic in non-physical arenas, where we're not sure where the edges and corners really end. Assuming ancient Platonisms are misdirected attempts to replace the Christian God, then Christians should be very uneasy about any talk of nonsupernatural necessities floating about the universe. But that aside, Openness theology involves a very fundamental misapplication of logic, given the above. Instead of letting logic rest naturally in the realm of the physical, it has no hesitation in assuming that the divine realm is clearly and distinctly quantifiable. By applying logic to the divine realm, Openness assumes it knows all the edges and possible negations. But this seems fundamental to misunderstanding the nature and abilities of logic.

7. *Revealing the Incomprehensible:* Openness advocates are not controversial in challenging those nonrevelational speculators who speak of the unspeakable: if God is wholly beyond human categories, then we couldn't speak of Him. But the Openness appeal to this thesis against those of us with revelational epistemologies is a bit odd— "Apart from revelation we cannot know that anything exists beyond our boundaries, and if, by revelation, we are informed of a transcendent existence, we can only understand it by use of our conditions" [i.e., univocity/Enlightenment literality].[37]

First, note how transcendence is ruled out *a priori*, since nothing can break the wall of literality (but see the first criticism above). Second, Openness theologians are quite confident that none of the "traditional" transcendence passages (e.g., Is. 58:8) "refer to character differences between God and humans, not ontological or epistemological differences. For Isaiah, God is incomparable to humans in that he loves those who would not."[38] But the fact is that in context no such ethical limits are set down there; instead the passage wide openly refers to various epistemological features: hearing, seeking, finding, knowing, and thoughts. And how would ethical or character differences not be species of epistemology and ontology? Such can

[37] Sanders, *Risks*, 37.
[38] Ibid., 22.

only be narrowed artificially. But third, various Scriptures reveal the truth of incomprehensibilities beyond our categories. Even on Openness terms, God could express to us in human language the fact that His being and knowledge is categorically different from ours without specifying its content in univocal terms. That sort of revelation would look like these:

+ "Oh, the depth of the riches both of the wisdom and knowledge of God! How *unsearchable* are His judgments and *His ways past finding out!* For who has known the mind of the Lord? Or who has become His counselor?" (Rom. 11:33, 34).

+ "[T]o know the love of Christ which *passes knowledge;* that you may be filled with all the fullness of God. Now to Him who is able to do exceedingly abundantly above all that we ask or think, according to the power that works in us" (Eph. 3:19, 20).

Ironically, given the Openness argument for univocity, the rhetorical question "who has known the mind of the Lord" actually gets answered. *We* know the mind of God, since God can only speak univocally to us—or as Sanders says, "All that is possible for us to know is what God is like in relation to us. . . . The Lord our Creator and Redeemer is what God is really like in relation to us."[39] And once Christians embrace this aspect of the Enlightenment project as much as Openness theologians have, it does not take long before the Trinity and the Incarnation are booted. They, too, are much more interesting and complex than the mathematical simplicities of Aristotle and Descartes. Time will tell.

Given all of the above, it's evident that Openness theology is deeply committed to Enlightenment criteria for metaphor and reasoning. And yet, for all their complaints about Hellenism, they don't hesitate to embrace its revival in the Enlightenment and analytic philosophy of the twentieth century. Note this telling statement from William Haskers:

> Many of us have also found our philosophical home in the analytic tradition. And it is simply a fact that the habits of thought engendered by that tradition are not particularly congenial to the theory of divine timelessness. . . . A possible comment on this is that the current preference for analytical modes of thought is merely a contingent fact about a segment of our philosophical community, and is no more to be given

---

[39] Ibid., 30.

unthinking allegiance than were the Platonic-mystical inclinations of some earlier generations of philosophers. The comment is just, but the problem is inescapable. One can only view the world, and God, from the place where one does in fact stand.[40]

One can reject Platonic categories of divine eternalism and still be amazed at such an admission. It not only historicizes and trivializes the entire Openness contribution, it also highlights the problem of so much contemporary Christian philosophy. We're still complacent enough not to try to clarify the biblical antithesis and peel away both Hellenistic and Enlightenment assumptions about modality, knowledge, and language. We spend so much time still aping the Baalists and calling what we're doing new and improved biblical theology.

If my criticisms above have any merit, then we are faced with a very powerful irony: Openness theology claims to allow for divine creativity and fresh aesthetic insights:

> If the classical view of divine foreknowledge is correct, there are positive things humans can do that God cannot do. We can enjoy novelty— new songs, fresh poems, original paintings, unanticipated twists in stories, spontaneous play, creative dances, and so on. We can wonder, experience adventure, and enjoy surprises when encountering the unexpected. Though the Bible is explicit in ascribing many of these experiences to God, the classical view rules them out. Is this not limiting God?[41]

The glory of new songs and fresh poems and creativity, though, depend upon the sort of metaphor and aesthetic dimension mathematically precluded by Openness methods. Its core assumptions about metaphor and reason are the very things that destroy genuine creativity. Descartes and Hobbes and Locke could not have inspired a poetic tradition (and did not); they were inherently hostile to it. Everything becomes mathematicized and tamed, including the Triune God. One cannot hold to Openness assumptions and grasp the depths of poetry. And no genuine artist could ever be impressed with Openness simplicities. On the other hand, historic Orthodoxy, stripped of any lingering Hellenism, is the very heart of beauty, goodness, and truth. Whereas Openness ends up denying new songs and fresh poems and

---

[40] Haskers, God, Time, 181.
[41] Boyd, Possible, 129.

creativity to *both God and man,* Christian orthodoxy has the metaphorical depth to embrace the divine mysteries to such an extent that God can control all things, preserve genuine human "give-and-take" freedom, and still be the transcendent model of true adventure, play, and creativity in ways "past finding out" (Rom. 11:33), ways that wonderfully "pass knowledge" (Eph. 3:19), such that human creativity can only shadow.

But to get there, we can't fawn after paganism, worrying, as Boyd does, that we are more and "more out of sync...with our culture."[42] Instead we must be willing to be fools before the narrow perspectives of both Hellenism and Enlightenment thought: "Let no one deceive himself. If anyone among you seems to be wise in this age, let him become a fool that he may become wise. For the wisdom of this world is foolishness with God" (1 Cor. 3:18–19).

[42] Ibid., 108.

3

Atlas Shrugged:
Worshipping in the Beauty of Holiness

R.C. Sproul, Jr.

Postmodernism, the current mask of skepticism and unbelief, has a host of different fields in which it seeks to spread its uncertainty. Though the term is itself a kind of power grab, the philosophical equivalent of "new and improved," it is neither new nor an improvement. It is instead just another narrative, like all the others that preceded it, telling us that we don't know what we're saying.

It makes its assault on literature under the guise of deconstructionism, arguing that there is no meaning inherent in a given text, and that the event of reading is the collision of the reader's and the writer's unknown, unknowable, yet all-powerful political and cultural presuppositions. That is, Shakespeare wrote and I enjoy *The Taming of the Shrew* only because we're a pair of reactionary misogynists. And Toni Morrison writes what she writes, and I don't enjoy it, only because she suffers under the brutal oppression of reactionary misogynists like me.

In the field of history, postmodernism gives us a clean slate, taking the essentially valid premise that the victors write the history books to an absurd extreme. It also gives us historical fiction. If history is just the imaginations of things past (by old white guys), why not write a different history? In *this* one the oppressed will be the heroes and the benefactors of mankind. The telegraph is as much the invention of an ancient tribe from Pago Pago as it is the work of Samuel Morse. Probably more so, because Samuel Morse was one of them, the bad guys.

Postmodernism, however, is a weed that not only sprouts its noxious presence like so much kudzu in a host of assorted fields of inquiry; it also attacks at the roots of civilization itself. It operates beneath the surface, destroying the soil that builds the world. Beneath civilization is the bedrock, that triad of virtues that civilization is supposed to be built upon goodness, truth, and beauty. And it even gets beneath the bedrock and seeks to ambush the foundation of the pillars, God Himself.

It was Plato who posited goodness, truth, and beauty as the ultimate goods. He described these three as the font of virtue, in the sense that all other virtues are only virtues insofar as they serve these three. These three alone, in the mind of Plato, are properly ends in themselves. They are to be pursued for their own sake. Courage is also a virtue, not in itself, but only because it serves goodness, truth, and beauty. Fidelity likewise. But these three are good because they are good. They are true because they are true. And they are beautiful because they are beautiful. These are the givens, much like all Euclidean geometry is built upon the presuppositions of the point, the line, and the plane.

Plato was, in a limited sense, right. He, by the common grace of the one true God, stumbled upon three of the fundamental attributes of God Himself. God, though Plato perhaps would not concede this, is the foundation upon which these pillars stand. He is the font of the font, and the end of the ends. Without Him, these three fall into boundless space. Such is the goal of postmodernism, that these three eternal virtues would go the way of all flesh. Postmodernism is modernity's destructive child, which has already successfully paved the university paradise and put up a polyglot.

Few of us, however, live in the university. Postmodernism, for all its apparent obtuseness, is not restricted to the ivory tower. The assault in our workaday world is more direct, less nuanced. We inhabit a world in which everyone is convinced of this unassailable truth, that there is no truth. It is perhaps our most widely held creed. Our epistemology is this, that there is no epistemology. We know only one thing, that we can know nothing. And this in turn vitiates any ethic. Even if we wanted to assert an objective ethic, to say X is good, non-X is bad, we cannot as long as there is no objective truth. With a relativistic epistemology, we cannot say that it is true that X is good. And so we have embraced as good the belief that there is no good. Everything is but a matter of point of view. And just as it would be false to affirm that there is such a thing as false, so it is wrong to affirm that there is such a thing as wrong. I know, I know. But you can't hold these folks to logical consistency, as if that had anything to do with truth. Affirm to the relativist, whether epistemological or moral or both, that the system contradicts itself and you receive not a puzzled look, but a happy smile. Consistency, after all, is the hobgoblin of little minds, and contradiction is the hallmark of truth (which, of course, doesn't exist).

In the Church, however, we are alarmed. If there is no truth, then Jesus isn't it. If there is no good, then not even the Father is good. When we finally realized that the dinosaurs of modernism that we were fighting had been dead for quite some time, we turned our attention to the Son that sat upon the throne. We have argued vociferously and compellingly that there is indeed truth, and that it can be known. We have argued with equal ardor that right and wrong are real and not mere personal or societal phantoms. But when it comes to beauty, we follow the beat of their drummer. When beauty is relegated to mere taste, when postmodernism insists that there is no objective transcendent standard for beauty, the Church has responded with a resounding "Amen."

The problem, however, is the same. We cannot put truth out to pasture because it is grounded in the very nature of God. When Jesus says, "I am the truth," He means it. He is not truth to some and not truth to others. He is truth immutably. When the heavenly angels sing "Holy, Holy, Holy is the Lord God of hosts," they are describing His character. They are not suggesting that He will seem righteous to some, and be righteous and wicked to others, and be wicked in the same time and in the same relationship. Neither are they praising God that He is holy now, while in the back of their minds worrying about what will happen when that all changes. He is immutably holy. And when the Scripture tells us to worship the Lord in the beauty of that holiness, it is likewise ascribing beauty not as a mere descriptive term, but as His very nature. His beauty is not like ours, subject to the vicissitudes of time. God is not in His heaven applying Retin-A to keep the wrinkles at bay. He is beauty immutably. If He is beauty, then our duty is to have our understanding of beauty reflect Him. We are not free to make up our own understanding anymore than we can make up our own sense of truth, or of goodness. We are no more to call that which is ugly beautiful than we are to call that which is evil good.

And neither is God. As the Church has wrestled with the

relationship of God to His world, so it has wrestled with the relationship of God to God. For instance, when the Scripture tells us that God is good, what is it telling us? Is it saying that there is a standard of righteousness that precedes God's own existence? Is it saying that goodness is something that transcends even God Himself? If so, from whence did this standard come? Is there a god above God, a creator of the measuring stick, by which God is found to be so pure? On the other hand, is goodness merely a creation of God? Does He have authority over goodness, such that tomorrow He could determine that it is wicked to give to the poor and righteous to steal from them? Is God *sub lego*, under law, or *supra lego*, above law? The Church has always answered that He is neither. Rather God is autonomous, a law unto Himself. God is not below law, such that He is good because He abides by some standard that He did not create. Neither is He above it such that He may change it at will. Good is good because it corresponds to God's character. And God is good because that is His character. He cannot call evil good, for this would be to contradict Himself.

The same principle applies to beauty. We do not say that God is beautiful because there is an eternal standard of beauty that transcends God, but to which He is favorably compared. Neither is beauty a mere creation of God's, with which He may, by right of ownership, do as He pleases. Beauty is beauty because God is beauty. He is, in a word, auto-aesthetica, beauty unto Himself.

He is so immutably. His goodness, His truth, His beauty precede the created order, and so in no way can be modified by it. And this is where it runs up against the Openness of God theologians.

Like postmodernism, Openness is not new. And like postmodernism, its disavowals of any relationship to its older cousins are just not true. Process theology grew out of the same graveyard of unbelief that was nineteenth-century liberalism. That is, the proponents of this idea that God changes came out of mainline, liberal institutions. Their tradition was one of unbelief. Like the arch-heretic Marcion who preceded them, their motivation was in part to distance themselves from the perceived nasty God of the Old Testament, and to cling to the sweet and tender God of the New. They had made a god in their own image, and when He didn't seem to match what they had created, they posited that He was at least trying.

The Openness theologians, however, come not from the ranks of rank unbelief, but from the Arminian wing of the Church. They dishonestly describe themselves as evangelicals, though they are in fact not even historical theists. Nevertheless, that is their "faith tradition."

One of the great troubles with Arminianism, or semi-Pelagianism, is that it wants to have it both ways. Man makes free decisions, such as choosing to embrace the gospel, and God knows the future. In the debates over this deviant view of the relationship between the will of man and the providence of God, many Reformed apologists have asked with greater and greater vigor, how can God know a future that is not settled? Openness theologians conceded the point and, in order to maintain the free will of man, jettisoned God's absolute foreknowledge of all future events. A small price to pay for freedom. They are simply Arminians who have chosen the door with the tiger.

God, according to these men, is of course to be excused. It is no fault of God's that He cannot know the unknowable. It hasn't happened yet, so how could He know? And these men will even argue that their conception of their God who knows not the future is even more grand than the omniscient knower-of-all-things who has always been the God of the Church. After all, their God has to be fast on His feet. He must adjust His plans and keep one step ahead of us, all without knowing what our next step will be.

But this god is not, in the end, too terribly grand. With the knowledge of the truth of what is yet future, we also must jettison the knowledge of beauty. Beauty becomes a beast in the hands of this ignorant God. And that ugliness will of necessity affect our worship. We cannot worship the Lord in the beauty of holiness if God does not know what is yet to come.

One of the reasons, I believe, that the Church has been so swift in abandoning any defense of the objective nature of beauty is that beauty is admittedly less easy to quantify than goodness or truth. Truth is that which corresponds to reality, and God has given all men rational and empirical faculties by which it might be known. Goodness is also comparatively easy to quantify. God has given us His Word, and that Word contains His law. And so we know that bad is any want of conformity to or transgression of the law of God.

But beauty, how do we measure that? If we seek to dissect beauty, to slice it thin and put it under the microscope, we will find that we will have killed it. One could certainly assign numbers to notes, and translate the Brandenburg Concerto into numbers, but everyone, even the greatest arithma-phile, recognizes that something significant is lost in the translation. There is something mysterious in beauty, just as there is much mysterious in God. Nevertheless, that God is beauty ends the debate over the relativity of beauty. If the speed of light is the constant in Einstein's universe, by which time and distance become relativized, so is God the necessary constant of beauty, both because He is beauty itself and because He is so immutably.

However mysterious beauty might be, like its opposite, we know it when we see or hear it. Even the crassest relativist knows he is lying when he claims that the random noises that escape from my heat pump are as beautiful as Pachelbel's Canon in D. We affirm the objectivity of beauty, at least in part, practically. We plant flowers instead of weeds; we hang paintings instead of inkblots, we put Bach on the stereo instead of the sounds of car wrecks.

And practicality is a big selling point for the Openness gurus. That is, they argue that part of what should appeal to us about this view is that it fits with our practice. We are told in the preface to *The Openness of God*, by Clark Pinnock and others, "We need a theology that is biblically faithful and intellectually consistent, and that reinforces, rather than makes problematic, our relational experience with God. The view of God presented in this book may seem new to those outside scholarly circles, where it is well known. But if we remember that it presents in a systematic way what most Christians already practice in their devotional lives, then it will not seem strange at all."

David Basinger, professor of philosophy at Roberts Wesleyan College is given the task in *The Openness of God* of explaining to the readers the practical implications of this view. While never addressing the issue of aesthetics or worship directly, he does address how this view affects our prayers, a vital part of our worship. His approach is to lay out the fundamentals of the classical view on a subject, such as prayer, and the view of the process theologians, and then try to place his own view in the safe confines of the reasonable middle. For those who hold to a fixed future, we of course have no reason to pray our petitions, because everything has already been decided. For the poor process crowd, there is again no reason to pray petitionally, because God can't do anything anyway. In the Openness view, when we pray, we are graciously invited by God to participate with Him in creating an unknown future. Where is this alleged middle ground?

Unlike proponents of specific sovereignty [the view that God has ordained whatsoever comes to pass], we do not believe that God can unilaterally ensure that all and only that which he desires to come about in our world will in fact occur. We maintain, rather, that since God has chosen to create a world in which we possess significant freedom, and since we can be significantly free only if he does not unilaterally control how this freedom is utilized, God voluntarily forfeits control over earthly affairs in those cases where he allows us to exercise this freedom.

However, unlike proponents of process theism, we maintain that God does retain the right to intervene unilaterally in earthly affairs. That is, we believe that freedom of choice is a gift granted to us by God and thus God retains the power and moral prerogative to inhibit occasionally our ability to make voluntary choices to keep things on track.

God's sovereignty and man's free will, in other words, is sort of like a money market savings account at the bank. It's really God's money, but He can only write three checks on it a month.

What does this do to our worship? Worship is that dance of beauty where we gather in the presence of God to renew covenant with Him. We begin that renewal in the context of remembering the great and gracious acts of God done on our behalf in the past. Just as God reminds the children of Israel before giving the law at Sinai that He is the one who brought them up out of the house of bondage, so we when we gather we remember God's great acts for us. Many of the Psalms of David, which were sung in the worship of the people of God from the time they were written, consist of retelling God's great deeds. But there's a problem. As we proclaim God's praises for His graces, we find in this view that He really hasn't done that much. We cannot praise Him in His sanctuary, for He has been passive. We cannot thank Him for confusing the enemies of Gideon, but rather should praise Gideon. We cannot praise Him for drying up the Red Sea; apparently He was surprised as Moses when it happened. Or at least, He did not know that the children of Israel would flee through His work safely, nor that the armies of Pharaoh would follow.

We are in the same boat. For what do we thank God in our day? Are we grateful to Him for the Christian who first told us of the work of Christ? By no means. He didn't know such would happen, much less bring it to pass. Do we thank Him for delivering us from all the dangers and uncertainties we have passed through? Not when they were also uncertainties to Him. Do I praise God for the great gift of the little blessings with which He has graced my home? Not a chance. My children exist merely because of decisions made by my dear wife and me, and the natural outworking thereof.

Our worship and our prayers, as we gather to renew covenant, however, do not center around the many blessings of God that flow out of that covenant, but rather from that which brings us into covenant with God, the work of Christ on the cross. We are gathering to remind ourselves that Jesus Christ, on Calvary, redeemed us such that we have peace with God. But here again we are left in the Openness view, with little to praise. The crucifixion of Christ did not happen in a vacuum. That event central to worship and to history happened in history, through the interconnected events of a host of human decisions. What if the Pharisees had gladly accepted the teaching of Jesus? Or suppose that Judas had freely chosen to not betray our Lord? Suppose that Pilate's uneasiness had caused him to merely rebuke Jesus? Suppose the crowds had, in an unanticipated fit of conscience, demanded that Barabbas be put to death instead of Jesus? Suppose Jesus had decided that He would prefer the simple life of being a carpenter? We are left with nothing for which we can praise God. Indeed, one can't help but wonder if somehow the Father were wringing His hands as He witnessed the cruelty pressed against His Son. We praise the Father for bringing to pass our redemption. But in the Openness view, He did no such thing. Our worship is not merely diminished, but utterly deflated. The beauty of the gospel is lost, for it is nothing but a series of random, unpredictable events.

Of course we also miss out on the delightful way in which He brought to pass the fulfillment of the prophecies concerning our Savior. What brings Joseph and Mary to Bethlehem but the rapacious tax of the Caesar? How do we have one person being a product of Bethlehem, Nazareth, and Galilee, save for the inter-working of a host of human decisions? The same applies, however, to all the prophecies of Scripture. When Daniel reveals the meaning of Nebuchadnezzar's nightmare in Daniel 2, he presents a very specific future. Medo-Persia would destroy mighty Babylon. Greece would follow as the next great world power. And then would come the Romans. How many human decisions went into all that brought to pass this succession of four great world powers? How clear was this prophecy? Daniel tells us,

"The dream is certain, and its interpretation is sure" (Dan. 2:45b). It appears that God knows the future after all.

Our worship begins with acknowledging our sins and God's many graces to us. The next step in the dance is remembering the work of Christ on our behalf, in fulfillment of all the promises, from Genesis 3:15 to Malachi 4:4–6. But we do not stop there, as God's revelation does not stop there. Finding ourselves having been blessed by the omnipotent, omniscient God of the universe, finding ourselves at peace with Him, we then look to the fullness of the future blessings of God. We worship by stepping into the fullness of time, and tasting of the consummation of the kingdom. Daniel gives us a glimpse of this, as he explains the last part of Nebuchadnezzar's dream,

> And in the days of these kings the God of heaven will set up a kingdom which shall never be destroyed; and the kingdom shall not be left to other people; it shall break in pieces and consume all these kingdoms, and it shall stand forever. Inasmuch as you saw that the stone was cut out of the mountain without hands, and that it broke in pieces the iron, the bronze, the clay, the silver and the gold—the great God has made known to the king what will come to pass after this. (Dan. 2:44–45a)

The beauty of worship reaches its apex in the certainty of the consummation of the kingdom. We rejoice because we know that all things will be made right, that we will be like Him, and that we will see Him as He is, because we know that on that great day every knee will bow and every tongue confess that Jesus Christ is Lord. We rejoice because we know that He will wipe away every tear. And it all reduces to a *maybe* in the Openness of God view. Instead of hearing His promise, we gather to hear God's hopes or dreams. Instead of coming to rest in His power we are called to gird up our loins to try to bring about His ends. Instead of finding peace in knowing what will come to pass, we gather to worry with the Not-So-Great Worrier in the sky. Yes, as they promise, we meet a god who is more accessible, more connected to us, because we meet not the Captain of the Lord's Hosts, but a god who is, as a prophet, one of their own, put it, "a slob just like us." We are not the adorned bride of the reigning King, but rather the random collection of followers of Him who is not the Lord of the Dance, but who is making things up as He goes along.

And there is the key to beauty and to worship—intentionality. It stands on the opposite end of the spectrum with randomness. Beauty requires an intentioned marrying of harmony and complexity. The universe is beautiful, and declares the glory of God, in part because of the dance of the stars, and the dance of the subatomic particles, and the dance of the subatomic particles in the dancing stars. Despite the claims of Heisenberg, these are not the random movements of purposeless matter. And history reflects the glory of God in much the same way, as God weaves together a staggering array of particulars, from the rise and fall of empires to the pair of socks that I am wearing, into a delicate dance of beauty. All these things come to pass not because God has let go, but because He hasn't.

In removing God from the scene in His role as the ultimate cause of whatsoever comes to pass, we are left with no ultimate cause. We are left with no intentionality, but only the random collision of time, space, and matter. Openness theologians are worse than materialist scientists who stretch our credulity to the limits of the universe by claiming that all reality is an accident. Instead they argue that all reality is an accident and that God has merely watched. They are deists who deny that God even wound up the clock. They have robbed God of His glory, and bid us to rejoice in it.

There is, however, good news. The Openness theologians at least claim to be open about their openness, finding even the Process theology that they say does not describe them as acceptable. Basinger argues,

> I do not consider our model to be logically superior to all others in the sense that I believe ours to be the only self-consistent, comprehensive model that can justifiably be claimed by its proponents to be a plausible perspective on the relationship between God and the world. Nor do I believe the Open model to be experientially superior in the sense that I believe it to be the only model that any thoughtful, sincere person could find reasonably satisfying. Just as not all children will agree on the most appealing parenting style, and not all students will agree on the most appealing teaching style, not all Christians will agree on the most appealing type of divine-human interaction. And I see no objective basis for denying that proponents of other models can justifiably continue to view their perspectives on the relationship between God and our world as the most fulfilling personally.

POTATO, POTAWTO

But there is a *profound* difference. The good news is that we need not bow down to the idol these men have created in their own fevered imaginations. We can pray with confidence that in His grace He will not allow His redeemed to fall into this damnable heresy. Indeed, as we continue to worship the God who not only knows but also determines the future, we can pray that He would destroy the idolatrous works of iniquity and the workers thereof. We can be confident not that our prayers will change the sovereign, efficacious will of God Most High, but that He will, as He has promised, vindicate His own name, to His everlasting glory. And when He has brought the dance of history to a close then we will dance with Him, at the great, final, and certain marriage feast of the Lamb.

TRUTH

4

Liberals in Drag

Ben R. Merkle

Contrary to the way they often speak, the advocates of the Openness of God view have not necessarily been plowing exciting new territory. As Solomon put it, "That which has been is what will be, that which is done is what will be done. There is nothing new under the sun. Is there anything of which it may be said, 'See this is new'? It has already been in ancient times" (Eccl. 1:9–10). The Preacher knew this well, having experienced his own share of vain follies, and his words speak to the matter at hand. The Openness of God doctrine is merely a re-hash of some of the more obnoxious parts of the theology of six-teenth-century Socinus. Or, more recently, the Openness of God view is a baptized version of what has been parading about the University of Chicago for the last fifty years under the heading of Process theology. This chapter will attempt to point out the truth of Solomon's saying, "there is nothing new under the sun." The Openness of God teaching is an old heresy.

SOCINIANISM

In the early years of the Reformation Calvin had great hope for the possibilities of the advance of Protestant doctrine within Poland. The Polish King, Sigusmund Augustus, had joyfully received regular en-couragement and advice from Geneva. In fact, Calvin dedicated his commentary on the Book of Hebrews to the King, who also had Calvin's *Institutes* read to him twice a week and expounded on by an Italian pastor.[1] At the time, many viewed Poland as having the possi-bility of growing into a thoroughly Protestant nation where Reformed

---

[1] Ronald Wallace, *Calvin, Geneva & the Reformation* (Eugene: Wipf and Stock Pub-lishers, 1998), 154.

theology could truly take root and thrive. Unfortunately, even within
the lifetime of Calvin, this proved not to be the case. The Polish people became quite taken with anti-Trinitarian theology, and soon
formed a strong Unitarian-Anabaptist community, later taking the
name of their most influential teacher, Faustus Socinus.

Faustus was born in Siena, Italy, in 1539. His uncle, Laelius Socinus,
had been an influential theologian, known for experimenting with
anti-Trinitarian teachings and other heretical whims. Laelius had
spent time in theological discussion with Calvin, Melanchthon, and
Bullinger. Calvin had warned him of the danger of his teachings, but
to no avail. Laelius died, unrepentant, in 1562, and Faustus proceeded
to pick up where his uncle had left off. Operating with a highly rationalistic hermeneutic, Faustus Socinus experimented with a number of
Christological heresies while living in Lyons, Florence, and Basel,
eventually settling in Poland with the already-formed Unitarian
church. Although he refused to be rebaptized by the church in
Poland, it wasn't very long before he was considered their most
famous spokesman.

Along with his anti-Trinitarian teachings, Socinus held to a Pela-
gian view of the atonement (the crucifixion served as an example for
us, but forgiveness was found through our own repentance and good
works), denying both predestination and foreknowledge. In the late
seventeenth century, Francis Turretin took many swings at the teachings of Socinus in his *Institutes of Elenctic Theology*. In fact, Turretin's *Institutes* reads like a cosmic game of tetherball, with Socinus being
swatted for a whirl on every other page. Although Socinus held to a
number of other heresies, it's his view of God's foreknowledge that is
the most relevant here. Turretin describes Socinus's position quite
well.

> Another question of greater importance refers to future contingent
> things, the knowledge of which the Socinians endeavor to wrest from
> God in order to establish more easily the indifference of free will (its
> freedom from all necessity, even from that which is usually placed on it
> by the foreknowledge of God). . . . they openly withdraw from him the
> knowledge of future contingencies as not being in the class of knowable
> things, saying either that he does not know them absolutely or only in-
> determinately and probably. Socinus says, "Since, then there is no rea-
> son, no passage of Scripture, from which it can be clearly gathered that
> God knew all things which happened before they happened, we must
> conclude that we are by no means to assert such a foreknowledge of

God, especially when both many reasons and sound testimony are not
wanting, utterly opposed to it."[2]

A denial of predestination was not enough for Socinus. If God still
had a perfect foreknowledge of the future, then the future was written
in permanent ink somewhere. How could a man's will have the sort of
freedom that Socinus required if the future was set in the concrete of
foreknowledge? For Socinus, a slave to his rationalism, the only sen-
sible thing to do was to deny the concrete. His god must lack even a
perfect foreknowledge.

PROCESS THEOLOGY

Socinus's teaching dominated Poland into the eighteenth century and
served as a precursor to the rationalistic criticism of the nineteenth
century. One particular sect that grew out of nineteenth-century criticism was Process theology, the brain-child of Alfred Whitehead
(1861–1947). Whitehead, the son of a vicar of the Church of England,
was a mathematician and philosopher of the early twentieth century.
Whitehead began his dabbling in theology by proposing his own theories on the nature of time and how events occur within time. For
Whitehead, process was fundamental. Time, instead of flowing like a
steady stream, "comes into being in little droplets."[3] At each moment
all other actual entities are intuitively felt (in Whitehead's terminology "prehended"). As the forming moment culminates, enjoying its
subjective immediacy, it then prehends all other actual entities. This
metaphysic, although not very exciting as conversation around the
coffee table, was applied vigorously to the area of theology by one of
Whitehead's students, Charles Hartshorne.

Although Whitehead had applied his speculation to theology, he
had always been a mathematician at heart, and his theological application never seemed to be the stuff that sermons are made of. Hartshorne, on the other hand, took the metaphysic of Whitehead and the
description of deity that Socinus had provided, and with the two
made a religion that any self-respecting, rationalistic, abortion doctor
could belong to. Hartshorne, although never coming close to

[2] Francis Turretin, *Institutes of Elenctic Theology* (Phillipsburg: Presbyterian and Reformed Publishing, 1992) v. 2, 208.
[3] John Cobb and David Griffin, *Process Theology* (Philadelphia: Westminster Press,
1976), 14.

pretending that Scripture was authoritative (or even relevant for that matter), decked Process theology in a Christian party dress. What had been philosophy with Whitehead was religion with Hartshorne.

Hartshorne clearly saw Process thought as a Socinian Revival.

> [H]ave we any other reason for rejecting that old Socinian proposition that even the highest conceivable form of knowledge is of the past-and-definite *as* the past-and-definite and of the future and partly indefinite *as* future and partly indefinite?... Is God all-knowing? Yes, in the Socinian sense. Never has a great intellectual discovery passed with less notice by the world than the Socinian discovery of the proper meaning of omniscience. To this day works of reference fail to tell us about this. ... As the Socinians said, once for all, future events, events that have not yet happened, are not there to be known, and the claim to know them could only be false.[4]

The nonexistence of the future is important for Process theologians for the same reason that the impossibility of foreknowledge was important for Socinus. A future in concrete means that in some way all actions are restricted. Since Process theology requires the same sort of autonomous will as Socinianism, Process theology has also sought the same solution by denying any knowledge of the future.

His exegesis, though claiming to belong ever so vaguely to Christianity, never depended on Scripture. Rather, Hartshorne and current Process adherents only concern themselves with the criticisms that they receive from philosophy, dismissing any appeals to Scripture as the rambling of ignorant fundamentalists. I'll describe Hartshorne's impression of God in the next section in order to draw comparisons to the Openness of God as we go, but it is critical to remember that the Socinians sacrificed the foreknowledge of God for the sake of being able to have a free will that has absolutely no competition. We will see both Process and Openness theologians do the same.

THE OPENNESS OF GOD

Although disposing of several of Process thought's more alarming accessories, several miscreants have snitched Process theology's major selling point, a denial of God's foreknowledge, in order to make room

---

[4] Charles Hartshorne, *Omnipotence and Other Theological Mistakes* (SUNP: Albany, NY, 1984) 26–27; 38–39.

for a rationalist's free will, given it a complete makeover, and plopped it down in the center of orthodoxy's camp. Under the guise of the Openness of God, this heresy has assumed the position of the third string basketball player, sprinting desperately about the court looking for reaffirming high fives and someone to tell him that he really does belong out here on the floor.[5] It's often confusing whether the authors of the Openness books are attempting to convince the rest of Christendom or themselves that they are really within the bounds of orthodoxy.

Both Openness proponents and Process philosophers begin their case with the accusation that the classical orthodox description of God's omnipotence and omniscience is some sort of Hellenistic love-child. "For it is our contention that the 'theological mistakes' in question give the word *God* a meaning which is not true to its import in sacred writings or in concrete religious piety. This result came about partly because theologians in medieval Europe and the Near East were somewhat learned in Greek philosophy and largely ignorant of any other philosophy."[6] Hartshorne then goes on to describe Plato's proposition in *The Republic* that to be perfect must mean to be completely unchanging and how, he believes, this platonic presupposition remains at the foundation of historical Christianity. John Sanders writes an entire chapter making this same charge in the book *The Openness of God*. When Sanders asks where the orthodox position comes from he gives his own explanation. "The answer, in part, is found in the way Christian thinkers have used certain Greek philosophical ideas."[7] It's odd how both these heresies seem to forget that it was classical orthodoxy that stood for the incarnation.

WHAT IS A REAL CHOICE?

From here both Process and Openness theologians begin to wax eloquent on the virtues of a mutable deity. Hartshorne begins with an ugly portrayal of the historical view of God. "Is it the highest ideal of power to rule over puppets who are permitted to think they make

---

[5] For an example of this behavior, see Pinnock's letter to *Christianity Today*, Feb. 9, 1998, available at http://www.christianityonline.com/ct/8t2/8t2043.html.

[6] Hartshorne, *Omnipotence*, 1.

[7] Clark Pinnock et al, *The Openness of God* (Downers Grove: InterVarsity Press, 1994), 59.

decisions but who are really made by another to do exactly what they do? For twenty centuries we have had theologians who seem to say yes to this question."[8] He is quite clear in his contempt for historical Christianity. "No theologian was ever more committed to the concept that I . . . am criticizing than the Christian Jonathan Edwards. And he thought, with considerable justification, that he represented the tradition."[9] Hartshorne refuses to worship an all-powerful God, and instead demands a god who will let *him* play too. "But how is it if God is the supreme, however benevolent, tyrant? Can we worship a God so devoid of generosity as to deny us a share, however humble, in determining the details of the world, as minor participants in the creative process that is reality?"[10]

This last quote describes the central connection between Process theology and the Openness of God, and, incidentally, the driving force behind both. Hartshorne asks to be allowed in on the "creative process." But his definition of this creative process includes the reason he wants in so badly. This creative process is *reality*. In other words, to be *real*, in the sense that your existence matters, means to be taking part in that culminating moment of the process, prehending all other actual entities, as it were. However, we must understand that at the culminating moment all players enter the moment on equal footing. The Holy Spirit may influence me, but it is just as likely that I will influence Him. If someone immutable were to step into our moment of prehension, it would ruin all of the fun. For God to enter the culminating moment as an immutable being would be like the bully down the street entering our game of marbles with the precondition that he couldn't lose any marbles. Obviously we wouldn't want to play marbles under these restrictions. After all, it wouldn't be a *real* game. Now if we reason to bigger and better things, we will see that a God of this nature would rob our lives of reality. Hartshorne requires a god whose marbles are at risk too.

So we see that to be a part of the process Hartshorne demands mutability. If one is not changed through the process then one was never in the process. Not only must this position elevate man to co-creator, but it must bring God down an infinite number of notches. "According

---

[8] Hartshorne, *Omnipotence*, 12.
[9] Ibid., 19.
[10] Ibid., 16.

to Whitehead, the basic relationship is 'prehension' which in the most concrete form (called 'physical prehension') is defined as 'feeling of feeling,' meaning the manner in which one subject feels the feelings of one or more other subjects. In other words, 'sympathy' in the most literal sense.... God is said to know the world by physical prehensions, in other words by feeling the feelings of all the subjects composing that world."[11] God must be another player in this culminating moment where we all influence each other. In order for God to be *real* he must be subject to being changed by me. He must be mutable.

On the Openness side, Pinnock, although skipping the physics and mathematics of Whitehead, jumps straight into an argument that parallels Hartshorne. For Pinnock, only an Open view gives us a God who allows our lives to be *real* and *meaningful*.

> We believe that the Bible presents an open view of God as living and active, involved in history, relating to us and changing in relation to us. We see the universe as a context in which there are real choices, alternatives and surprises. God's openness means that God is open to the changing realities of history, that God cares about us and lets what we do impact him. Our lives make a difference to God—they are truly significant.[12]

Again there is this assumption that unless God is in some way affected by my choices, then my choices can't be *real* or *significant*.

Augustine dealt with this foolishness when he addressed Cicero's same concern. "Now, against the sacrilegious and impious darings of reason, we assert both that God knows all things before they come to pass, and that we do by our free will whatsoever we know and feel to be done by us only because we will it.... But it does not follow that, though there is for God a certain order of all causes, there must therefore be nothing depending on the free exercise of our own wills, for our wills themselves are included in that order of causes which is certain to God, and is embraced by His foreknowledge, for human wills are also causes of human actions; and He who foreknew all the causes of things would certainly among those causes not have been ignorant of our wills."[13]

[11] Ibid., 27–8.

[12] Pinnock, *Openness*, 104.

[13] Augustine, *The City of God* (Peabody: Hendrickson Publishers, 1995) Nicene and Post Nicene Fathers, vol. 2, 91.

DIVINE INFLUENCE

In Process thought, God's ability to control history is limited to His ability to influence or urge us: "the power of God is persuasive, not controlling."[14] At that moment of prehension, a man feels the divine will urging him one way or another, but what the man does with that urge is entirely up to him. The possibility of man rejecting the urges of God exists because otherwise our choices wouldn't be real. "God did not bring about creatures such as us, with our great capacity for discordant self-determination and destructive instrumental value, simply because freedom is in itself a great value, but because beings capable of the values we enjoy must necessarily have these other capacities."[15]

Openness advocates give a similar description of divine interactions with this world. God doesn't manhandle Christians, He *urges* them. "The contention, rather, is only that God, as a *general rule*, must allow choice to be voluntary in the sense that it is free from coercive divine manipulation."[16] God doesn't have a plan for our lives. As John Sanders puts it—he has goals. "It is God's desire that we enter into a give-and-take relationship of love, and this is not accomplished by God's forcing his blueprints on us. Rather, God wants us to go through life together with him, making decisions together. Together we decide the actual course of my life."[17] But Sanders points out that there is a hitch. "Regarding the leading of the Spirit, the risk model implies that we may or may not fail to understand the Spirit's direction. We may not understand what God expects of us in a particular instance. We may not accurately grasp the divine wisdom God attempts to give us for some problem. God will do all he can to help us, but since God is dependent on us for some things there is no guarantee that we will properly appropriate the divine wisdom. . . . The deeper our personal relationship with God develops, however, the better we experience his love, which enables us to better understand how we should live and better give ourselves in loving service to God. In so doing we follow his leading."[18] Sanders makes the same point as Process theology, only

---

[14] Cobb and Griffin, *Process*, 69.

[15] Ibid., 74–75.

[16] David Basinger, *The Case for Freewill Theism* (Downers Grove: Intervarsity Press, 1996), 36.

[17] Sanders, John, *The God Who Risks* (Downers Grove: Intervarsity Press, 1998), 276–77.

[18] Ibid., 278.

Sanders removes all of the heady philosophical terminology and re-places it with evangelical Christianese. Instead of "prehending all ac-tualities," we have a "personal relationship."

Interestingly, both Openness and Process theologians see this shift in thinking as a move from a masculine bias of our perception of God to a more feminine way of conceiving of Him. Pinnock alludes to this in a footnote as he describes how God, instead of clinging to His right to dominate, would rather invite us all to be His partners.[19] In his footnote he points out that this is a conception that feminists are more likely to embrace, "having experienced the male dominating power."[20] Hartshorne devotes several pages to this same point. "The feminist's complaint that they have been asked to worship a male deity seems pertinent and well founded.... Much more appropriate is the idea of a mother, influencing, but sympathetic to and hence influenced by, her child and delighting in its growing creativity and freedom."[21]

Openness theologians frequently try to distinguish themselves from Process theologians on the question of how much power God can wield by insisting that Openness describes a God that, though usually limiting His interaction with us to that of urging, is still capa-ble of, and sometimes does use, actual coercion. We are free because He chooses to give us the room to make free choices, but at any point, if things get hairy, He can interrupt our freedom to straighten things out. We are like the small child, sitting on the lap of his father who has allowed us to take the steering wheel and given us the thrill of com-plete control of the family station wagon. We are *really* steering. But at any moment, if we should steer onto the shoulder or cross the cen-terline, our father could right our mistake, though robbing us of the privilege of being in *real* control: "Freewill theists acknowledge that God does not control much of what occurs. However, unlike process theists, they are adamant in their belief that this is the result of a moral choice, not an external restriction."[22]

William Hasker, while discussing the relationship between how much power God can exert and how much foreknowledge God has, puts it this way—"Formally the two theories [Process and Openness] are in agreement here; God knows what is logically possible for him to

[19] Pinnock et al, *Openness*, 113.
[20] Ibid., 192.
[21] Hartshorne, *Openness*, 58.
[22] Basinger, *Freewill*, 36.

know, and this does not include what depends on the future free actions of his creatures. But according to free will theism, God is able to
know quite a lot more than according to process theism, because he is
able to do more to ensure the completion of his plans."[23] According to
Hasker, the Open God can know more than the Process God because
He has a freer hand in controlling our lives. But even this distinction
is called into question by Openness theologian David Basinger. In his
essay *Divine Power: Do Process Theists Have a Better Idea?*, Basinger suggests that the limitations put on God by Process theists are actually
inconsistent with the premises of Process theism. In the end Basinger
concludes that it is consistent with the premises of Process theism
that the possibility exists of God controlling on the same level as the
Open God, rather than simply influencing our decisions. "In short,
while there may well be good reasons why the process God *would*
never control our behavior through psychological manipulation, I see
no reason to deny that such control is possible."[24] With this it would
seem possible that the Process God and the Open God are both capable of the same influence (although Basinger would strongly deny it).

DIFFERENCES

One of the quite comic things about reading books from the Openness genre is the fact that Openness authors all feel an obligation to
explain, quite frequently, why the theology that they are advocating is
not Process theology. The effect is reminiscent of the panic-stricken
boy who, upon merely seeing the face of his mother, immediately ex-
claims, "I wasn't playing with matches, honest I wasn't." The very denial of the charge is enough to make us all a bit nervous.

Openness writers tend to distance themselves from Process theologians by essentially saying, "Yes, it's true that the God we are describing acts a lot like the God of Process theology, but the difference
is that our God doesn't *have* to act like that, He *chooses* to." The God
of Process theology is not ontologically separated from creation, but is
necessarily dependent on it. Openness advocates hold that God is separate from creation, but *chooses* to let Himself be dependent on it. Although, in the end, this distinction is far from sufficient to distance

[23] Pinnock et al, *Openness*, 199.
[24] Nash, Ronald, *Process Theology* (Grand Rapids: Baker Book House, 1987), 208.

Openness from Process, it must be admitted that this is a distinction. Openness theologians are quite critical of Process thought and do a good job of showing how a God who is ontologically dependent on creation is no God. Pinnock writes "Process theology denies ontological independence, maintaining that God needs the world as much as the world needs God. This drops out the crucial distinction between God and the world so central to the scriptural portrayal. It makes God too passive, able only to experience the world and to organize the elements that present themselves to him. The Bible describes God as more present to the world than that, as a deity working out salvation in history and moving all things forward to a new creation."[25]

To someone holding to the classical view of God's sovereignty this last quote can be quite frustrating. When one hears a proponent of Openness critiquing another position for making God "too passive" and insisting rather that we must believe in a God who is moving all things, a believer in God's sovereignty can only hear the pot calling "Black!" to every passing kettle. Distinctions like these can be hard to see to those who are some distance from the one holding the position in question. For instance, some time ago, while I was downtown doing evangelism, I ran into an odd-looking character who was getting ready to perform in a Drag show in one of the night clubs that evening. He was willing to talk, but when we began discussing the Bible's condemnation of homosexuality he stopped me to explain that he wasn't homosexual, he was merely a transgender-illusionary-artist. This distinction, though quite laughable for most of us, seemed the difference of night and day to this young man.

But, upon further consideration, both the drag queen and the Openness advocates have a point. Perhaps there is a difference between being a practicing homosexual and a drag queen, and a similar divide exists between Process and Openness. However, this doesn't remove the charge that Openness is Process theology's kid sister, because this point isn't a *consistent* point. If a man condemns homosexuality but then wears a dress and struts about to fulfill other men's homosexual fantasies, we have every right to question his self-professed distance from the gay crowd. The Openness authors find themselves in a similar awkward position, maligning God's sovereignty in an attempt to eke out their own autonomous wills, while claiming to be a

---

[25] Pinnock et al, *Openness*, 112.

member in good standing of Orthodoxy. And we must put the challenge to them: take off the dress or admit that you like boys.

Openness attempts to maintain its distances from Process by refusing to deny *creatio ex nihilo*, the doctrine that God created all things out of nothing. In many ways this doctrine refers to the very godness of God. When Paul wants to differentiate between the idols of the Athenians and the God of the Bible, it's God's creation that he appeals to. When Job questions God, God rebukes Him by pointing out His creative power. It's this Creator-creature divide that demands that we be worshippers and God be worshipped. Therefore, we ought to commend the Openness crowd for holding on to this vital attribute of God. But this attempt to cling to the remnants of orthodoxy puts the idea of Openness in a difficult bind. They now have a foot on the dock and one on a departing ocean liner. They must pick either Process or Orthodoxy, or they must fall into the salty sea. Their current straddle can't be maintained.

The reason is quite simple. Process philosophers have already shown what the price is for a man who wants a distant God. Whitehead was a brilliant philosopher, and he knew just what he was doing when he pieced together his cosmology. In order to achieve the sort of autonomy that he demanded, the destruction of *creatio ex nihilo* was absolutely necessary. Cobb and Griffin begin their introduction to Process theology by quoting Whitehead. "Whitehead noted that 'whatever suggests a cosmology, suggests a religion.'"[26] Whitehead knew that a religion is shaped by and depends upon its cosmology. Process theology takes what it thinks is true about life in this world (primarily, the fact that our wills are autonomous) and then reasons from these presuppositions to the cosmology that *must* exist to support this conclusion. They conclude, and rightly so, that this sort of will demands a god who didn't make us. They see clearly that they must step wide and clear of the idea of a creating God, because a creating God is necessarily a controlling God. "Process theology rejects the notion of *creatio ex nihilo*, if that means creation out of *absolute* nothingness. That doctrine is part and parcel of the doctrine of God as absolute controller."[27] Notice that even Process theists see no middle ground in this debate. God either created out of nothing and is

---

[26] Cobb and Griffin, *Process*, 13.
[27] Ibid., 65.

absolute controller of all or He didn't create out of nothing and He isn't all powerful. *Creatio ex nihilo* requires a sovereign God. To try and stand with a foot in both camps is to play the part of the heterosexual drag queen. And, unfortunately for the Openness advocate, to shift the metaphor, the man who stands between two armies gets shot at by both sides.

It's also interesting that the way the Openness theists set their priorities, in one very central way the Process God is better than the Openness God. If this ability to give creatures these "real" choices makes a god a better god, then wouldn't a god who is ontologically built that way be better than a god who just tries to act like that most of the time? For instance, if we assume that moral behavior is a virtue, then which kind of god would be a better god, a god who has moral behavior built into his ontology or a god who attempts to be moral most of the time, but sometimes falls a little short? Obviously, we would all conclude that the god who has moral perfection built into his very being is a better god. If, as Openness advocates assert, the mutability of God is a virtue, then a god whose mutability is built into his ontology (i.e., the god of Process theology) would seem to be a better god.

THE END OF THE ROAD

In order to distance themselves from Process theology, Openness proponents are forced to cram all sorts of inconsistencies into their theology. Process theologians, being completely free of the restraints of orthodoxy, have the luxury of being able to run their premises out to their logical conclusion. In many ways Process conclusions are the *reductio* that Openness is unwilling to swallow.

For instance, in both Process and Openness thinking freedom of choice is the test for a valid existence. Our lives aren't genuine if we aren't making *free* choices. Hartshorne, the Process theologian, takes this premise to its logical end. Because choice is the *sine qua non* of a valid existence, then infants, who give us no reason to believe that they are making any real choices, are certainly not to be considered valid life. "People are much more conscious of the process of decision making than the other animals need be supposed to be; but when it comes to that, how conscious is an infant in determining its activities? If chimpanzees have no freedom, how much freedom has an infant, which by every test that seems applicable is much less intelligent than an adult chimpanzee? (One would never guess this fact from what 'pro-lifers' say about a fetus being without qualification a person, so loose is their criterion for personality)."[28] Hartshorne later points out—"Physiologists know that its [a young child's] brain cells must have been matured definitely beyond the state of the newly born, or of a fetus, which some physiologist has compared to the brain cells of a pig."[29] The life of the fetus, for the Process theologian, has the equivalent worth of the life of a pig. Why? Because physiologists can tell us that this baby isn't making decisions, and its decision making ability, its ability to make "free" choices, are the measure of its worth. Hartshorne goes on to point out that in "nearly every society until recent centuries it was taken for granted that killing of human adults is a vastly more serious matter than even infanticide (if the latter is done by the parent or parents). This is enough to show that the idea of a fetus as a person in the full sense is not so plainly true that it can be used as a noncontroversial premise for political or moral conclusions."[30]

On the other hand, Christianity says that the child is a real life. Why? Because God decreed it so. Our choices are real and worthwhile because God decreed that they would be and the baby is real because God decreed that it would be. Openness advocates may side with classical orthodoxy on the issue of abortion, but they do so despite, and not because of, their premises. After all, only those who make choices are truly living a "real" existence.

OAKLAND AND MIAMI

While it is true that advocates of God's Openness are not conveying the exact same message as what has been taught by Process theologians, the Openness of God is certainly drinking from the same spring. Openness advocates attempt to distance themselves from Process theology by drawing a huge spectrum and setting orthodoxy (always portrayed as just a rehash of the Hellenistic ultra-transcendent god with no real interaction with this world) on one side and Process

---

[28] Hartshorne, *Omnipotence*, 13. Advocates of Process theology also make this point effectively in their dialogue with Open theists in Cobb and Pinnock, *Searching for an Adequate God* (Grand Rapids: Eerdmans, 2000), 21ff.

[29] Hartshorne, *Openness*, 100.

[30] Ibid., 101.

theology (an ultra-immanent god that isn't really a god) on the other. Then, after we have become thoroughly horrified at our only two options, we are supposed to be delighted to discover that Openness places itself in the exact middle, with a God who is both transcendent and immanent. Those of us who thought this was accomplished at Nicea are obviously still suffering from Hellenistic brainwashing.

Of course to place Hellenism and classical orthodoxy side by side on the spectrum is somewhat like calling Salt Lake City and Boston two cities in the Northeast. And to call Openness the happy medium between Calvinism and Process theology is similar to describing Oakland as lying halfway between San Francisco and Miami. Openness is truly Process theology's kid sister. Many of the Openness authors give hearty praise to the work that Process theists have done and even concede the heavy influence that Process thought has had on their own opinions. In his critique of Process theology, Pinnock devotes an entire paragraph to the wonderful insights that he has received from Hartshorne. So perhaps Mr. Pinnock ought to have the last word in this chapter.

> He [Charles Hartshorne] has taught me that thinking of God as literally *all*-powerful divests the finite universe of a degree of power. He has pressed the point that God, though unchanging in his character, is certainly able to change in response to a changing creation. In my theology, at least, God has used process thinkers to compel me to change certain ideas which I had and bring them up to scriptural standards.[31]

---

[31] Nash, *Process*, 317.

5

Open Theism and Divine Foreknowledge

John M. Frame

Open theists deny that God knows the future exhaustively. In their view, God is often ignorant about what will happen,[1] sometimes even mistaken.[2] He "expresses frustration"[3] when people do things He had not anticipated. He changes His mind when things don't go as He had hoped.[4] In these contentions, Open theists admittedly differ from "the classical view of God worked out in the western tradition"[5] that prevailed from the early Church fathers to the present with a few exceptions (such as the Socinian heresy.)[6] This classical view has been the position of all Christian theological traditions: Eastern Orthodox, Roman Catholic, and all forms of Protestantism.[7] It affirms that God

---

[1] Clark Pinnock, "Systematic Theology," in Pinnock, et al., *The Openness of God* (Downers Grove: InterVarsity Press, 1994), 121–24.

[2] John Sanders, *The God Who Risks: A Theology of Providence* (Downers Grove: InterVarsity Press, 1998), 132–33.

[3] Pinnock, *Openness*, 122.

[4] Richard Rice, "Biblical Support for a New Perspective," in ibid., 26–35.

[5] John Sanders, "Historical Considerations," in ibid., 59.

[6] For the connection between Open theism and Socinianism, see Robert B. Strimple, "What Does God Know?" in John Armstrong, ed., *The Coming Evangelical Crisis* (Chicago: Moody Press, 1996), 140–41, and Ben Merkle's essay in the present volume. Sanders doesn't mention the Socinians in his "Historical Considerations," Pinnock, *Openness*, 59–100.

[7] Gregory Boyd, in *The God of the Possible* (Grand Rapids: Baker, 2000), 116, says, "No ecumenical creed of the orthodox church has ever included an article of faith on divine foreknowledge," implying that the whole matter is an open question for Christianity. If by "ecumenical" creed we mean creeds like the Apostles' and Nicene that are accepted by all branches of Christianity, Boyd here makes a correct historical observation. But those ecumenical creeds are rather brief. They don't include articles on justification, for example. If we move ahead to the Reformation period, however, we encounter the Westminster Confession of Faith, which says that "In [God's] sight all things are open and manifest, His knowledge is infinite, infallible, and

has complete knowledge of everything that happens in the past, present, and future. Thus Open theism denies the historic Christian view of God's omniscience. The present article will discuss the major issues in the controversy between the classical view and the Open view.

LIBERTARIANISM

Why this radical divergence from the almost universal consensus of professing Christians? Open theists offer various reasons for their position, but the most fundamental, in my judgment, is that the classical view is inconsistent with human freedom in the libertarian sense. Since Open theists (also called "freewill theists") want to affirm human freedom in this sense, they must abandon the classical view of God's omniscience.

A free act in the libertarian sense[8] is an act that is utterly uncaused, undetermined. It is not caused by God, nor by anything in creation, nor even by the desires and dispositions of the one who performs the act. Such causes may "influence" or "incline" us to a certain choice, but they never determine a choice, if that choice is free in the libertarian sense. At the moment of choice, on this view, we are always equally able to choose or not to choose a particular alternative.[9] For this reason, libertarian freedom is sometimes called "liberty of indifference," for up to the very moment of choice nothing is settled; the will is indifferent.[10]

---

independent upon the creature, so as nothing is to Him contingent, or uncertain" (2.2), and the Confession reinforces this view of God's knowledge with its view of God's decree (3), creation (4), providence (5), free will (9), and effectual calling (10). For the Reformed tradition, at least, the extent of God's foreknowledge is not an open question.

[8] There are, besides libertarianism, other theological senses of *freedom* and *free will*. *Moral* freedom, for example, is freedom from the bondage of sin, given by God's grace (John 8:32-36, Rom. 6:7, 18-22, 8:2). *Compatibilist* freedom (so called because it is compatible with determinism) is the freedom to act according to one's own nature and desires. Scripture affirms the existence of freedom in these senses, but not in the libertarian sense.

[9] Open theist William Hasker defines libertarian freedom as the view that *"an agent is free with respect to a given action at a given time if at that time it is within the agent's power to perform the action and also in the agent's power to refrain from the action."* Hasker, "A Philosophical Perspective," in OG, 136-37. Italics his.

[10] For a longer discussion of libertarian freedom, see R.K. McGregor Wright, *No Place for Sovereignty* (Downers Grove: InterVarsity Press, 1996), 43-62.

Now if people are free in the libertarian sense, then human decisions are radically unpredictable. Even God cannot know them in advance. If in 1930 God knew that I would be writing this article in
2000, then I would not be writing it freely. I could not avoid writing
it. So if my writing is a free choice in the libertarian sense, even God
cannot have been certain of it in advance. Libertarian freedom excludes the classical view of God's foreknowledge.[11]

On this view, the future is of such a nature that it *cannot* be known
exhaustively. So Open theists claim that on their view God is indeed
omniscient, in the sense that He knows everything that can be known.
That He lacks exhaustive knowledge of the future is no more of a limitation than His inability to make a square circle. Just as His omnipotence enables Him to do everything that can be done, so His omniscience enables Him to know everything that can be known. That
includes knowledge of the past and present, but not the future, so
Open theists name their view *presentism*.[12]

For Open theists, therefore, libertarian freedom is a fundamental
premise, a standard by which all other theological statements are
judged. Typically, Open theists do not argue the case (such as there is)
for libertarian freedom; rather, they assume it.[13] It is their *presupposition*. So God *cannot* have exhaustive knowledge of the future. Pinnock
says,

> However, omniscience need not mean exhaustive foreknowledge of all
> future events. If that were its meaning, the future would be fixed and
> determined, much as is the past. Total knowledge of the future would
> imply a fixity of events. Nothing in the future would need to be decided.
> It also would imply that human freedom is an illusion, that we make no
> difference and are not responsible.[14]

[11] Traditional Arminianism tries to hold both libertarianism and exhaustive divine
foreknowledge. In this respect, Open theism is more logical than traditional Arminianism, but it pays a high theological price for its superior logic.

[12] Sanders, *The God Who Risks*, 198–99.

[13] I may have missed something, of course, but in the major writings of the Open
theists I have yet to find a serious *argument* for libertarian freedom. These authors
express much distaste for views like Calvinism that deny such freedom, and they
speak glowingly of the freshness, spontaneity, creativity, newness, etc., that libertarianism brings us. They also mention some Scripture passages that I will discuss
below, but there is always a great leap from the text to the libertarian conclusion.
They also suggest (see following note) that libertarianism is necessary to moral
responsibility, but they offer no argument to that effect.

[14] Pinnock, *Openness*, 121.

He is saying that God cannot know the future exhaustively, because if He did we would not have libertarian freedom.

In my view, however, libertarianism is both unscriptural and incoherent.[15] Scripture does speak of God determining the choices of human beings. In Proverbs, the writer declares, "To man belong the plans of the heart, but from the LORD comes the reply of the tongue.... In his heart a man plans his course, but the LORD determines his steps" (Prov. 16:1, 9).[16] God's counsel, indeed, brings *everything* to pass: Christians are predestined to eternal life "according to the plan of Him who works out everything in conformity with the purpose[17] of his own will" (Eph. 1:11; compare Rom. 11:36, Lam. 3:37–38).[18]

Open theist Gregory Boyd seeks to mitigate the implications of the fact that Jesus predicted Judas' betrayal (Jn. 6:64, 70–71, 13:18–19, 17:12). But he concedes the heart of the matter:

[15] For a more thorough discussion of God's sovereign control over free agents and the inadequacies of libertarianism, see my forthcoming *Doctrine of God* (Phillipsburg: Presbyterian and Reformed Publishing), especially Chapters 4, 8 (with 15 arguments against libertarianism), 14, and 16. I can only scratch the surface in this article, because I must focus on the issue of divine foreknowledge rather than on divine sovereignty in general. Much should be added, however, concerning election, reprobation, effectual calling, regeneration, and illumination, all of which presuppose God's full sovereignty over human decisions. See also various Reformed systematic theologies on these subjects.

[16] For more examples, see Exod. 34:24, Num. 23—24, Judg. 7:22, 1 Kgs. 13:1–3, Ezra 6:22, Jer. 1:5, Dan. 1:9. God also foreordains sinful actions (Exod. 3:9, 4:21, 7:3, Deut. 2:30, Josh. 11:18–20, 1 Kgs. 12:15, Ps. 105:24, Is. 6:9–10, 63:17, Rev. 17:17), including the betrayal and crucifixion of Jesus (Lk. 22:22, Jn. 6:64, 70–71, 13:18–19, 17:12, Acts 2:23, 4:28, 13:27). Human actions begin in the heart (Mt. 7:15–20, Lk. 6:43–45), and the human heart is in God's hands (Ps. 33:15, Prov. 21:1). People with sinful hearts *cannot* please God (Rom. 8:8). Their wills are not, therefore, indifferent to righteousness or sin. Faith, the human decision to believe in Christ, is a gift of God (Jn. 6:37, 44, 65, Acts 13:48, 16:14). Those who believe are "appointed to eternal life" (Acts 13:48). Plainly God's appointment implies that their choice was not indifferent.

[17] The reference to God's purpose clearly indicates that God *knows* what He is doing. If God's plan governs all things past, present, and future, then His knowledge extends just as broadly.

[18] Incredibly, neither Sanders, *The God Who Risks*, nor Gregory Boyd, *God of the Possible*, lists Ephesians 1:11 in the Scripture index. Boyd doesn't list Romans 11:36 or Lamentations 3:37–38 either. Sanders discusses the general contexts of the Romans and Lamentations passages, but he does not mention the indications there of the universality of God's controlling plan.

Scripture elsewhere teaches that a dreadful time may come when God discerns that it is useless to strive with a particular individual or a group of people any longer. At this point, he withdraws his Spirit from these people, hardens their hearts, and thus seals their destinies (e.g., Gen. 6:3; Rom. 1:24–27).[19]

Clearly Judas' decision to betray Jesus was not free in the libertarian sense. He was not then equally able to choose either alternative. Boyd implies that many human decisions are not free in this sense.

But what human decisions *are* free in the libertarian sense? Scripture never teaches libertarianism or even mentions it explicitly. Libertarians do try to derive it from the biblical view of human responsibility, but Scripture itself never does that. Judas is fully responsible for his betrayal of Christ, though we saw above that it was not a free act in the libertarian sense.

Nor does Scripture ever judge anyone's conduct, as we might expect on the libertarian view, by showing that the conduct was uncaused.[20] If only uncaused actions were morally or legally responsible, how could anyone prove moral or legal guilt? For it is impossible to prove that any human action is uncaused. Indeed, courts today as in biblical times rightly assume the opposite of libertarianism: that morally responsible actions (as opposed, for example, to accidents or insane behavior) are determined by motives. Lack of a motive diminishes or abrogates responsibility. So libertarianism, which Open theists regard as the foundation of moral responsibility, actually destroys moral responsibility.[21]

---

[19] Boyd, *Possible*, 38.

[20] Since Scripture never mentions libertarian freedom it obviously does not place upon it the value that Arminians and Open theists ascribe to it. Open theists place such a high value on libertarian freedom that they are willing to sacrifice almost any other theological concept to accommodate it. It is the grid that governs what other theological statements are and are not acceptable. But they have no justification in valuing so highly a concept that Scripture doesn't even mention.

[21] Calvinists and other anti-libertarians often make this point in colorful ways. James H. Thornwell says, "As well might a weather-cock be held responsible for its lawless motions as a being whose arbitrary, uncontrollable will is his only law," *Collected Writings II* (Edinburgh: Banner of Truth, 1974), 180. R.E. Hobart, arguing a secular form of determinism, says, "In proportion as [a person's action] is undetermined, it is just as if his legs should suddenly spring up and carry him off where he did not prefer to go," in "Free Will as Involving Determinism and Inconceivable Without It," *Mind* 43 (January 1934), 7.

These considerations show, in my view, that libertarian freedom does not exist. Therefore it provides no barrier to our confession that God knows the future exhaustively. And so important is libertarianism to the Open theist position that without it, the Open theist position entirely lacks credibility.

DIVINE IGNORANCE IN SCRIPTURE?

Nevertheless, we should also consider the Open theist contention that Scripture itself reveals a God who is sometimes ignorant about the future. Pinnock says,

> Many believe that the Bible says that God has exhaustive foreknowledge, but it does not. It says, for example, that God tested Abraham to see what he would do and after the test says through the angel, "Now I know that you fear God" (Gen. 22:12). This was a piece of information God was eager to secure. In another place Moses said that God was testing the people in order to know whether they actually love him or not (Deut. 13:3).

He also mentions Jeremiah 32:35 ("nor did it enter my mind that they should do this abomination") and the verses in which God hopes that "perhaps" His people will listen (Jer. 26:3, Ezek. 12:3, etc.). Throughout this discussion, Pinnock returns several times to talk about the importance of libertarian freedom, to the extent that the reader is entitled to ask if Pinnock is reading these texts through a libertarian lens.

As I indicated earlier, other Open theists also discuss passages in which, on their view, God is uncertain, changes His mind, is frustrated, discovers new information, and so on. In this article I cannot deal exhaustively with this list of passages, but I will suggest some principles that bear on their interpretation:[22]

1. Typically, passages in which God "finds out" something occur in *judicial* contexts. In Genesis 3:9, God asks Adam, "where are you?" This is not a request for information.[23] In this verse God begins His judicial cross-examination. Adam's responses will confirm God's indictment, and God will respond in judgment and grace. But the

---

[22] For a more thorough discussion, see my *Doctrine of God*, especially Chapter 22.

[23] If it were, it would show God's ignorance of the present, not the future. But Open theists usually claim that God knows the present exhaustively.

same judicial context exists in other texts where God "comes down" to "find out" something. See Genesis 11:5, 18:20–21,[24] 22:12, Deuteronomy 13:3, Psalms 44:21, 139:1, 23–24. When God draws near, He draws near as the judge. He conducts a "finding of fact" by personal observation and interrogation, then renders His verdict and sentence (often, of course, mitigated by His mercy). So none of these passages entail divine ignorance.

2. God's "remembering" and "forgetting" are also judicial categories in Scripture, because they are covenant categories. For God to "remember" His covenant simply means for Him to carry out its terms. So God "remembered" Noah and the earth's creatures in Genesis 8:1 (compare 9:15–16, Exod. 6:5).[25] God's "forgetting" is either His delay in fulfilling the covenant's terms (Ps. 9:18, 13:1), or His administration of the curse to covenant breakers (Jer. 23:39).

3. When God says that something "never entered my mind" (Jer. 7:31, 19:5, 32:35) He is not confessing ignorance, but describing His standards for human behavior (still another judicial point). Note the context of Jeremiah 7:31:

> They have built the high places of Topheth in the Valley of Ben Hinnom to burn their sons and daughters in the fire—something I did not command, nor did it enter my mind.

The contexts of 19:5 and 32:35 are similar. "Mind" here is *heart* in Hebrew, often in Scripture the locus of *intentions* (compare 2 Chr. 7:11, Neh. 7:5). God is saying here that the horrible human sacrifice of

---

[24] If in Genesis 3:9, 11:5, and 18:20–21 God's "finding" presupposes divine ignorance, then it is ignorance about the present, not only of the future. Open theists don't (to my knowledge) use these verses as examples of divine ignorance, because they believe that God does have exhaustive knowledge of the present. But if Genesis 11:5 and 18:20–21 can be explained without assuming divine ignorance, the same is certainly true of the other passages.

[25] Douglas Wilson comments on Genesis 8:1, "then God remembered Noah": "Does God smack His forehead in this passage? 'Oh, yeah! *Noah!*' Or in Exodus 6:5: 'Man, that was close! I almost forgot. The *covenant!*" See Wilson, "Foundations of Exhaustive Knowledge," chap. 9 of this book. Neither Sanders nor Boyd in the books previously cited includes Genesis 8:1 or Exodus 6:5 in his Scripture index. Sanders (not Boyd) describes the rainbow of Genesis 9:14–16 as God's "reminder to himself," suggesting at least that God might otherwise have forgotten His plan. But such an idea impugns, not God's knowledge of the future, but His knowledge of the *past*, despite the Open theists' affirmations that God's knowledge of the past is exhaustive.

Topheth is utterly contrary to His holy standards. God was not at all ignorant of these practices or of the danger that Israel would be tempted to sin in this way. He explicitly forbade human sacrifice in Leviticus 18:21 and Deuteronomy 18:10. So in the intellectual sense, these practices *did* enter His mind.

4. Some passages do say that God changes His mind in response to circumstances. Often Scripture says that God "relents" from a judgment He had planned, or regrets a course of action He had taken[26] (Gen. 6:6, 18:16–33, Exod. 32:9–14, 1 Sam. 15:35, Joel 2:13–14, Amos 7:1–6, Jonah 4:1–2). Paradoxically, however, this divine changeability is part of God's unchangeable covenant purpose.[27] God says to Jeremiah,

> If at any time I announce that a nation or kingdom is to be uprooted, torn down and destroyed, and if that nation I warned repents of its evil, then I will relent and not inflict on it the disaster I had planned. And if at another time I announce that a nation or kingdom is to be built up and planted, and if it does evil in my sight and does not obey me, then I will reconsider the good I had intended to do for it. (Jer. 18:7–10)

This principle means that many prophecies[28] are conditional. The nature of their fulfillment depends on human responses.

This conclusion, in itself, is congenial to Open theists. But what this implies is simply that God does not intend such conditional prophecies to be revelations of His unchanging purpose. Contrary to Open theists, God does have an unchanging purpose, described in Ephesians 1:11 and other texts noted earlier. That purpose is unchanging, but it ordains change, including the divine relentings mentioned in the above passages. God has decreed eternally that many of His purposes will be accomplished through created means, including intercessory prayer and the responses of people to conditional prophecies.

---

[26] In these passages, *relent* is typically the Hebrew *nacham*, which can also be translated "be grieved" or "be sorry."

[27] Indeed, it is part of the meaning of God's covenant name *Yahweh*. Notice how Joel 2:13 and Jonah 4:1–2 refer to the exposition of the divine name in Exodus 34:6, 7.

[28] Not all, of course. Some prophecies explicitly exclude such conditions, as Jeremiah 7:15, Amos 1:3, 6, 9, Isaiah 45:23, etc. Sometimes God guarantees the unconditional fulfillment of a prophecy by oath, as Psalm 110:1, Isaiah 14:24, 54:9, etc. (compare Ezek. 5:11, 14:16, etc.) For an excellent account of conditional prophecy by a Reformed Old Testament scholar, see Richard Pratt, "Historical Contingencies and Biblical Predictions," available at www.thirdmill.org.

5. There are some ways in which God does experience change when He enters the temporal world. The incarnation of Christ is the clearest example, mysterious as it is. Jesus grew in wisdom and stature (Lk. 2:52) even though He was omniscient (Jn. 2:24–25, 16:30, 21:17). He responded to events: rejoicing at this, angry at that. At one time He is rested, at another weary. He is born in Bethlehem and grows up in Nazareth. It was not merely the human nature of Jesus that underwent these changes, but the *person* of Jesus, the God-man.

But in a sense, God always experiences change of this kind when He is present in the world. When God met Moses in the burning bush, He said one thing, then another. When God acts in the world, in providence and redemption, His actions are temporally successive. He does one thing, then something else. He does what is appropriate in each situation, responding to one situation one way, to another another way. This is, as Open theists emphasize, a kind of change.

Those who defend God's changelessness against Open theism sometimes describe these temporal successions as "anthropomorphic." Of course in one sense everything we say about God is anthropomorphic, because we are using human language. But I don't think the term *anthropomorphic* quite captures this temporal involvement of God in history. *Anthropomorphic* suggests that God does not *really* act in a temporally successive way. But in Scripture, God is really present in history, doing one thing, then another.[29]

The error of Open theism is not in claiming that God's actions in history are temporal and responsive, or even that in the temporal world there is a kind of "give and take" between God and His creatures. Open theists err, rather, in denying that in addition to God's immanence in the world He also exists transcendently, governing everything in the world by His comprehensive decree.

So God is both fully omniscient *and* responsive to creatures. We may be grateful to the Open theists for showing how pervasive in Scripture is the theme of divine responsiveness. But our conclusion should not be to deny God's exhaustive sovereignty and foreknowledge. Rather, we should see Him as even more sovereign than we had

---

[29] God "responds" to creation even when there are no human beings around. After He creates light in Gen. 1, He responds by evaluating it as good and by naming the light and the darkness. We can see that any time God acts in history, in the creation, He will act responsively. In God's acts within creation, there is always "give and take."

thought before: ruling not only from a timeless transcendent realm, but also as temporally omnipresent, existing in and with all the changing events of nature and history, using the give and take of history to accomplish His unchangeable eternal purpose, ruling immanently as the Lord.

GOD'S EXHAUSTIVE KNOWLEDGE OF THE FUTURE

We have seen, therefore, that the divine responsiveness noted in Scripture does not refute belief in God's eternal decree and exhaustive foreknowledge. But does Scripture give positive testimony to God's exhaustive foreknowledge?

Scripture typically shows us God's knowledge of the future by the phenomenon of prophecy. One aspect of prophecy is the prediction of future events. Indeed, one test of a true prophet is that his predictions must come true (Deut. 18:22). In Isaiah, God challenges the gods of the other nations to foretell the future, knowing that only He is able to do this (Is. 41:21–23, 42:9, 43:9–12, 44:7, 46:10, 48:3–7).

Open theists agree that there is a predictive element in prophecy, but they insist that this predictive element does not imply that God has exhaustive foreknowledge. To show this, they enumerate three types of prophecy:

> A prophecy may express God's intention to do something in the future irrespective of creaturely decision. If God's will is the only condition required for something to happen, if human cooperation is not involved, then God can unilaterally guarantee its fulfillment, and he can announce it ahead of time...
>
> A prophecy may also express God's knowledge that something will happen because the necessary conditions for it have been fulfilled and nothing could conceivably prevent it. But the time God foretold Pharaoh's behavior to Moses, the ruler's character may have been so rigid that it was entirely predictable...
>
> A prophecy may also express what God intends to do *if* certain conditions obtain.[30]

I agree that in Scripture there are prophecies of all these kinds. I discussed conditional prophecies earlier, and of course I concede that

---

[30] Rice, *Openness*, 51.

God can announce His own actions independent of creaturely deci-sion.[31] The second kind of prophecy that Rice mentions ought to be troubling to Open theists, because (as I mentioned earlier in regard to Boyd's interpretation of Judas) it suggests that some human decisions (Pharaoh's, in the quote from Rice) are morally responsible even though they are clearly not free in the libertarian sense. It is odd to see Open theists speaking of "necessary conditions" for someone's behav-ior and using terms like "rigid" and "entirely predictable"—determin-istic language, in support of a libertarian view of things! Of course, for Open theists, Pharaoh and Judas harden themselves before their hardening becomes irreversible, that is, before God hardens them. Nevertheless, even the Open theists must admit that, once the hard-ening has taken place, God holds these people responsible for actions they could not have avoided.

I believe, however, that, besides prophecies of these kinds, there are others that (1) do not *merely* state divine intentions but depend for their fulfillment on human choices, (2) imply that God's decision de-termines those human choices, and (3) are not merely conditional.

Consider, as examples, the early prophecies of the history of God's people, given by God to Noah (Gen. 9:26–27), Abraham (Gen. 15:13–16), Isaac (Gen. 27:27–29, 39–40), Jacob (Gen. 49:1–28), Balaam (Num. 23—24), and Moses (Deut. 32:1–43, 33:1–29). Here God an-nounces (categorically, not conditionally) many centuries ahead of time the character and history of the patriarchs and their descen-dants. These prophecies anticipate countless free decisions of human beings, long before any had the opportunity to form their own char-acter.

In 1 Samuel 10:1–7, the prophet Samuel tells King Saul that after he leaves Samuel he will meet three men, and later a group of prophets. Samuel tells him precisely what the three men will be carrying and the events of the trip. Clearly God through Samuel anticipates in detail the free decisions of the unnamed men and prophets, as well as the events of the journey. Compare a similarly detailed account of an en-emy's war movements in Jeremiah 37:6–11.

In 1 Kings 13:1–4, God through a prophet tells the wicked King Jer-oboam that God will later raise up a faithful king, Josiah by name.

---

[31] On my view, of course, creaturely decisions are themselves the result of God's decisions.

This prophecy occurs three hundred years before the actual birth of King Josiah. Compare references in Isaiah 44:28—45:13 to the Persian King Cyrus over a hundred years before Cyrus's birth.[32] Many marriages, many combinations of sperm and egg, many human decisions are necessary in order for these precise individuals to be conceived, born, and raised to the throne, and to fulfill these prophecies. These texts assume that God knows how all these contingencies will be fulfilled. The same is true of Jeremiah 1:5, in which God knows Jeremiah before he is in the womb and appoints him as a prophet. Compare also the conversation between Elisha and the Syrian Hazael in 2 Kings 8:12, and the detailed future chronology in Daniel 9:20–27 of the affairs of empires and the coming of the Messiah.

Scripture is not unclear as to how God gets this extraordinary knowledge. God knows, as I said earlier, because He controls all the events of nature and history by His own wise plan. God has made everything according to His wisdom (Ps. 104:24), and He works out everything in conformity with the purpose of His will (Eph. 1:11). Therefore, God knows all about the starry heavens (Gen. 1:15, Ps. 147:4, Is. 40:26, Jer. 33:22) and about the tiniest details of the natural world (Ps. 50:10–11, 56:8, Mt. 10:30). "God knows" is an oath-like utterance (2 Cor. 11:11, 12:2–3) that certifies the truth of human words on the presupposition that God's knowledge is exhaustive, universal, and infallible. God's knowledge is absolute knowledge, a perfection; so it elicits religious praise (Ps. 139:17–18, Is. 40:28, Rom. 11:33–36).

So God "knows everything" (1 Jn. 3:20). And,

> Nothing in all creation is hidden from God's sight. Everything is uncovered and laid bare before the eyes of him to whom we must give account. (Heb. 4:13)

Does that knowledge include exhaustive knowledge of the future? Given the inadequacy of the Open theist arguments, the strong emphasis in Scripture on God's unique knowledge of the future, and the biblical teaching that God's plan encompasses all of history, we must say yes.

---

[32] I am assuming, of course, that Scripture is accurate in its account of when these events take place. If Scripture is God's Word, then we must assume such accuracy, contrary to the usual approach of liberal Bible critics.

6

Open Theism's Attack on the Atonement

John MacArthur, Jr.

More than a decade ago a controversial article in *Christianity Today* heralded the rise of Open theism. The article, "Evangelical Megashift," was written by Robert Brow, a prominent Canadian theologian. Brow described a radical change looming on the evangelical horizon—a "megashift" toward "new-model" thinking, away from classical theism (which Brow labeled "old-model" theology).[1] What the article outlined was the very movement that today is known as the "Open" view of God, or "Open theism."

Although Brow himself is a vocal advocate of Open theism, his 1990 article neither championed nor condemned the megashift. In it, Brow sought merely to describe how the new theology was radically changing the evangelical concept of God by proposing new explanations for biblical concepts such as divine wrath, God's righteousness, judgment, the atonement—and just about every aspect of evangelical theology.

The Quest for a Manageable Deity

Brow's article portrayed new-model theology in benign terms. He saw the movement as an attempt to remodel some of the more difficult truths of Scripture by employing new, friendlier paradigms to explain God.

According to Brow, old-model theology casts God in a severe light. In old-model evangelicalism, God is a stern magistrate whose judgment is a harsh and inflexible legal verdict; sin is an offense against His

---

[1] Robert Brow, "Evangelical Megashift," *Christianity Today* (19 Feb. 1990), 12–14.

divine law; God's wrath is the anger of an indignant sovereign; hell is a relentless retribution for sin; and atonement may be purchased only if payment in full is made for sin's judicial penalty.

In new-model theology, however, the God-as-magistrate model is set aside in favor of a more congenial model—that of God as a loving Father. New-model thinkers want to eliminate the negative connotations associated with difficult biblical truths such as divine wrath and God's righteous retribution against sin. So they simply redefine those concepts by employing models that evoke "the warmth of a family relationship."[2] For example, they suggest that divine wrath is really nothing more than a sort of fatherly displeasure that inevitably provokes God to give us loving encouragements. God is a "judge" only in the sense of the Old Testament judges ("such as Deborah or Gideon or Samuel")[3]—meaning He is a defender of His people rather than an authority who sits in judgment over them. Sin is merely "bad behavior" that ruptures fellowship with God, and its remedy is always correction, never retribution. Even hell isn't really a punishment; it is the ultimate expression of the sinner's freedom, because according to new-model thought, "assignment to hell is not by judicial sentence"[4] —so if anyone goes there, it is purely by choice.

Gone are all vestiges of divine severity. God has been toned down and tamed. According to new-model theology, God is not to be thought of as righteously indignant over His creatures' disobedience. In fact, Brow's article was subtitled "Why you may not have heard about wrath, sin, and hell recently." He characterized the God of new-model theology as a kinder, gentler, more user-friendly deity.

Indeed, one of the main goals of the Open-theism megashift seems to be to eliminate the fear of the Lord completely. According to Brow, "No one would deny that it is easier to relate to a God perceived as kindly and loving."[5]

Of course, the God of old-model theology is also unceasingly gracious, merciful, and loving (a fact one would not be able to glean from the gross caricature new-model advocates like to paint when they describe "old-model orthodoxy"). But old-model theologians teach that there is more to the divine character than beneficence. God is also

[2] Ibid., 12.
[3] Ibid., 13.
[4] Ibid.
[5] Ibid., 14.

holy, righteous, and angry with the wicked every day (Ps. 7:11). He is fierce in His indignation against sin (cf. Ps. 78:49; Is. 13:9–13; Zeph. 3:8). Fear of Him is the very essence of true wisdom (Job 28:28; Ps. 111:10; Prov. 1:7; 9:10; 15:33). And "the terror of the Lord" is even a motive for our evangelism (2 Cor. 5:11). "our God is a consuming fire" (Heb. 12:29; cf. Deut. 4:24), and "It is a fearful thing to fall into the hands of the living God" (Heb. 10:31).

Nonetheless, Open theists are determined to eliminate or explain away every feature of the divine character *except* those that are instantly "perceived as kindly and loving." They want nothing to do with a God who demands to be feared. Their theology aims to construct a manageable deity, a god who is "easier to relate to"—a quasi-divine being who has been divested of all the features of divine glory and majesty that might provoke any fear or dread in the creature. Instead, they have made Him into a kindly, nonthreatening, heavenly valet.

REDEFINING THE ATONEMENT

Above all, the new-model god never demands any payment for sin as a condition of forgiveness. According to the new-model view, if Christ suffered for our sins, it was only in the sense that He "absorb[ed] our sin and its consequences"—certainly not that He received any divinely-inflicted punishment on our behalf at the cross. He merely became a partaker with us in the human problem of pain and suffering. (After all, earthly "pain and suffering" are just about the *worst* consequences of sin new-model theologians can imagine.)

The most disturbing line in Robert Brow's article is an almost incidental, throwaway remark near the end, in which he states that according to new-model theology, "the cross was not a judicial payment," but merely a visible, space-time expression of how Christ has *always* suffered because of our sin.[6]

In other words, according to new-model theology, the atoning work of Christ was not truly substitutionary; He made no ransom-payment for sin; no guilt was imputed to Him; nor did God punish Him as a substitute for sinners. None of His sufferings on the cross

---

[6] Ibid. For a reply to the erroneous suggestion that God "suffers" at the hands of His creatures, see the chapter by Phil Johnson in this volume.

were administered by God. Instead, according to the new model, *atonement* means that our sins are simply "forgiven" out of the bounty of God's loving tolerance; our relationship with God is normalized; and Christ "absorbed the consequences" of our forgiveness (which presumably means He suffered the indignity and shame that go with enduring an offense).

So what *does* the cross mean according to new-model theologians? Many of them say Christ's death was nothing more than a public display of the awful consequences of sin—so that rather than offering His blood to satisfy *God's* justice, Christ was merely demonstrating sin's effects in order to fulfill a *public* perception of justice.[7] Other new-model theologians go even further, virtually denying altogether the need for any kind of ransom for sin.[8] Indeed, the entire concept of a payment to expiate sin's guilt is nonsense if the Open theists are right.[9]

---

[7] This is a version of Grotius's governmental atonement theory discussed later in this chapter. See also Appendix 1 ("How Are We to Understand the Atonement?") in John MacArthur, *The Freedom and Power of Forgiveness* (Wheaton: Crossway, 1998), 197–203 for a more thorough critique of Grotius's view of the atonement.

[8] John Sanders, a leading proponent of Open theism, begins his discussion of the cross by writing, "I understand sin to primarily be alienation, or a broken relationship, rather than a state of being or guilt." With such a definition of sin, what need is there of any propitiation? Indeed, Sanders goes on to characterize the cross as a public display of God's willingness to "suffer the pain, foregoing revenge, in order to pursue the reconciliation of the broken relationship." In other words, the "cost of forgiveness" in Sanders' system is a sacrifice God makes pertaining to His personal honor and dignity, rather than a price He demands in accord with His perfect righteousness. So Sanders believes God ultimately *relinquishes* the rightful claims of His justice and holiness rather than *satisfying* them through the atoning blood of Christ. That is the typical view of Open theism toward the atonement. *The God Who Risks* (Downers Grove: InterVarsity, 1998), 105.

[9] Open theist David Basinger suggests that the believer's own free will choice—rather than Christ's atonement—is what "bridges" the "initial separation between God and humans." Clark Pinnock, et al., *The Openness of God* (Downers Grove: InterVarsity, 1994), 173–75.

Basinger moreover describes the gap "between God and humans" without any reference to sin whatsoever; it is merely "an initial inability for God and humans to interact to the extent possible" [ibid.]. He depicts the gospel as "'good news'—the joy and excitement of being properly related to God" [ibid.]. Utterly missing from his discussion of Open theism's evangelistic ramifications is any reference to the cross of Christ or the meaning of atonement. No wonder—for if Basinger and other Open theists are right, the cross is really superfluous as far as divine forgiveness is concerned. The crucifixion of Christ becomes little more than a melodramatic display of sentiment, not a ransom for anything.

Thus new-model theologians have rather drastically remodeled the doctrine of Christ's atonement, and in the process they have fashioned a system that is in no sense truly evangelical, but is rather a repudiation of core evangelical distinctives. It is surely no overstatement to say that their emasculated doctrine of the atonement obliterates the true meaning of the cross. According to Open theism, the cross is merely a demonstrative proof of Christ's "willingness to suffer"—and in this watered-down view of the atonement, He suffers *alongside* the sinner, rather than *in the sinner's stead.*

It is my conviction that this error is the bitter root of a corrupt tree that can never bear good fruit (cf. Mt. 7:18–20; Lk. 6:43). Church history is rife with examples of those who rejected the vicarious nature of Christ's atonement and thereby made shipwreck of the faith.

SOCINIANISM REDUX

In fact, the "new-model" innovations described in Robert Brow's 1990 article—and the distinctive principles of Open theism, including the Open theist's view of the atonement—are by no means a "new model." They all smack of Socinianism, a heresy that flourished in the sixteenth century.

Like modern Open theism, sixteenth-century Socinianism was an attempt to rid the divine attributes of all that seemed harsh or severe. According to Socinianism, love is God's governing attribute; His love essentially overwhelms and annuls His displeasure against sin; His goodness makes void His wrath. Therefore, the Socinians contended, God is perfectly free to forgive sin without demanding a payment of any kind.

Moreover, the Socinians argued, the idea that God would demand a payment for sins is contradictory to the very notion of forgiveness. They claimed that sins could be either remitted or paid for, but not both. If a price must be paid, then sins are not truly "forgiven." And if God is really willing to *pardon* sin, then no ransom-price should be necessary. Moreover, according to the Socinian argument, if a price is demanded, then grace is no more gracious than any legal transaction, like the payment of a traffic ticket.

That argument may seem subtly appealing to the human mind at first. But biblically it falls far short. In fact, it is completely contrary to what Scripture teaches about grace, atonement, and divine justice. It hinges on definitions of those terms that ignore what Scripture clearly teaches.

Grace is *not* incompatible with the payment of a ransom. It was purely by grace that God Himself (in the person of Christ) made the payment we owed. In fact, according to 1 John 4:9–10, this is the consummate expression of divine grace and love—that God willingly sent His Son to bear a world of guilt and die for sin in order to propitiate His righteous indignation, fully satisfy His justice, and thereby redeem sinners: "In this was manifested the love of God toward us, because that God sent his only begotten Son into the world, that we might live through him. Herein is love, not that we loved God, but that he loved us, and sent his Son *to be the propitiation for our sins*" (emphasis added). Christ came to be "the Lamb of God, which taketh away the sin of the world" (Jn. 1:29). That language is a plain reference to the Old Testament sacrificial system, deliberately evoking the concept of expiation, which in the Jewish sacrificial system involved the payment of a blood-price, a penalty for sin.

Furthermore, anyone who studies what Scripture has to say about the forgiveness of sin will see very quickly that the shedding of Christ's blood is the *only* ground on which sins may ever be forgiven. There can be no forgiveness unless the ransom-price is paid in blood. Remember, that is the very thing both Socinians and Open theists deny. They say forgiveness is incompatible with the payment of a penalty—sins that must be paid for haven't truly been remitted. But Hebrews 9:22 clearly refutes their claim: "Without shedding of blood [there] is no remission."

The Biblical Doctrine of Substitutionary Atonement

On the cross, God made Christ a *propitiation*—a satisfaction of the divine wrath against sin (Rom. 3:25). The sacrifice Christ rendered was a payment of the penalty for sin assessed by God. Christ offered Himself on the cross *to God*. He "loved us, and hath given himself for us an offering and a sacrifice *to God* for a sweetsmelling savour" (Eph. 5:2, emphasis added). His death was a sacrifice offered to appease God's justice. It was the only way God could remain just while justifying sinners (Rom. 3:26). It was the only way He could forgive sin without compromising His own justice and holiness.

Scripture expressly teaches this. Christ died in our place and in our stead. He "was once offered to bear the sins of many" (Hebrews 9:28). He "bore our sins in His own body on the tree" (1 Pet. 2:24). And as He hung there on the cross, he suffered the full wrath of God on our behalf. "Surely he hath borne our griefs, and carried our sorrows: yet we did esteem him stricken, smitten of God, and afflicted. But he was wounded for our transgressions, he was bruised for our iniquities: the chastisement of our peace was upon him; and with his stripes we are healed." (Is. 53:4–5). "The LORD hath laid on him the iniquity of us all" (v. 6). "Christ hath redeemed us from the curse of the law, being made a curse for us" (Gal. 3:13). These are principles established in the Old Testament sacrificial system, not concepts borrowed from Greek and Roman legal paradigms, as Open theists are so fond of claiming.

It was *God* who decreed and orchestrated the events of the crucifixion. Acts 2:23 says Christ was "delivered by the determinate counsel and foreknowledge of God." God's hand and His counsel determined every facet of Christ's suffering (Acts 4:28). According to Isaiah 53:10, "it pleased the LORD to crush him; *he* hath put him to grief." That same verse says Jehovah made His Servant "an offering for sin." In other words, *God* punished Christ for sin on the cross and thereby made Him a sin offering. All the wrath and vengeance of the offended Almighty was poured on Him, and He became the sacrificial Lamb who bore His people's sin.

This is the whole gist of the book of Hebrews as well. "It is not possible that the blood of bulls and of goats should take away sins" (Heb. 10:4). Verse 10 says "we are sanctified through the offering of the body of Jesus Christ once for all." Verse 12 says His death was "one sacrifice for sins for ever." Very clearly those verses are teaching that Christ was sacrificed as a blood atonement to meet the demands of God's righteousness. No wonder many find that a shocking truth. It *is* shocking. And it is profound. It ought to put us on our faces before God. Any "new model" that diminishes or denies the truth of Christ's vicarious suffering at God's own hand is a seriously flawed "model."

What do you think of when you ponder Christ's death on the cross? Open theism reasserts the old liberal lie that He was basically a martyr, a victim of humanity—put to death at the hands of evil men. But Scripture says He is the lamb of God, a Victim of divine wrath.

What made Christ's miseries on the cross so difficult for Him to bear was not the taunting and torture and abuse of evil men. It was that He bore the full weight of divine fury against sin. Jesus' most painful sufferings were not merely those inflicted by the whips and nails and thorns. But by far the most excruciating agony Christ bore was the full penalty of sin on our behalf—God's wrath poured out on Him in infinite measure. Remember that when He finally cried out in distress, it was because of the afflictions He received from *God's own hand*: "My God, my God, why hast thou forsaken me?" (Mk. 15:34). We cannot even begin to know what He suffered. It is a horrible reality to ponder. But we dare not follow Open theism in rejecting the notion that He bore His Father's punishment for our sins, for in this truth lies the very nerve of genuine Christianity. It is the major reason the cross is such an offense (cf. 1 Cor. 1:18).

Scripture says, "[God] hath made [Christ] to be sin for us, who knew no sin; that we might be made the righteousness of God in him" (2 Cor. 5:21). Our sins were imputed to Christ, and He bore the awful price as our substitute. Conversely, His righteousness is imputed to all who believe, and they stand before God fully justified, clothed in the pure white garment of His perfect righteousness. In other words, this is the meaning of what happened at the cross for every believer: *God treated Christ as if He had lived our wretched, sinful life, so that He could treat us as if we had lived Christ's spotless, perfect life.*

Deny the vicarious nature of the atonement—deny that our guilt was transferred to Christ and He bore its penalty—and you in effect have denied the ground of our justification. If our guilt wasn't transferred to Christ and paid for on the cross, how can His righteousness be imputed to us for our justification? Every deficient view of the atonement must deal with this same dilemma. And unfortunately, those who misconstrue the meaning of the atonement invariably end up proclaiming a different gospel, devoid of the principle of justification by faith.

The Battle for the Atonement

The atonement has been a theological battleground ever since Anselm of Canterbury (1033–1109) first began to focus the clear light of Scripture on this long-neglected and often misunderstood aspect of redemption. The early Church, consumed with controversies about the Person of Christ and the nature of the Godhead, more or less took for granted the doctrine of the atonement. It was rarely a subject for debate or systematic analysis in early Church writings. But when Church fathers wrote about the atonement, they employed biblical terminology about ransom and propitiation.

Few would argue that the Church fathers had a fully-formed understanding of the atonement as a penal substitution, but Augustus Hodge pointed out that the idea of vicarious atonement was more or less implicit in their understanding, even if it was "often left to a remarkable degree in the background, and mixed up confusedly with other elements of truth or superstition."[10] Specifically, some of the fathers seemed confused about the nature of the ransom Christ paid —especially on the question of to whom the ransom was due. Some of them seemed to think of it as a ransom paid to Satan, as if Christ paid a fee to the devil to purchase release for sinners. That view is often called the *ransom theory* of the atonement.

Nonetheless, according to Hodge, "With few exceptions, the whole church from the beginning has held the doctrine of Redemption in the sense of a literal propitiation of God by means of the expiation of sin."[11] Selected Church fathers' comments about the ransom of Christ should not be taken as studied, conscientious doctrinal statements but rather as childlike expressions of an unformed and inadequate doctrine of the atonement. Philip Schaff, commenting on the lack of clarity about the atonement in early Church writings, said, "The primitive church teachers lived more in the thankful enjoyment of redemption than in logical reflection upon it. We perceive in their exhibitions of this blessed mystery the language rather of enthusiastic feeling than of careful definition and acute analysis."[12] "Nevertheless," Schaff added, "all the essential elements of the later Church doctrine of redemption may be found, either expressed or implied, before the close of the second century."[13]

Until Anselm, no leading theologian really focused much energy on systematizing the biblical doctrine of the atonement. Anselm's work on the subject, *Cur Deus Homo?* (*Why Did God Become Man?*), offered compelling biblical evidence that the atonement was not a ransom paid *by* God to the devil but rather a debt paid *to* God on behalf of

---

[10] A. A. Hodge, *The Atonement* (Memphis: Footstool, n.d.), 267.

[11] Ibid., 269.

[12] Phillip Schaff, *History of the Christian Church* (Grand Rapids: Eerdmans, 1970 reprint), 2:584.

[13] Ibid.

sinners, a satisfaction of divine justice. Anselm's work on the atonement established a foundation for the Protestant Reformation and became the very heart of evangelical theology. The doctrine Anselm articulated, known as the *penal substitution theory* of the atonement, has long been considered an essential aspect of all doctrine that is truly evangelical. Historically, all who have abandoned this view have led movements *away* from evangelicalism.

A close contemporary of Anselm's, Peter Abelard, responded with a view of the atonement that is virtually the same as the view held by some of the leading modern Open theists. According to Abelard, God's justice is subjugated to His love. He demands no *payment* for sin. Instead, the redeeming value of Christ's death consisted in the power of the loving example He left for sinners to follow. This view is sometimes called the *moral influence theory* of the atonement. Abelard's view was later adopted and refined by the Socinians in the sixteenth century (as discussed above).

Of course, as is true with most heresies, there is a kernel of truth in the moral influence theory. The atoning work of Christ *is* the consummate expression of God's love (1 Jn. 4:9–10). It is also a motive for love in the believer (vv. 7–8, 11). But the major problem with Abelard's approach is that he made the atonement *nothing more* than an example. If Abelard was correct, Christ's work on the cross accomplished nothing objective on the sinner's behalf—so that there is no real propitiatory aspect to Christ's death. That essentially makes redemption from sin the believer's own responsibility. Sinners are "redeemed" by following the example of Christ. "Salvation" reduces to moral reform motivated by love. It is a form of works-salvation.

Abelard's view of the atonement is the doctrine that lies at the core of liberal theology. Like every other form of works-salvation, it is a different gospel from the good news set forth in Scripture.

A third view of the atonement was devised by Hugo Grotius (1583–1645) during the Arminian controversy in Holland. Known as the *governmental theory* of the atonement, this view is something of a middle road between Abelard and Anselm. According to Grotius, Christ's death was a public display of God's justice, but not an actual payment on behalf of sinners. In other words, the cross shows what punishment for sin would look like if God recompensed sin. But no actual vicarious payment of the sinner's debt was made by Christ.

Grotius, like Abelard and the Socinians, believed God could forgive sin without any payment. But Grotius said the dignity and authority of God's law still needed to be upheld. Sin is a challenge to God's right to rule. If God simply overlooked sin, He would in effect abrogate His moral government of the universe. So Christ's death was necessary to vindicate God's authority as ruler, because it proved His willingness and His right to punish, even though He ultimately relinquishes the claims of His justice against repentant sinners. Christ's death therefore was not a substitute for anyone else's punishment, but merely a public example of God's moral authority and His hatred of sin.

In other words, unlike Abelard, Grotius saw that the death of Christ displayed the wrath as well as the love of God. Like Abelard, however, Grotius believed the atonement was exemplary rather than substitutionary. Christ did not actually suffer in anyone's place. The atonement accomplished nothing objective on the sinner's behalf; it was merely a symbolic gesture. Christ's death was an example only. And redemption therefore hinges completely on something the sinner must do. So the governmental theory also results inevitably in works-salvation.[14]

New-model Open theists seem to halt between two wrong opinions —sometimes echoing Grotius's governmentalism; sometimes sounding suspiciously Abelardian.[15] But one thing all Open theists would agree on is this: Anselm and the penal substitution view of the atonement are obsolete, part of an outdated model they can hardly wait for the evangelical movement to shed.

---

[14] Most governmentalists stress repentance as a human free will decision. Charles Finney, a conscientious defender of Grotius's view of the atonement, preached a message titled "Making a New Heart," in which he argued that regeneration (and particularly the change of heart that involves removal of the stony heart and implantation of a heart of flesh—cf. Ezekiel 36:26) is something each sinner must accomplish for himself. Moreover, in his *Systematic Theology*, Finney wrote,

[Sinners] are under the necessity of first changing their hearts, or their choice of an end, before they can put forth any volitions to secure any other than a selfish end. And this is plainly the everywhere assumed philosophy of the Bible. That uniformly represents the unregenerate as totally depraved [a voluntary condition, not a constitutional depravity, according to Finney], and calls upon them to repent, *to make themselves a new heart*" (Minneapolis: Bethany House, 1994), 249 (emphasis added).

[15] In his article "From Augustine to Arminius: A Pilgrimage in Theology," Clark Pinnock recounted his own retreat from the penal substitution view via a route that took him from Anselm to Grotius to Barth. Pinnock, ed. *The Grace of God, the Will of Man: A Case for Arminianism*, (Grand Rapids: Zondervan, 1990).

EVANGELICALISM? HARDLY

Clearly, Brow, Pinnock, Greg Boyd, and most other leading advocates of new-model Open theism want to be accepted as evangelicals. Near the end of his article, Brow wonders aloud if new-model thinking has any place under the evangelical umbrella. Does it provide a more helpful picture of God's good news, or is it "another gospel"?[16]

Earlier generations of evangelicals would have answered that question without hesitation by declaring that Open theism's message is "another gospel" (Gal. 1:8–9). Indeed, that is precisely how they *have* answered whenever Socinians, unitarians, liberals, and various other peddlers of New Theologies have raised these very same challenges to the "old model."

Unfortunately, the major segment of this generation of evangelicalism seems to lack the will or the knowledge to decide whether Open theists are wolves in sheep's clothing or true reformers.[17] But let it be clearly stated: by any definition of evangelicalism with historical integrity,[18] Open theism opposes the very core truths that evangelicals stand for. And by any truly *biblical* definition, they are heretics, purveyors of a different gospel. Both of these charges are substantiated by Open theism's abandonment of substitutionary atonement alone.

In fact, the only significant difference between today's Open theists and the Socinians of yesteryear is that the Socinians denied the deity of Christ, whereas Open theists ostensibly do not. But in effect, Open theists have denied the deity of *God Himself* by humanizing Him and trying to reconcile Him with modern standards of political correctness.

---

[16] Brow, *Megashift*, 14.

[17] The Baptist General Conference's recent refusal to clarify their doctrinal statement and rule out Open theism's deficient view of divine omniscience is clear evidence that modern evangelicals are vacillating and ambivalent on these issues.

[18] Quite simply, the label *evangelical* has historically been used to identify those who hold to both the formal and material principles of the Reformation—*sola Scriptura* (Scripture as the supreme authority) and *sola fide* (justification by faith alone). Although in recent years much broader and more complex definitions have been proposed, the history of the evangelical movement is inextricably linked with a resolute defense of those two vital principles. Absolutely essential to the doctrine of justification by faith is the truth of a vicarious atonement, where the guilt of the sinner is imputed to Christ and paid for, while the merit of Christ is imputed to the believer as the sole ground of acceptance with God. All who have denied substitutionary atonement have either been far outside the historic evangelical mainstream, or they have led movements that quickly abandoned evangelical distinctives.

In "Evangelical Megashift," Robert Brow claims that "the wind of [new-model theology's] influence blows in through every crack when we read C.S. Lewis's Chronicles of Narnia stories."[19] Lewis was no theologian, and there's no doubt that his views were squidgy on the question of eternal punishment. He held other views that make old-model evangelicals shudder. But one wonders if he really would have been in sympathy with Open theists' quest for a tamed and toned-down deity.

In the Narnia Chronicles, Aslan, the fierce but loving lion, represents Christ. His paws are frighteningly terrible, sharp as knives with the claws extended, but soft and velvety when the claws are drawn in.[20] He is both good *and* fearsome. When the children in Lewis's tale looked at him, they "went all trembly."[21] Mr. Beaver says of him, "He's wild, you know. Not like a *tame* lion."[22] And Lewis as narrator observes, "People who have not been in Narnia sometimes think a thing cannot be good and terrible at the same time."[23]

That same basic false assumption was the starting point for the heresy of Open theism. New-model theologians began with the assumption that God could not be good and terrible at the same time, so they set out to divest Him of whatever attributes they didn't like. Like the Socinians and liberals who preceded them, they have set out on a misguided quest to make God "good" according to a humanistic, earthbound definition of "good." They are devising a god of their own making.

In the final book of the Narnia series, a wicked ape drapes a lion skin over a witless ass and pretends the ass is Aslan. It is a sinister and dangerous pretense, and in the end it leads countless Narnians astray. The god of Open theism is like an ass in an ill-fitting lion's skin. And it is leading many away from the glorious God of Scripture.

God is both good *and* fearsome. His wrath is as real as his love. And though He has "mercy for thousands, forgiving iniquity and transgression and sin, [He] will by no means clear the guilty" without satisfying His own justice and wrath (Exodus 34:7).

---

[19] Brow, *Megashift*, 12.

[20] C.S. Lewis, *The Lion, the Witch, and the Wardrobe* (New York: MacMillan, 1950), 125.

[21] Ibid., 123.

[22] Ibid., 180.

[23] Ibid., 123.

True evangelicals will never relinquish those truths. And those who cannot stomach God the way He has revealed Himself have no right to the label "evangelical." These are issues worth fighting for, as both Church history and Scripture plainly prove. The rise of Open theism is a grave threat to the cause of the true gospel. May God raise up a new generation of evangelical warriors with the courage and conviction to contend for the truth of substitutionary atonement.

7

God Without Mood Swings

Phillip R. Johnson

Perhaps the most difficult biblical dilemma for those of us who affirm the classic view of an utterly sovereign and immutable God is the problem of how to make sense of the various divine affections spoken of in Scripture. If God is eternally unchanging—if His will and His mind are as fixed and constant as His character—how could He ever experience the rising and falling passions we associate with love, joy, exasperation, or anger?

Classic theism teaches that God is *impassible*—not subject to suffering, pain, or the ebb and flow of involuntary passions. In the words of the Westminster Confession of Faith, God is "without body, parts, or *passions,* immutable" (2.1).

God without passions? Can such a view be reconciled with the biblical data? Consider Genesis 6:5–6: "God saw that the wickedness of man was great in the earth, and that every imagination of the thoughts of his heart was only evil continually. And it repented the LORD that he had made man on the earth, and *it grieved him at his heart*" (emphasis added). In fact, Scripture frequently ascribes changing emotions to God. At various times He is said to be grieved (Ps. 78:40), angry (Deut. 1:37), pleased (1 Kgs. 3:10), joyful (Zeph. 3:17), and moved by pity (Judg. 2:18).

Classic theism treats such biblical statements as *anthropopathisms*—figurative expressions ascribing human passions to God. They are the emotional equivalent of those familiar physical metaphors known as *anthropomorphisms*—in which hands (Exod. 15:17), feet (1 Kgs. 5:3), eyes (2 Chr. 16:9), or other human body parts are ascribed to God.

We know very well that God is a Spirit (Jn. 4:24), and "a spirit hath not flesh and bones" (Lk. 24:39)—so when Scripture speaks of God as having body parts, we naturally read such expressions as figures of speech. Almost no one would claim that the biblical tropes ascribing physical features to God are meant to be interpreted literally.[1]

But the texts that assign *emotions* to God are another matter. Many Christians are loathe to conclude that these are meant to be taken figuratively in any degree.[2]

After all, one of the greatest comforts to any believer is the reassurance that God loves us. But if love is stripped of passion, we think it's a lesser kind of love. Doesn't the doctrine of divine impassibility therefore diminish God's love?

To complicate matters further, when we try to contemplate how any of the divine affections can be fixed and constant, we begin to imagine that God is inert and unfeeling.

Fearing such inferences, some veer to the opposite extreme and insist instead that God is even *more* passionate than we are. In one of those ubiquitous Internet theological forums, a minister who hated the doctrine of divine impassibility wrote, "The God of the Bible is much *more* emotional than we are, not less so!"

Someone else sarcastically replied, "Really? Does your god have even bigger mood swings than my mother-in-law?"

The point was clear, even if made indelicately. It is a serious mistake to impute any kind of thoughts to God that are cast in the same mold as human passions—as if God possessed a temper subject to involuntary oscillation.

In fact, a moment's reflection will reveal that if God is "subject to like passions as we are" (cf. Jas. 5:17), His immutability is seriously undermined at every point. If His creatures can literally make Him change His mood by the things they do, then God isn't even truly in control of His own state of mind. If outside influences can force an

---

[1] Presumably, even most Open theists would not claim that God has a physical body. Recently, however, I corresponded with a pastor from a well-known evangelical church in the United Kingdom who told me he believes God *does* have a physical form. He worships a corporeal deity, a being not unlike the gods one reads about in Greek mythology. And this pastor, like so many Open theists, had the temerity to insist that it is the God of classic theism who is derived from Greek thought!

[2] Nicholas P. Wolterstorff, Professor of Philosophical Theology at Yale Divinity School, says he rejected the doctrine of impassibility after the death of his own son. Shattered by grief, Wolterstorff concluded that God could not possibly be unmoved by human tragedy. "I found that picture [of God as blissfully unperturbed by this world's anguish] impossible to accept—*existentially* impossible. I could not live with it; I found it grotesque." ["Does God Suffer?" *Modern Reformation* (September/October 1999), 45.]

involuntary change in God's disposition, then what real assurance do we have that His love for us will remain constant? That is precisely why Jeremiah cited God's immutability and impassibility as the main guarantee of His steadfast love for His own: "It is of the LORD's mercies that we are not consumed, because his compassions fail not" (Lam. 3:22). God Himself made a similar point in Malachi 3:6: "For I am the LORD, I change not; therefore ye sons of Jacob are not consumed."

Still, many find the doctrine of divine impassibility deeply unsatisfying. After all, when we acknowledge that an expression like "the ears of the Lord" (Jas. 5:4) is anthropomorphic, we are recognizing that God has no physical ears. So if we grant that the biblical expressions about divine affections are anthropopathic, are we also suggesting that God has no real affections? Is He utterly unfeeling? If we allow that God's grief, joy, compassion, and delight are anthropopathic, must we therefore conclude that He is really just cold, apathetic, and indifferent?

THE ALTERNATIVE GOD OF OPEN THEISM

That is precisely the way most Open theists—and even some who reject Open theism—have misconstrued the doctrine of divine impassibility. A recent article in *Christianity Today* asserted that the doctrine of impassibility is actually just an outmoded relic of Greek philosophy that undermines the love of God.

> If love implies vulnerability, the traditional understanding of God as impassible makes it impossible to say that "God is love." An almighty God who cannot suffer is poverty stricken because he cannot love or be involved. If God remains unmoved by whatever we do, there is really very little point in doing one thing rather than the other. If friendship means allowing oneself to be affected by another, then this unmoved, unfeeling deity can have no friends or be our friend.[3]

Open theist Richard Rice similarly exaggerates the doctrine of impassibility. According to him, here is the view of God that has dominated Church history:

[3] Dennis Ngien, "The God Who Suffers," *Christianity Today* (3 February 1997), 38. The article's subtitle distills the message: "If God does not grieve, then can he love at all? An argument for God's emotions."

God dwells in perfect bliss outside the sphere of time and space.... [H]e remains essentially unaffected by creaturely events and experiences. He is untouched by the disappointment, sorrow or suffering of his creatures. Just as his sovereign will brooks no opposition, his serene tranquility knows no interruption.[4]

Elsewhere, Rice claims classic theists commonly dismiss the biblical terminology about divine affections as "poetic flights essentially unrelated to the central qualities that the Old Testament attributes to God." Instead, according to Rice, the God of classic theism "is made of sterner stuff. He is powerful, authoritarian and inflexible, so the tender feelings we read of in the prophets are merely examples of poetic license."[5] To hear Richard Rice tell it, the God of historic mainstream Christianity is aloof, uncaring, unfeeling, and utterly indifferent to His creatures' plight.

By contrast, Rice depicts the God of Open theism as a God of fervent passion, whose "inner life"[6] is moved by "a wide range of feelings, including joy, grief, anger, and regret."[7] According to Rice, God also experiences frustrated desires, suffering, agony, and severe anguish. Indeed, all these injuries are *inflicted* on Him by His own creatures.[8]

Clark Pinnock agrees. "God is not cool and collected but is deeply involved and can be wounded."[9] Pinnock believes the essence of divine love and tenderness is seen in God's "making himself vulnerable within the relationship with us."[10]

And so the Open theists want to set a stark dichotomy before the Christian public. The two clear and only options, according to them, are the tempestuously passionate God of Open theism (who is subject to hurts that may be inflicted by His creatures), and the utterly indifferent God they say goes with classic theism (who, at the end of the day, "looks a lot like a metaphysical iceberg.")[11]

---

[4] Clark Pinnock, Richard Rice, John Sanders, William Hasker, David Basinger, *The Openness of God* (Downers Grove: InterVarsity, 1994), 12.

[5] Ibid., 25.

[6] Ibid., 23–24.

[7] Ibid., 22.

[8] Ibid., 24.

[9] Ibid., 118.

[10] "An Interview with Clark Pinnock," *Modern Reformation* (November/December 1998), 37.

[11] Ibid.

Consider carefully what the Open theists are saying: Their God can be wounded; His own creatures may afflict Him with anguish and woe; He is regularly frustrated when His plans are thwarted; and He is bitterly disappointed when His will is stymied—as it regularly is.[12] Open theists have placed God in the hands of angry sinners, because *only* that kind of God, they claim, is capable of true love, genuine tenderness, or meaningful affections of any kind.

In fact, since the God of classic theism is *not* capable of being hurt by His creatures, Open theists insist that He is also incapable of being "relational." He is too detached, unfeeling, apathetic, and devoid of all sensitivity. According to Open theism, those are the inescapable ramifications of the doctrine of divine impassibility.

That is, frankly, Open theism's favorite cheap-shot assault on classic theism. It has great appeal for their side as far as the typical Christian in the pew is concerned, because no true believer would ever want to concede that God is callous or uncaring.[13]

And the sad truth is that these days the doctrine of divine impassibility is often neglected and underemphasized even by those who still affirm classic theism. Many who reject the other innovations of Open theism are wobbly when it comes to impassibility. They have been too easily swayed by the caricatures, or else they have been too slow to refute them.[14]

[12] In their zeal to avoid what they wrongly imagine makes God *apathetic*, they have replaced Him with a god who is merely *pathetic*.

[13] According to Pinnock, the doctrine of impassibility is "the most dubious of the divine attributes discussed in classic theism" [Pinnock, et al., *The Openness of God*, 118]. Impassibility has certainly proven to be a much easier target for Open theists than the other aspects of God's immutability.

[14] For example, Wayne Grudem's mostly-superb *Systematic Theology* quickly dismisses the doctrine of impassibility. Grudem writes, "I have not affirmed God's impassibility in this book.... God, who is the origin of our emotions and who created our emotions, certainly does feel emotions" (Grand Rapids: Zondervan, 1994), 166. Grudem seems to think the Westminster Confession's statement that God is "without...passions" means to portray God as utterly apathetic. He therefore agrees with the critics of classic theism who claim the doctrine of impassibility makes God cold and unfeeling. What Grudem doesn't discuss is the nature of God's "emotions" and how they differ from human passions. His entire discussion of divine immutability is marred by this, and it even seems to cause him to take a weak stance on the question of whether God actually changes His mind.

SORTING OUT SOME OF THE DIFFICULTIES

To be perfectly frank, impassibility is a difficult doctrine, both hard to understand and fraught with hazards for anyone who handles it carelessly. And dangers lurk on both sides of the straight and narrow path. While the radical-Arminian Open theists are busily lampooning the doctrine of divine impassibility by claiming it makes God an iceberg, a few hyper-Calvinists at the other end of the spectrum actually seem prepared to agree that God *is* unfeeling and cold as ice.[15] Obviously, people on both sides of the Open theism debate are confused about this doctrine. And that is to be expected. After all, we are dealing with something we cannot possibly comprehend completely. "For who hath known the mind of the Lord?" (Rom. 11:34).

We must begin by acknowledging that we are all too prone to think of God in human terms. "You thought that I was just like you," God says in Psalm 50:21. "I will reprove you and state the case in order before your eyes" (NASB). "My thoughts are not your thoughts, neither are your ways my ways, saith the LORD. For as the heavens are higher than the earth, so are my ways higher than your ways, and my thoughts than your thoughts" (Is. 55:8–9). Again and again, Scripture reminds us that the affections of God are ultimately inscrutable (cf. Eph. 3:19; Rom. 11:33).

To cite just one example, consider that God's love never wavers and never wanes. That alone makes it utterly unlike any human love we have ever experienced. If we consider how the Bible *defines* love rather than how we *experience* the passions associated with it, we can see that human love and divine love both have all the same characteristics, which are spelled out in detail in 1 Corinthians 13. But notice that not one characteristic in the biblical definition of love has anything

[15] I have a thick file of Internet correspondence from various ultra-high Calvinists who insist that the optative expressions ascribed to God in Scripture (see note 20) are utterly meaningless because they are anthropopathisms. One man whose ultra-ism had got the better of him wrote me, "God has no desires and no affections, no true delight or grief, and certainly no sorrow over anything that comes to pass—because His mind is pure, sovereign, irresistible will. You yourself acknowledge that the verses that talk about divine affections are anthropopathic. Why can't you see that such expressions teach us nothing whatsoever about how God *really* thinks?" That man and the Open theists have far more in common than he would care to admit. Both are convinced that the doctrine of impassibility makes God utterly cold and unfeeling. Both are wrong, however. While anthropomorphisms are not to be taken as wooden, literal truths, they certainly are meant to convey *some* truth about the mind and heart of God (as we shall note again near the end in this chapter).

whatsoever to do with passion. Real love, we discover, is nothing at all like the *emotion* most people refer to when they mention "love."

That's why we must let Scripture, not human experience, shape our understanding of God's affections. Those who study the matter biblically will quickly discover that God's Word, not merely classic theism, sets the divine affections on an infinitely higher plane than human passions. We can learn much from the anthropopathic expressions, but to a large degree the divine affections remain hidden in impenetrable, incomprehensible mystery, far above our understanding.

We cannot completely grasp what Scripture means, for example, when it tells us that the eternally unchanged and unchanging God became so angry against Israel at Sinai that He threatened to annihilate the entire nation and essentially void the Abrahamic covenant:

> And the LORD said unto Moses, I have seen this people, and, behold, it is a stiffnecked people: Now therefore let me alone, that my wrath may wax hot against them, and that I may consume them: and I will make of thee a great nation. And Moses besought the LORD his God, and said, LORD, why doth thy wrath wax hot against thy people, which thou hast brought forth out of the land of Egypt with great power, and with a mighty hand? (Exod. 32:9–11)

Two things are perfectly clear from such an account: First, we are not to read this passage and imagine that God is literally subject to fits and temper tantrums. His wrath against sin is surely something more than just a bad mood. We *know* this passage is not to be interpreted with a wooden literalness.

How can we be so sure? Well, Scripture clearly states that there is no actual variableness in God (cf. Jas. 1:17). He could not have truly and literally been wavering over whether to keep His covenant with Abraham (Deut. 4:31). Moses' intercession in this incident (Exod. 32:12–14) could not *literally* have provoked a change of mind in God (Num. 23:19). In other words, a strictly literal interpretation of the anthropopathism in this passage is an impossibility, for it would impugn either the character of God or the trustworthiness of His Word.

Nonetheless, a second truth emerges just as clearly from this vivid account of God's righteousness anger. The passage destroys the notion that God is aloof and uninvolved in relationship with His people. Even though these descriptions of God's anger are not to be taken literally, neither are they to be discarded as meaningless.

In other words, we can begin to make sense of the doctrine of impassibility only *after* we concede the utter impossibility of comprehending the mind of God.

The next step is to recognize the biblical use of anthropopathism. Since our thoughts are not like God's thoughts, His thoughts must be described to us in human terms we *can* understand. Many vital truths about God cannot be expressed *except* through figures of speech that accommodate the limitations of human language and understanding.[16]

The anthropopathisms must then be mined for their meaning. While it is true that these are figures of speech, we must nonetheless acknowledge that such expressions mean *something* we were meant to understand. Specifically, they are reassurances to us that God is not uninvolved and indifferent to His creation.

However, because we recognize them as metaphorical, we must also confess that there is something they *do not mean*. They do not mean that God is literally subject to mood swings or melancholy, spasms of passion or temper tantrums. And in order to make this very clear, Scripture often stresses the constancy of God's love, the infiniteness of His mercies, the certainty of His promises, the unchangeableness of His mind, and the lack of any fluctuation in His perfections. "With [God there] is no variableness, neither shadow of turning" (Jas. 1:17). This absolute immutability is one of God's transcendent characteristics, and we must resist the tendency to bring it in line with our finite human understanding.

WHAT DOES IMPASSIBILITY MEAN, THEN?

What about the charge that impassibility turns God into an iceberg? The complaint turns out to be bogus. In truth, mainstream classic theism has *always* denied that God is cold and remote from His

---

[16] Open theists must concede this point if they are honest. Unless they are willing to argue that God has physical features (like that British pastor mentioned in note 1), they themselves tacitly acknowledge that figurative language is regularly employed throughout Scripture to describe God. Yet inconsistently, they insist on a hermeneutic that interprets every reference to divine passions in a rigorously literal sense. Since both sides already understand and agree that true knowledge of God far surpasses the limitations of human thought and language, there is simply no good reason for Open theism's stubborn refusal to allow for anthropopathism where Scripture is dealing with a subject as mysterious and incomprehensible as the divine affections.

creation. One of the earliest Church fathers, Justin Martyr, said any view of God that sees Him as apathetic amounts to a kind of atheistic nominalism:

> If any one disbelieves that God cares for [His creation], he will thereby either insinuate that God does not exist, or he will assert that though He exists He delights in vice, or exists like a stone, and that neither virtue nor vice are anything, but only in the opinion of men these things are reckoned good or evil. And this is the greatest profanity and wickedness.[17]

God isn't like a stone or an iceberg. His *immutability* is not *inertia*. The fact that He doesn't change His mind certainly doesn't mean He is devoid of thought. Likewise, the fact that He isn't subject to involuntary passions doesn't mean He is devoid of true affections. What it *does* mean is that God's mind and God's affections are not like human thoughts and passions. There's never anything involuntary, irrational, or out of control about the divine affections. Here's how J.I. Packer describes the doctrine of impassibility:

> This means, not that God is impassive and unfeeling (a frequent misunderstanding), but that no created beings can inflict pain, suffering and distress on him at their own will. In so far as God enters into suffering and grief (which Scripture's many anthropopathisms, plus the fact of the cross, show that he does), it is by his own deliberate decision; he is never his creatures' hapless victim. The Christian mainstream has construed impassibility as meaning not that God is a stranger to joy and delight, but rather that his joy is permanent, clouded by no involuntary pain.[18]

Notice Packer's emphasis: God's affections are never passive and involuntary, but rather always active and deliberate. Elsewhere, Packer writes,

> [Impassibility is] not impassivity, unconcern, and impersonal detachment in face of the creation; not insensitivity and indifference to the distresses of a fallen world; not inability or unwillingness to empathize with human pain and grief; but simply that God's experiences do not come upon him as ours come upon us, for his are foreknown, willed and

---

[17] *First Apology* (c. 150), 28.
[18] J.I. Packer, "God," in Sinclair Ferguson and David Wright, eds., *New Dictionary of Theology* (Downers Grove: InterVarsity, 1998), 277.

chosen by himself, and are not involuntary surprises forced on him from outside, apart from his own decision, in the way that ours regularly are.[19]

R.L. Dabney saw the doctrine in a similar light. He described God's affections as "active principles"to distinguish them from mere passive emotions. He wrote,

> These are not passions, in the sense of fluctuations or agitations, but none the less they are affections of his will, actively distinguished from the cognitions in his intelligence. They are true optative functions of the divine Spirit [expressions of God's spiritual desires and wishes].[20] However anthropopathic may be the statements regarding God's repentings, wrath, pity, pleasure, love, jealousy, hatred, in the Scriptures, we should do violence to them if we denied that he here meant to ascribe to Himself active affections in some mode suitable to his nature.[21]

Note that both Packer and Dabney insist, and do not deny, that God has true affections. Both, however, see the divine affections as always active, never passive. God is the sovereign initiator and instigator of all His own affections—which are never uncontrolled or

[19] "Theism for Our Time," in Peter T. O'Brien and David G. Peterson, *God Who Is Rich in Mercy* (Grand Rapids: Baker, 1986), 16.

[20] The question of whether God can in any sense "desire" what He does not sovereignly bring to pass further complicates the whole question of divine impassibility but is too involved to deal with fully in this chapter. It is worth noting, however, that Scripture often imputes unfulfilled desires to God (e.g., Deut. 5:29; Ps. 81:13; Is. 48:18; Ezek. 18:31–32; Mt. 23:13; Lk. 19:41–42). And the question of what these expressions mean involves the very same issues that arise out of the debate over impassibility.

Specifically, we know that expressions of desire and longing from the heart of God cannot be taken in a simplistically literal sense without compromising the sovereignty of God. After all, Scripture says God accomplishes *all* His pleasure (Is. 46:10); He works *all things* after the counsel of His own will (Eph. 1:11). Nothing can ever frustrate Him in an ultimate sense. Therefore the yearning God expresses in these verses must to some degree be anthropopathic. At the same time, we must also see that these expressions mean *something*. They reveal an aspect of the divine mind that is utterly impossible to reconcile with the view of those who insist that God's sovereign decrees are equal to His "desires" *in every meaningful sense*. Is there no sense in which God ever wishes for or prefers anything other than what actually occurs (including the fall of Adam, the damnation of the wicked, and every evil in between)? My own opinion—and I think Dabney would have agreed—is that those who refuse to see any true expression of God's heart whatsoever in His optative exclamations have embraced the spirit of the hyper-Calvinist error.

[21] "God's Indiscriminate Proposals of Mercy," in *Discussions*, 3 vols. (Edinburgh: Banner of Truth, 1982 reprint), 1:291.

arbitrary. He cannot be made to emote against His will, but He is always the source and author of all His affective dispositions.

Jonathan Edwards made another helpful distinction. He wrote,

> The *affections* and *passions* are frequently spoken of as the same; and yet, in the more common use of speech, there is in some respect a difference. *Affection* is a word that, in its ordinary signification, seems to be something more extensive than *passion*, being used for all vigorous lively actings of the will or inclination; but *passion* for those that are more sudden, and whose effects on the animal spirits are more violent, and the mind more overpowered, and less in its own command.[22]

Edwards was suggesting that *passions* are involuntary and non-rational, whereas *affections* are volitions and dispositions that are under the control of the rational senses.

Given such a distinction, it seems perfectly appropriate to say that whereas God is "without passions," He is surely not "without affections." In fact, His joy, His wrath, His sorrow, His pity, His compassion, His delight, His love, His hatred—and all the other divine affections—epitomize the very perfection of all the heartfelt affections we know (albeit imperfectly) as humans. His affections are absent the ebb and flow of changeableness that we experience with human emotions, but they are real and powerful *feelings* nonetheless. To suggest that God is unfeeling is to mangle the intent of the doctrine of impassibility.

So a proper understanding of impassibility should not lead us to think God is unfeeling. But His "feelings" are never passive. They don't come and go or change and fluctuate. They are active, sovereignly-directed dispositions rather than passive reactions to external stimuli. They differ in this way from human passions.

Furthermore, God's hatred and His love, His pleasure, and His grief over sin—are as fixed and immutable as any other aspect of the divine character (Num. 23:19; 1 Sam. 15:29; Mal. 3:6; Jas. 1:17).[23] If God

---

[22] Jonathan Edwards, *Treatise Concerning the Religious Affections* (Edinburgh: Banner of Truth, 1961 reprint), 26–27 (italics added).

[23] Someone with whom I once corresponded on these issues raised the question whether *all* God's affections, including the negative ones, are eternally and equally unchanging: "Is the Holy Spirit endlessly and permanently grieved?"

Careful reflection will reveal that God's holy hatred of sin *must be* an immutable affection in the very same sense that His love is unchanging and unwavering. Surely we are not to imagine that His hatred of sin diminishes or grows stronger at varying times. He hates evil with a perfect hatred. And His utter loathing for sin is the main

appears to change moods in the biblical narrative—or in the outworking of His Providence—it is only because from time to time in His
dealings with His people, He brings these various dispositions more
or less to the forefront, showing us all the aspects of His character.
But His love is never overwhelmed by His wrath, or vice versa. In fact,
there is no change as we know it in Him at all.

How can that be? We don't know. As humans we can no more imagine how God's affections can be eternally free from change than we can
comprehend infinity itself. In Dabney's words, "Can we picture an
adequate conception of [God's affections]? No; 'it is high; we cannot
attain to it.' But this is the consistent understanding of revelation, and
the only apprehension of God which does not both transcend and violate man's reason."[24] God's affections, like every other aspect of His
character, simply cannot be understood in purely human terms. And
that is why Scripture employs anthropopathic expressions.

Dabney also gave a wise word of caution about the danger of brush-
ing aside the *meaning* of biblical figures of speech. While he acknowledged the widespread use of anthropopathism in Scripture, he was
not willing to evacuate such metaphors of their common-sense implications. These may be figurative expressions, Dabney argued, but
they are not devoid of meaning. Citing some verses that speak of
God's delight and His wrath, Dabney asked, "Is all this so anthropopathic as not even to mean that God's active principles here have an
objective? Why not let the Scriptures mean what they so plainly strive
to declare?"[25]

Unlike the modern Open theists, Dabney saw clearly *both sides* of
what the Scriptures strive to declare: God is unchanging and unchangeable, but He is not devoid of affection for His creation. His
impassibility should never be set against His affections. His immuta-

---

gist of what Scripture refers to when it says the Holy Spirit is "grieved" by our sin.
(The expression does not mean the Almighty is literally made to suffer.) So God's
hatred of sin is a divine affection that is permanent, fixed, eternal. The *manifestation*
of that hatred may change, however, which is why we perceive that the Holy Spirit is
grieved with this or that particular act of sin on particular occasions (cf. 2 Sam.
11:27).

This argues for the doctrine of eternal punishment. Since God's *mind* is eternally
unchanging, the dispositions that color His attitude toward sin (grief, wrath, hatred,
etc.) *must* be as eternal and unwavering as His love. The eternality of His wrath is
seen in the biblical descriptions of hell.

[24] Dabney, "Indiscriminate," 293.
[25] Ibid., 292.

bility does not rule out personal *involvement* with His creatures. Transcendence isn't incompatible with immanence.

God is not a metaphysical iceberg. While He is never at the mercy of His creatures, neither is He detached from them. His wrath against sin is real and powerful. His compassion for sinners is also sincere and indefatigable. His mercies are truly over all His works. And above all, His eternal love for His people is more real, more powerful, and more enduring than any earthly emotion that ever bore the label "love." Unlike human love, God's love is unfailing, unwavering, and eternally constant. That fact alone ought to convince us that God's affections are not like human passions.

In fact, isn't that a basic principle of Christianity itself? Anyone who imagines the divine affections as fluid, vacillating passions has no biblical understanding of the steadfastness and faithfulness of our God. That is why I object so strongly to Open theism's denial of God's impassibility. In the name of making God more "relational," they have undermined the constancy of His love; they have divested Him of yet another of His incommunicable attributes, and they have taken another giant step further toward refashioning Him in the image of His creatures. Who can tell where the campaign to humanize God will end?[26]

---

[26] Wolterstorff, who rejects impassibility, admits that the denial of this doctrine is like a thread that, when pulled, unravels our entire understanding of God. "Once you pull on the thread of impassibility, a lot of other threads come along.... One also has to give up immutability (changelessness) and eternity. If God *responds*, then God is not metaphysically immutable; and if not metaphysically immutable, then not eternal" ["Does God Suffer?", 47].

8

Trinity, Time, and Open Theism: A Glance at Patristic Theology

Peter J. Leithart

The basic historical claim of Open theism is that classical theism has been deeply infected by Hellenistic philosophical categories, which have distorted the biblical revelation of God. As John Sanders explains, "The early church fathers lived in the intellectual atmosphere where Greek philosophy (especially middle Platonism) dominated."[1] Though Sanders is careful to say that "the early fathers did not sell out to Hellenism," he concludes that they contributed to the development of a "classical" theology that "functions as a preunderstanding that rules out certain interpretations of Scripture that do not 'fit' with the conception of what it is 'appropriate' for God to be like, as derived from Greek metaphysics." As a result, "the Greek metaphysical system 'boxed up' the God described in the Bible" and adversely shaped "Christian understandings of the nature of God, the Trinity, election, sin, grace, the covenant, the sovereignty of God, salvation and the incarnation."[2] This rhetoric has an obvious appeal to Christians who are striving to be consistently biblical in their view of God.

It must be admitted that the charge is not *altogether* false. Far from it. The best-known truisms of historical theology cluster here: the

---

[1] John Sanders, "Historical Considerations," in Clark Pinnock, ed., *The Openness of God: A Biblical Challenge to the Traditional Understanding of God* (Downers Grove: InterVarsity, 1994), 59–60.

[2] Ibid., 60. See the similar statements of Clark Pinnock in his interview with *Modern Reformation* (available at www.alliancenet.org) and William Hasker's summary of his position, originally published by the *Christian Scholar's Review* 28:1 (Fall 1998) and available at www.opentheism.org.

Alexandrian fathers Clement and Origen were deeply affected by forms of Platonic philosophy; Augustine confessed that the writings of the Platonists were crucial in the development of his theology; Aquinas set out to adapt Aristotle to the Christian faith, but at least occasionally the adaptation went in the opposite direction.[3] Certainly some of the characteristic Christian ways of thinking about God's relation to creation, time, and space employ ideas first formulated by Greek philosophers.[4] Even today, the work of purging theology of pagan Greek elements remains an unfinished task.

From these incontestable facts, however, the argument can proceed in a variety of directions, especially at this level of generality. As Sanders points out, the process was both a Christianization of Hellenism and a Hellenization of the Church,[5] and sorting out where each was going on would require a lifetime's study. Suffice it to say, in general, that it is possible for terminology and concepts from one system to be adapted into a new system without distorting the new perspective. Indeed, this was going on, necessarily so, in the New Testament itself, where words loaded with Hellenistic cultural baggage were put to the service of the Hebraic gospel.[6] To judge the evidence that Open theists offer, one would have to ask in detail whether the Greek skin confined the gospel wine, or whether the wine burst the skins.

Some writers, at least, have argued that in some important respects the latter process occurred during the early centuries of the Christian Church, and specifically in theology proper, the doctrine of God. That is to say, Greek philosophical concepts did not set the limits for the

---

[3] Sanders provides the most extensive historical survey from the perspective of Open theism, tracing the influence of Hellenistic ideas from the Church fathers through the present. My examination, by contrast, will be limited to a narrow set of questions that arise in considering the theology of the patristic period.

[4] While warning that "there is no such thing as *the* Greek view of time," G.E.R. Lloyd recognizes that the contrast of a timeless eternal realm and a temporal and changing realm is a "recurrent motif in Greek metaphysical speculation on time." More particularly, Lloyd credits Parmenides as the first to distinguish clearly between changeless being and mutable appearances, finds in Plato the first clear distinction between "everlastingness" and "eternity," and notes that Plato anticipated Augustine in saying that "time and the created universe came into being together" "Views on Time in Greek Thought," in L. Gardet et al., *Cultures and Time* (Paris: Unesco Press, 1976), 117, 129, 137–18, 145.

[5] Sanders, "Historical Considerations," 59–60.

[6] "Gospel" itself, in fact, being one such word. See the discussion in J. Louis Martyn, *Galatians* (Anchor Bible #33A; New York: Doubleday, 1997), 127–128.

Christian understanding of God; rather, the gospel changed the way Greek terms were understood. John Zizioulas, for example, has examined the use that the Cappadocians made of Greek philosophy, and argues that they fundamentally reshaped the philosophical system and terminology they inherited. According to Zizioulas, Greek philosophy was "monistic," meaning that reality is basically "one." A simple way to think about this is to consider the process of "abstraction": Take a specific thing and think about what categories it can be fit into, beginning with the most specific and moving to the most general. A cat is a feline, a mammal, an animal, a living thing, and so on. The most general thing you can say about anything is that it "exists," and you can say this about everything that does exist. Everything can be put into the box labeled "being." For many philosophers, however, "being" is not just a category of classification but a philosophical principle. Though not material, it is the reality in which every existing thing "participates," or it simply *is* everything.

As Zizioulas points out, on these assumptions, any kind of relation and interaction between things is fundamentally impossible. If the cat and the mouse are both ultimately part of one reality of Being, then at some level they are not really enemies but merely points where "Being" is chasing itself about the barn (which is also part of Being!). Applied to theology, a monist view can lead in one of several directions. On the one hand, the gods may be powerful but limited beings, subordinate to the larger reality of "Being," like the gods of Greek myths—colorful personalities but not absolute. On the other hand, one might identify "God" with "Being," but this means that "God" cannot really relate to anything, since relating to anything is just relating to other "parts" of Himself. God is absolute, but at the cost of making Him impersonal—He is not a god whom we can love, to whom we can pray. For Aristotle, the unmoved something behind the world in motion is "thought thinking itself," hardly a vision of god that inspires intimacy and loyalty. On monist assumptions, the notion of an absolute but personal Being is nonsense.

In several respects, the Greek theologians demolished this conception of reality. By affirming the biblical doctrine of creation, they insisted that there is a real difference between God and the world. It is therefore possible for the two to relate, interact, and engage in mutual acts of giving and love. Meditating on the revelation of God in Jesus and on the New Testament's witness to that event, moreover, the

Greek Fathers recognized that God had revealed Himself to be Tri-une. Real difference is not merely a feature of God's relation to the world; there is real difference within God, and that means that God is eternally and essentially personal.

With both of these doctrines, the Greek fathers broke with the mo-nism of earlier philosophy. It is not the case that everything can be classified under one category of "Being," for there is a fundamental and unbridgeable gap between "being-Creator" and "being-creature." From the doctrine of the Trinity, they concluded that ultimate reality is not simply one; it is no more one than it is three, nor any more three than it is one. Plurality and relation, love and communion, replaced static and monistic "Being" as the basic ontological realities. In for-mulating the doctrine of creation and even more the doctrines of the Trinity and incarnation, the fathers employed philosophical terminol-ogy. But though the words remained the same, their meanings had ba-sically changed.[7] The wine left the wineskins unrecognizable.

Summarizing Zizioulas's discussion has accomplished two things. First, it displays some of the complexities of the Christian reception of Greek philosophy and indicates that it would be a distortion to say that classical theism is Hellenism in Christian garb. The Athenian trappings are obvious enough, but in significant ways Christian theo-logians were completely at home in Jerusalem. Second, the discussion focuses our attention on that area in the doctrine of God where Chris-tian theology departed most dramatically from the prevailing cultural and philosophical outlook, that is, the doctrine of the Trinity.[8] The simple fact that the Church fathers formulated the doctrine of the Trinity shows that Greek philosophy did not function as a straight-jacket that theologians were unable to escape. If Greek philosophy had exercised veto power, we would all be Arians.

It is frequently claimed, however, that some formulations of the Trinity, especially that of Augustine, were also framed in Hellenistic terms. According to Sanders, Augustine's doctrine of God betrays

---

[7] John Zizioulas, *Being As Communion: Studies in Personhood and the Church* (Crest-wood, NY: St. Vladimir's Seminary Press, 1993), 27–65. See the similar judgment of T.F. Torrance: "in making use of Greek thought-forms Christian theology radically transformed them in making them vehicles of fundamental doctrines and ideas quite alien to Hellenism"—*The Trinitarian Faith* (Edinburgh: T&T Clark, 1988), 68.

[8] Pinnock, in fact, makes the Trinity a centerpiece of his systematic theological presentation of Open theism (*Openness of God*, 107–109).

Hellenistic assumptions at many turns, as "neo-Platonic notions . . . vied with Augustine's biblical sensibilities for preeminence in his thinking." Specifically, Sanders charges that Augustine's emphasis on God's "immutability, simplicity and spirituality" as "the three most important divine attributes" was inspired by Neoplatonic conceptions.[9] Sanders goes on to trace the effects of these alien influences on Augustine's view of man, sin, predestination, and covenant.

On the Trinity, Sanders repeats standard criticisms of Augustine. First, Augustine used "psychological analogies" to explain the doctrine of the Trinity. That is, he discovered a created image of the Trinity in the triad of intellect, will, and memory in the human mind. As a result, Augustine encouraged the view that "the nature of the Trinity is known by turning within ourselves and examining our faculties." Since the true self is found "in the individual's inherent faculties . . . , not in our relations with others," God's nature too is conceived as basically unitarian: "The essence of God is to be alone." Second, Sanders charges that Augustine made "divine substance rather than the tripersonal God the highest ontological principle. The substance of God is what is ultimately real, not the relationships between the Father, Son and Spirit—let alone the relationships between the triune God and creatures." This affected the way that Augustine conceived of God's relation with creation, since reducing God to divine substance "makes God a remote deity, perilously close to being impersonal." Thus, "God's 'relationship' to creation [is] seen in mechanistic terms rather than in personalistic and covenantal categories."[10] Though we will see the connection more fully below, it is evident already that the issues of God's relation to time and space are linked to conceptions of the Trinity.

Sanders is not the only contemporary writer who makes such claims, and Colin Gunton, among others, has attributed the errors of Augustine's Trinitarian theology to the influence of Greek philosophy. Gunton claims that Augustine ignored the history of Jesus as the place where the Tri-unity of God is revealed, betraying his Neoplatonic distrust of the material and temporal world. According to Gunton, this tendency to separate God and the world arises in other parts of

---

[9] Anyone who has read *Confessions* will have noted that immutability is fundamental to Augustine's doctrine of God.

[10] Sanders, "Historical Considerations," 80–85.

Augustine's Trinitarian theology as well. Augustine described Old Testament theophanies (appearances of God) as being mediated through angels. For Gunton, this is problematic: It means that the self-enclosed God does not have any kind of immediate contact with the world, and we are left with an unknown God working through angels, rather than the Father relating to the world through His two "hands," the Son and Spirit. Like Sanders, Gunton also criticizes Augustine for employing psychological analogies of the Trinity, still another retreat from the world of time and matter: "The crucial analogy for Augustine is between the inner structure of the human mind and the inner being of God, because it is in the former that the latter is made known, this side of eternity at any rate, more really than in the 'outer' economy of grace." Psychological analogies tend to end in modalism, the heretical view that God is not really three but only reveals Himself in three modes. By their very nature, Trinitarian images taken from the human soul cannot capture the idea of three persons. Memory, understanding, and will are operations of one mind, not three distinct persons or subsistences. If this is the master analogy for the Trinity, then the persons are not persons at all but merely activities of the one God.

Such charges are something of a cliche in Augustine studies, and they are not groundless. Augustine did make statements that, especially in isolation, seem to imply that God is more fundamentally One than He is Three, that the substance is the real deity, and that the Persons are merely activities of the One God. Yet, I believe that Augustine's Trinitarian theology can be defended against many of these criticisms, and pursuing this issue in more detail will provide us with a modest test case for the claim that classical theism is indebted to Greek ideas. In the end, I hope that these considerations will also provide a further weapon or two in the battle with Hellenism that the Church fathers began but never completed.

Books 2–4 of Augustine's treatise *On the Trinity*[11] are principally concerned with the "sendings" or "missions" of the Son and Spirit, that is, with the incarnation of the Son and the pouring out of the Spirit at Pentecost. Augustine had good reason to address these issues

---

[11] All quotations from Augustine's treatise are taken from the translation by Edmund Hill (Brooklyn: New City Press, 1991).

at length. Earlier work on the Trinity had emphasized the unity of God, and to balance this emphasis on the oneness of God, theologians had placed a corresponding stress on the economy of redemption, in which the persons were manifested. In a number of writers, this emphasis on economy led to subordinationism. Their reasoning went like this: If the Son and Spirit were "sent" by the Father, then the Son and Spirit must be less than the Father.[12]

Living after the Council of Nicea, Augustine did not have the luxury of being fuzzy about these matters. He had to make it clear that the Son is coeternal and consubstantial with the Father, and in Books 2–4, he critically examined the bases for earlier subordinationism. The fact that the Son and Spirit are sent, Augustine argued, tells us about their origin but nothing about their ontological status. Someone may be sent without being inferior (2.7–11). According to many earlier theologians, the theophanies were appearances of the Son, and this too was sometimes spoken of in ways that smelled of subordinationism. But Augustine argued that the Bible gives too little evidence for us to decide which Person of the Trinity is manifested. The Son may well have appeared, but "this does not mean that God the Father never appeared to the fathers in this sort of guise" (2.32). If the Father Himself appeared to Old Testament saints, there was no basis in the Old Testament for subordinating the Son to Him.

But this led to a further question: If the Son and Spirit were "sent" before Christmas and Pentecost, what is unique about their sendings in the New Covenant? Augustine had already distinguished clearly between the sendings or missions of the Son and Spirit and the eternal procession of Son and Spirit, and he answers this question on the basis of that distinction. After spending most of Book 4 dealing with the work of redemption in a highly speculative numerological manner, he came to the key passage in 4.29:

[12] Tertullian claimed, for example, that at creation, "the Word receives its shape and form, its sound and voice, when God says Let there be light. This is the complete nativity of the Word, when it proceeds from God." Though Tertullian was not a modalist, he suggested that the Word comes to complete expression only in the economy. Elsewhere, he wrote, "We must understand the Father as the invisible in the fullness of his majesty, but we must acknowledge the Son as visible in the measure of his derivation." The Son, it seems, is not inherently the invisible God, but, because He is derived and secondary, is inherently visible. Both quotations are from Hill's introduction to *On the Trinity* in ibid., 41–43.

Just as being born means for the Son his being from the Father, so his being sent means his being known to be from him. And just as for the Holy Spirit his being the gift of God means his proceeding from the Father, so his being sent means his being known to be from him.

Augustine was doing two things here. First, he insisted that the sendings are not about "becoming" but about "becoming known." The Son was eternally generated from the Father, and the Spirit eternally proceeded from Father and Son, and that was true before Christmas and Pentecost. Second, he was able to isolate what is distinctive about the arrival of the Son and Spirit in the "fullness of time." What is new is that the Son is sent to become known as the Son of the Father, to be a mediator who reveals the knowledge of God the Father to us. Prior appearances did not have *this* purpose, i.e., to reveal the Father and to reveal the relation of Father and Son. The Spirit, likewise, had appeared before Pentecost, but at Pentecost it was revealed that He is the Spirit of the Father and the Son.

Contrary to Gunton and Sanders, therefore, Augustine does not ignore redemptive history in favor of "inner" and "mental" revelations of the Trinity. Indeed, he does not even introduce the psychological analogies of the Trinity until Book 9 of his treatise, in what he admits is a speculative effort to refine his grasp of what he has learned from Scripture and history. And it is not only that Augustine spent a great deal of space dealing with history, but it is also evident that he believed that the history of Jesus and the Spirit, of Christmas and Pentecost, are the prime locus of the revelation of the Trinity. The whole purpose of the Son being "sent" into time is to reveal the Father and the Son's origin from the Father. Time is, for Augustine, the medium in which the inner life of the Godhead is revealed, for in the progression of time the real differences of Father, Son, and Spirit are manifest to men. History does not create the Persons, but history is the stage on which the Persons are revealed. Augustine's classical theism thus does not present us with a distant and noninteractive God, a God enclosed within Himself, a God removed from history, a God whose nature is "to be alone." Rather, his classical *Trinitarian* theism presents us with a God whose eternal interpersonal character is unfolded in time and in interaction with the world.

If "sendings" in history reveal the inner life of God, then the inner reality of God is not some kind of completely static "being." That would be nothing less than death.[13] But God is "life," and in the inner relations of the Trinity the life of God is a life in "motion." The dynamic of redemptive history reveals an inner dynamism that is the *life* of God.[14] According to Gerald Bray, this is precisely where Augustine's Trinitarian theology leads. Though borrowing from the converted Neoplatonist Marius Victorinus, Augustine's conception of divine being as movement "owes its origin to the picture of an active God revealed in the Old Testament, as well as to Christian statements about the origin of the second and third persons of the Trinity." Bray is here referring to the patristic view that the Father "eternally begets" His Son, and the Spirit eternally proceeds from the Father and the Son (or, in the East, from the Father). If this means anything, it means that the inner life of God is active, and that an eternal "process" of generation and procession is inherent in God's Trinitarian being. Classical theism is Trinitarian, and for that reason departs from the assumption of "all previous theology," which assumed that "the divine being was static." Bray concludes, "It is ... of the utmost importance to grasp that Augustine did *not* believe in a static God."[15]

To be sure, theologians (including Augustine) did not always grasp the implications of the doctrine of the Trinity, and indeed Western theology has not always been decisively Trinitarian. The trajectory of a Trinitarian theology, however, is toward a conception of God's being as necessarily and eternally "ecstatic," as the Father eternally begets the Son that both is and is not Himself, and the Spirit eternally proceeds as the eternal gift of the Father to the Son and of the Son to the Father.[16]

In this, Augustine was in accord with the Trinitarian theology of

[13] See the stimulating comments on the connections between immobility and death in Karl Barth, *Church Dogmatics* (Edinburgh: T&T Clark, 1957), II/1, 494.

[14] Though not directly related to the Trinity, the classic definition of God's eternity from Boethius highlights the fact that God's being is life: "eternity is the total, simultaneous and complete perfection of unlimited life" (*Consolation of Philosophy*, 5.6; quoted in Barth, *Church Dogmatics*, II/1, 610–611). Barth goes on to argue that this "now" of perfect possession of life is untouched by the instability of the created temporality, but yet because it is life it is not only a "standing" but also a "flow," but notes that the implications of Boethius's definition were never "properly exploited."

[15] Gerald Bray, *The Doctrine of God* (Contours of Christian Theology; Downers Grove: InterVarsity Press, 1993), 169–170. See also J.N.D. Kelly, *Early Christian Doctrines*, rev. ed. (San Francisco: Harper and Row, 1978), 270–271.

[16] See the rather ecstatic expression of this in Catherine Mowry LaCugna, *God For Us; The Trinity and Christian Life* (San Francisco: Harper Collins, 1973), 354.

Athanasius and the Cappadocians. T.F. Torrance explains their view
in a passage that is worth quoting at some length:

> the Greek notion of *energia* ... was also Christianized under the trans-
> forming impact of the biblical conception of the creative and providen-
> tial activity of the living God. In contrast, especially to the Aristotelian
> view of God who is characterized by an "activity of immobility" ... and
> who moves the world only as "the object of the world's desire" ..., the
> Athanasian view of God was one in which activity and movement were
> regarded as intrinsic to his very being as God. ... God is never without
> his activity..., for his activity and his being are essentially and eter-
> nally one. The act of God is not one thing, and his being another, for
> they coinhere mutually and indivisibly in one another. Hence far from
> God being inactive in his inner being, it belongs to the essential and
> eternal nature of his being to move and energise and act. It was this dy-
> namic conception of God that marked so distinctively the Christian un-
> derstanding of the incarnation as the personal embodiment in space
> and time of God's providential and redemptive interaction with man-
> kind. Thus the Nicene theologians thought of Jesus Christ as one with
> God the Father in *act* as well as in *being,* for he incarnated the *active pres-
> ence* of God himself in human history, and constituted in all he was and
> did the free outgoing movement of the divine being in condescension
> and love toward mankind. This saving *philanthropia* ... —Athanasius'
> favorite word for God's active love toward us—was the very antithesis
> of the Aristotelian *eros* ..., the immanent desire for itself whereby the
> unmoved Mover timelessly affects the world. Whereas with the Aris-
> totelian conception of this inertial relation of God to the cosmos, there
> could be no idea of any creation of being out of nothing or of any be-
> ginning of time, the Judaeo-Christian conception of the living and act-
> ing God established the doctrine of the creation of all things out of
> nothing, and laid the foundation for a very different conception of mo-
> tion in created reality as well.[17]

---

[17] *The Trinitarian Faith*, 73–74. Similarly, in his "Third Oration," Gregory of
Nazianzen insists that, in contrast to Hellenists, Christians do not believe in either a
divine Anarchia or Polyarchia but in Monarchia. He hastens to add that this is "a
Monarchy that is not limited to one Person, for it is possible for Unity if at variance
with itself to come into a condition of plurality; but one which is made of an equality
of Nature and a Union of mind, and an identity of motion, and a convergence of its
elements to unity—a thing which is impossible to the created nature—so that
though numerically distinct there is no severance of Essence. Therefore Unity having
from all eternity arrived by motion at Duality, found its rest in Trinity. This is what
we mean by Father and Son and Holy Ghost" (see Philip Schaff and Henry Wace,
eds., *A Select Library of Nicene and Post-Nicene Fathers of the Christian Church* [second
series; Grand Rapids: Eerdmans, 1983], 7.301).

Focusing on the Trinity, in short, enables us to affirm in the strongest possible way that God is eternally personal, relational, and active, without making him dependent in any way on the creation.

According to Zizioulas, the doctrines of Trinity and creation were the two pillars of the Cappadocians' anti-Hellenistic program. We have dealt with the Trinity at some length, and in closing I offer some not-quite-historical observations on the doctrine of creation. In a brilliant essay,[18] Rowan Williams has explored the pastoral and social implications of the classical affirmation that God is independent of the creation, "outside" the continuum of time and space in such a way that creation is one-sidedly dependent upon Him. Williams begins with a critique of feminist theologian Sallie McFague. McFague argues that the notion of a God who makes something wholly different from Himself "generates and legitimates monarchical control over the world," and encourages imitation of such an indifferent God. In order to ground a "theology for an ecological nuclear age," McFague argues, it is necessary to blur the Creator-creature distinction, and insist that God's interests are "bound up with the world's." For McFague, the world must be seen as God's body.[19] Though differing on many points, McFague shares with Open theism the insistence that God is a player within the give-and-take of history, rather than living in a safe haven outside.[20]

This seems to be a liberating perspective, but in the end is the opposite. Over against the feminist claim, Williams points out that creation is not a process by which God manipulates and controls a world that has other plans for itself. Rather, the doctrine of creation teaches that "prior to God's word, there is nothing to impose on." To speak of creation is thus to say that everything that is is because God freely

18 "On being a Creature," in Rowan Williams, *On Christian Theology* (Challenges in Contemporary Theology; Oxford: Blackwell, 2000), 63–78.

19 Williams brilliantly shows how McFague's theology, for all her trendy maneuvering, is still locked in problematics that owe their existence to Descartes. If, he argues, the world is God's body, then our bodies are God's body; and that means that our bodies are not ours. In this paradigm, "I" am still estranged from my body; dualism reemerges in the midst of a theological project designed to attack dualism.

20 Of course, the spatial terms "inside" and "outside" are metaphorical, and it is clear that God is both within and without, transcendent and immanent. Here, I am using the metaphors in a more specific sense: To say that God is "outside" is to deny that He is dependent on creation, even as He moves and exists "inside" it; to say that God is "inside" means that God is to some extent dependent upon creation. I believe, too, that this captures the intent of Williams's usage.

speaks it, and to speak of providence is to say that God continuously speaks ever-new situations into being. Open theism, by contrast, implies that there is a creation independent of God's moving and willing, a creation to which God has to respond, and correspondingly a God who is "dependent upon the world in certain respects."[21] It thus suggests that God has in fact made a world "that then needs to be actively governed, subdued, bent to the divine purpose away from its natural course." But the doctrine of creation says that creation has no "natural course," but rather that "God's sovereign purpose *is* what the world is becoming." Though intending to secure freedom, Open theism pictures men as beings with autonomous inclinations that have to be overcome if God's purposes are to be realized. This God, not the God of classical theism, is the coercive God.

Open theists are correct about the need to purge the doctrine of God of Hellenistic viruses, but that does not require abandoning classical theism. Rather, we should follow more consistently the trajectory of those features of classical theism that pose the most profound challenge to Hellenism, namely, creation and the Trinity. The problem, after all, was the wineskins, not the wine.

---

[21] Richard Rice, "Biblical Support for a New Perspective," in *The Openness of God*, 16.

9

Foundations of Exhaustive Knowledge

Douglas J. Wilson

Many professing Christians today are uncomfortable with the biblical teaching of God's attributes as they have been traditionally defined. In particular, among some there is increasing discomfort with saying things like God is "immutable" or "impassible" or "omniscient." Such terms seem to the modern mind very much like artificial theological constructs. Consequently, if someone begins to maintain that such concepts and ideas came to us through the fevered inventions of medieval scholastics, and not from the Bible, the charge may be easily believed. But is it *true?*

The rejection of a traditional view of God may feel "progressive," "modern," "postmodern," or something—or at any rate, something recent. But the whole matter of God's foreknowledge is one of the ultimate questions, and of course these are therefore perennial issues. We must heed the warning of Solomon; there really is nothing new under the sun, and this certainly applies to the question of whether God knows the future choices of free agents. As we have seen elsewhere in this volume, in the time of the Reformation, this very "modern" rejection of classical theism was articulated by a man named Socinus. He and his "Socinian" followers argued in many of the same ways that we observe in our debates today. Because we do not have a comprehensive grasp of church history, many modern Christians tend to breathlessly discover things that are as old as dirt. The Church has been around this block before, and these questions have been raised—and answered—before.

In its modern dress, one early phrase used in rejecting the traditional understanding of God's knowledge and foreknowledge was the phrase "dynamic omniscience." It certainly sounds better to speak of "dynamic omniscience" rather than divine ignorance, but unless we are careful, we will soon find ourselves as ignorant as the "god" we profess to worship.

The descriptions are varied—free will theism, Openness of God, and so forth—but the essential point is constant. God's knowledge is interactive, and He *learns* as the future unfolds. In this view, God can know (if He wants to) everything which can be known, but the future choices and decisions of free-willed individuals are considered to be in the realm of the unknowable, not the realm of the unknown. Consequently, God does not know these choices because they are not considered to be genuine objects of knowledge. Future choices are not considered objects of knowledge, just as round squares are not genuine objects of knowledge.

Given a certain view of free will, genuinely free choices cannot be objects of genuine knowledge before those choices are actually made. Consequently, God cannot really know those future events that are controlled by such free wills. This means He does not know any of those things that He does not directly control or anticipate. Appeal is made to those passages that represent God as discovering, searching, or responding to those choices man apparently makes apart from God's control.

Although adherents of this view can use the term "omniscience," their understanding of the term is radically different than what we understand the Scripture to teach. The differences are so radical that, when taken out to their logical conclusion, they bring us to another god entirely.

What we *say* matters. What we confess is important, and, as we will see, important for our eternal salvation. The gospel concerns both the person and work of our Lord Jesus. Our salvation is found, not just in the fact that Jesus died on the cross, but also in what we confess about the *identity* of the One who died. "For there is one God and one Mediator between God and men, the Man Christ Jesus, who gave Himself a ransom for all, to be testified in due time, for which I was appointed a preacher and an apostle—I am speaking the truth in Christ and not lying—a teacher of the Gentiles in faith and truth" (1 Tim. 2:5–7). Christ is our High Priest, and He is God's apostle (Heb. 3:1). As our High Priest, He represents us to God, and as God's apostle, He represents God to us. Because He is Jehovah, He is our Savior. How we understand these things is very important.

We must deal with *knowledge, foreknowledge, and the gospel,* and we will address them in this order. I want first to address the question of epistemology. How do we as Christians know what we know? How are we to come to understand doctrinal truth? Next we will consider what the Bible teaches about God's knowledge or omniscience and how this relates to His foreknowledge of all future events. Last, we will turn to examine how these issues affect the gospel of our salvation.

REASON AND SUBMISSION

First is the question of epistemology. How do we know what is *true?* Those who reject what the Bible teaches about the nature of God because it conflicts with their ideas of "reason" have a problem with rationalism—the conviction that we cannot be required to submit to a doctrine that does not make good sense to *us.* This rationalism has entirely too high a view of the powers of human reason when dealing with revelations given to us from the mind of God Himself. Note that the problem is not with reason as properly understood, but rather with carnal reason as an idol.

Throughout Scripture we find a clear contrast between the philosophy of the natural man and the mind of Christ. When such passages are brought to bear on the various doctrines of the rationalist, the response is usually to shrug them off. And yet this is not sufficient; indeed, it is not *reasonable.* The Word of God may cut the tree of autonomous human reason down level with the ground, and yet we will still find the rationalist doing his best to sit in the shade.

The apostle Paul did not have a high view of the immorality of the natural man, or of the intellectual vanity that it invariably produced.

This I say, therefore, and testify in the Lord, that you should no longer walk as the rest of the Gentiles walk, in the futility of their mind, having their understanding darkened, being alienated from the life of God, because of the ignorance that is in them, because of the blindness of their heart; who, being past feeling, have given themselves over to lewdness, to work all uncleanness with greediness. But you have not so learned Christ, if indeed you have heard Him and have been taught by Him, as the truth is in Jesus: that you put off, concerning your former conduct, the old man which grows corrupt according to the deceitful lusts, and be renewed in the spirit of your mind, and that you put on the

new man which was created according to God, in true righteousness
and holiness. (Eph. 4:17–24)

Paul is very plain about it. We did not come to Christ through our
reason, but rather through putting off our pseudo-reason and *submitting*. For this reason, the epistemology that is foundational to free will
theism poses a very serious threat to the gospel. God has given us the
gift of reason to enable us to receive, understand, and obey His truth.
He has *not* given us reason to sit in judgment above His truth. Reason
may legitimately seek to understand in order to obey. Reason may not
deliberate on whether or not obedience makes sense.

When a man buys a computer, he also routinely receives an operating manual. This is designed to enable him to understand how to
operate the computer—it is *not* designed to teach him how the computer operates. When we read the Bible, our reason must seek to understand how God wants us to operate. What must we believe? What
must we do? The Bible was not given so that we could come to understand the mechanics of how God operates.

For this reason, the will to obedience must come prior to understanding—*credo ut intelligam*. "I believe in order that I might understand." Like Ezra, we should prepare our hearts to seek the law of
God, in order to understand and obey (Ezra 7:10). Rationalists consistently maintain that a truth need not be accepted if it makes no
sense to "reason." But does this not excuse those who are perishing?
The *gospel* makes no sense to them.

> For the message of the cross is foolishness to those who are perishing,
> but to us who are being saved it is the power of God. (1 Cor. 1:18)

The unregenerate are in need of the gospel, but the very thing that
provides the only hope of salvation is nonsense to them. The gospel is
veiled to those who are perishing (2 Cor. 4:3). The reply may be that
the gospel makes no sense to the perishing because their thought processes are distorted by sin, and they are unwilling. This is correct—
that is their problem. But this shows us how human thought processes, clouded as they can be by sin, *cannot* be the court in which we
settle what is true and what is false. If our reason has been renewed by
the Holy Spirit, it becomes possible for us to see in Scripture, with the
eyes of our reason, what God has revealed to us. Prior to this work,
the Bible remains spiritual gibberish because the natural man does

not understand the things of the Spirit; they are spiritually discerned (1 Cor. 2:14). This blindness does not excuse unbelievers. The gospel makes no sense to them. We may therefore conclude that the court of autonomous human reason is a worthless court when it comes to spiritual things. The wisdom of man is God's stupidity (1 Cor. 1:18–25).

Are the adherents of Openness theism willing for the biblical truth? Are they willing to submit to the clear teaching of Scripture on this subject of omniscience and the gospel? If they are unwilling (in the name of reason), then they need to take care lest they wind up losing the very thing they set in the place of the Bible's clear teaching. Autonomous reason, like Dagon, must necessarily fall. We always wind up losing the thing we worship in place of God.

> For I determined not to know anything among you except Jesus Christ and Him crucified. I was with you in weakness, in fear, and in much trembling. And my speech and my preaching were *not with persuasive words of human wisdom*, but in demonstration of the Spirit and of power, *that your faith should not be in the wisdom of men* but in the power of God. However, we speak wisdom among those who are mature, yet *not the wisdom of this age*, nor of the rulers of this age, who are coming to nothing. But we speak the wisdom of God in a mystery, the hidden wisdom which God ordained before the ages for our glory, which none of the rulers of this age knew; for had they known, they would not have crucified the Lord of glory. (1 Cor. 2:2–8)

In this passage, Paul is talking about the gospel—Christ and Him crucified. After referring to the cross, he immediately contrasts his message with that of human wisdom. Human wisdom, on its own, *would not* come up with the folly of the cross. In contrast to human wisdom, Paul speaks the wisdom of God, which is the cross of Christ. The wisdom of the cross was ordained, he says, before the ages. Had the rulers of that age known of the preordained wisdom of God in the cross, they would not have fulfilled it by crucifying Christ. But they did *not* know, and they were God's instruments in securing our salvation. The plain teaching of this text is not just that the cross saves sinners. It is that the cross was ordained before the ages, and that this affirmation causes problems for human wisdom. Paul glories in the fact that it does. The cross saves some sinners and baffles others. The "reason" that both sets of sinners hold in common is not competent to judge these things. All our thoughts must be submissive to Christ

(2 Cor. 10:4–5); we must love God with all our minds (Mt. 22:37); and we must never presume that God needs our counsel (Rom. 11:34–35). When the apostle with wonder asks, "Who has been His counselor?" he is not expecting someone in the back row to raise his hand.

Of course, we must understand what God is telling us before we can obey it; that is why He has given us reason. But we have no obligation at all to reconcile various truths philosophically in our minds before we can accept them. Reason can receive the information, seeking to understand what God has said. It has no authority to contrast this received truth with other revealed truth and determine how to tailor one or the other so that they may make good, plausible sense to the natural man.

We also may acknowledge that God does not contradict Himself. *True* reason is as much a part of His character and being as His holiness or kindness. But He is the judge of whether or not He has contradicted Himself—we most certainly are not. We know that God is holy because He has revealed Himself as such. The fact of evil in the world He governs is troubling to us, but He is the Judge and we are not. We know that God is kind because it is revealed in Scripture. Three-year-olds are murdered in His world, but He is the judge of whether this is consistent with His kindness, and we are not. And we know that God *knows everything,* including the future, because He has told us He does. This causes some interesting philosophical puzzles on the nature of eternity and time, but He is Judge of whether this is at all contradictory. He has told us in His Word that these things are so, and He has not resolved them for us, and this should be sufficient for us. We may be baffled by all this, but God is the foundation of all reason and order, and the problem does not perplex *Him.* But a man attempting to determine what the everlasting God may or may not do in history as He inhabits eternity is like a June bug trying to do quantum physics. If God were to come down to *explain,* as Job wanted Him to, I can just imagine any one of us trying to follow the argument. What a hilarious thought experiment! After the first two premises, our brains would blow up.

Some might want to respond that this proposed humility actually relieves us of any responsibility we have to make sense. Actually, whenever we speak, we are required by Scripture to make sense. Those who receive the limits on human reason set by Scripture know that this is not an argument for speaking nonsense, but rather an

admonition to us so that we might learn when we need to shut up—
so that we might *avoid* speaking nonsense. "Such knowledge is too
wonderful for me; it is high, I cannot attain it" (Ps. 139:6). Those who
do not admit, as David did, that God's knowledge of our actions is
"too wonderful" have begun to speak nonsense in the name of avoid-
ing nonsense. As he approaches the blackboard to solve the great
problem, a haughty June bug is likely to say some pretty silly things—
and he can't even hold the chalk.

Those who insist on grasping the ungraspable have completely
missed a central message of Ecclesiastes.

> He has made everything beautiful in its time. Also He has put eternity
> in their hearts, except that *no one can find out the work that God does from*
> *beginning to end.* (Eccl. 3:11)

We have a longing to understand because God has put eternity into
our hearts. But when we overstep our bounds, when we pry into such
things, we find that we cannot find them out. Our lives are lived out
under the sun, and we must acknowledge the limitations of our reasoning. The wise and great Solomon knew that the ways of God are
inscrutable, and this knowledge should affect everything we do. His
exhortation concerning vows before God can be applied to our theological reasoning as well—the principles involved are the same.

> Walk prudently when you go to the house of God; *and draw near to hear*
> rather than to give the sacrifice of fools, for they do not know that they
> do evil. Do not be rash with your mouth, and let not your heart utter
> anything hastily before God. *For God is in heaven, and you on earth; there-*
> *fore let your words be few.* (Eccl. 5:1–2)

If we disregard this we can muddle our way through into a pre-
tended wisdom. We think we can understand how an eternal God
interacts with us, living as we do in a world full of change. But we *can-*
not understand it. In our lives, "time and chance happen to them all"
(Eccl. 9:11). But God is sovereign over time, and sovereign over
chance. He is always and eternally the Lord.

> I know that whatever God does, it shall be forever. Nothing can be
> added to it, and nothing taken from it. *God does it that men should fear be-*
> *fore Him.* (Eccl. 3:14)

Objections to the biblical doctrine of God's exhaustive omniscience are at root philosophical, not exegetical. Moreover, they are *vain* philosophy, refusing to learn the lesson that God intended—i.e., that men should fear before Him. Nevertheless, some professing Christians are coming to reject this biblical doctrine, but for various reasons they still want to affirm the Bible is (mostly) true, or authoritative, or important to them in their faith community, or whatever. The Bible still has to be dealt with. Thus it becomes necessary for them to make the Bible fit somehow with this philosophy. As will be discussed below, certain verses isolated from their context do fit in this scheme—with ease—but we all know that isolated verses fit with *anything*. Shakespeare put it well in the *Merchant of Venice*: "In religion, what damned error, but some sober brow will bless it and approve it with a text, hiding the grossness with fair ornament?"

The rationalistic method of determining truth cannot be distinguished in principle at all from liberalism, higher criticism, and unbelieving textual criticism. A conservative with this method may think the liberals have made the wrong judgments, but by sharing their method he affirms their *right to judge*. History shows us that on this issue of rationalism, those who share the methods of unbelievers come at some point to share their unbelief. Ideas have consequences—and destinations.

Submissive reason tells us we must take the Bible—all of it—as our only ultimate and infallible authority. It is admitted all round that the primary audience of the writers of Scripture were the people whom the writers specifically addressed. That is, the book of Ephesians was written *to* the Ephesians. But is the Bible *for* us as well? The answer is *yes*. The authority of Scripture must be paramount throughout all ages.

> For assuredly, I say to you, till heaven and earth pass away, one jot or one tittle will by no means pass from the law till all is fulfilled. Whoever therefore breaks one of the least of these commandments, and teaches men so, shall be called least in the kingdom of heaven; but whoever does and teaches them, he shall be called great in the kingdom of heaven. (Mt. 5:18)

The standard must always be Scripture—all of it. The church was formed to exist "throughout all ages" (Eph. 3:21), and the church is built on "the foundation of the apostles and prophets" (Eph. 2:19–22).

Throughout all the ages, the Word of God is to be our guide. Jesus quoted Deuteronomy to this effect: "Man shall not live by bread alone, but by every word that proceeds from the mouth of God" (Mt. 4:4).

A continuity of doctrine and obedience is assumed in the last great commission which Christ gave to the church. "Go therefore and make disciples of all the nations, baptizing them in the name of the Father and of the Son and of the Holy Spirit, teaching them to observe all things that I have commanded you; and lo, I am with you always, even to the end of the age. Amen" (Mt. 28:19–20). We are to teach obedience to what Christ said both to do and to *think*. To this end, we must turn to what the Bible teaches.

For Christians, this continuity of doctrinal teaching is built on the firm foundation of the sufficient Word of God. Man's thoughts, man's reason, man's doctrines, and to use Orwell's phrase, man's "smelly little orthodoxies," are not the standard. We do not discover God or invent Him. *God reveals Himself.*

WHAT THE BIBLE SAYS

With this said about the role of reason, what does the Bible teach directly about God's omniscience? We will begin with passages addressing God's knowledge generally and then proceed to discuss the passages that talk of His exhaustive knowledge of the future. In both cases, Scripture abounds with references to the closely related doctrines of the exhaustive omnipresence and omniscience of God.

> "Can anyone hide himself in secret places, so I shall not see him?" says the LORD; "Do I not fill heaven and earth?" says the LORD. (Jer. 23:24)

The answer to the first rhetorical question is obvious—*no*. The answer to the second is equally obvious. No one can hide himself away from God. In this passage from Jeremiah, the prophet is ruthlessly contrasting the worthless prophecies of man with the genuine Word of God. The inventors of vain humanistic words are ignorant. The living God who speaks *knows everything*. No secret place excludes Him; if a place exists in heaven, or if it is in earth (and scripturally, there are no *other* places), then God fills that place. The implication is obvious; God does not fill such places ignorantly. He is *there* and nothing is hidden from Him.

And there is no creature hidden from His sight, but all things are naked and open to the eyes of Him to whom we must give account. (Heb. 4:13)

This teaches that God's knowledge of us is total and immediate, i.e., there is no mediator between God and the "facts." All things are naked and open before Him; there is no refuge from His knowledge. If something is created, i.e., it is a *creature,* then it cannot be hidden from the eyes of God. Every creature is in full view of the Lord, and He watches us intelligently. He is not gazing at us absent-mindedly, or looking off in the middle distance. We must give an account to Him in the light of what He observes, and He observes everything.

For every beast of the forest is Mine, and the cattle on a thousand hills. I know all the birds of the mountains, and the wild beasts of the field are Mine. (Ps. 50:10–11)

When Jesus teaches us that not a sparrow falls to the ground apart from the will of the Father, He could have pointed to the passage above to echo His point. God knows every bird of the mountains. His knowledge of the universe is much more than a grand, broad knowledge—it extends down to minute particulars. God knows far more than the correct number of galaxies; He knows all the movements of the mockingbird in your backyard—every dive, every step, every movement, every turn of the eye, every tug at a tuft of grass. *God knows.*

Are not two sparrows sold for a copper coin? And not one of the them falls to the ground apart from your Father's will. But the very hairs of your head are all numbered. (Mt. 10:29–30)

We are of course missing the point of the Lord's doctrine if we say, "Yes, God knows all about the sparrows, but where does the Bible say He keeps track of swallows?" Jesus is giving us one blunt example in order to show us the extremities of God's knowledge. He *invites* us to extend His teaching into every nook and cranny of the universe. If one were to say that God knows the position and velocity of every atom in the planet Jupiter, the point would *not* be to claim He is ignorant about the atoms of Neptune.

Because we are worth more than many sparrows, we should not be surprised to find that God keeps an eye on us as well.

Does He not see my ways, and count all my steps? (Job 31:4)

How many steps have I taken today? I do not know, but God most certainly does. *He counts them.* The Lord does not look away from us for a moment. He counts all our steps. Elihu agrees with Job concerning what God knows.

For His eyes are on the ways of man, and He sees all his steps. (Job 34:21)

This truth cannot be limited to important individuals like Job. This is generally true about everyone in the human race. The Lord sees all men in this way.

For the ways of man are before the eyes of the LORD, and He ponders all his paths. (Prov. 5:21)

No place in the universe stands apart from the Lord—not even the secret enclaves of our hearts. If God gazes upon Hell and Destruction (for He is the Lord of both), then how much more does He look upon our hearts? God sees everything outside and everything inside.

Hell and Destruction are before the LORD; so how much more the hearts of the sons of men. (Prov. 15:11)

God knows everything about us. He knows when we brush our teeth; He knows when we take a nap; He knows when we sit down to the dinner table, and what we are thinking at all times: "for You, only You, know the hearts of all the sons of men." (1 Kgs. 8:39b)

You know my sitting down and my rising up; you understand my thought afar off. You comprehend my path and my lying down, and are acquainted with all my ways. For there is not a word on my tongue, but behold, O LORD, You know it altogether. (Ps. 139:2–4)

We live out our lives in full view. God as He reveals Himself in Scripture is an "in your face" God. This makes sinners nervous (which it should), but the Bible does not tailor truth to make us all feel better about ourselves.

The LORD looks from heaven; He sees all the sons of men. . . . He fashions their hearts individually; He considers all their works. (Ps. 33:13, 15)

God forms each individual heart, and He *ponders* everything we do. Our actions are weighed in His balances, and our motives are held in His hands.

"Can anyone teach God knowledge, since He judges those on high" (Job 21:22)? This is a rhetorical question, with the expected answer of "No one." No one can teach God knowledge. But if free will theism is the case, then lots of people can teach God knowledge. If Openness theology is the case, then every time someone makes a free choice, then he is surprising God. He is *teaching* Him something. Even if what he teaches God is nothing more than certain unrevealed aspects of his own personality, the fact remains that God is learning something which a creature originated. Even some of the pagans knew this to be false:

> for in Him we live and move and have our being, as also some of your own poets have said, 'For we are also His offspring.' (Acts 17:28)

The pagan poet quoted above knew that the environment of all creatures is *God*. Not surprisingly, the judgment of God at the last day is dependent upon this exhaustive knowledge.

> Therefore judge nothing before the time, until the Lord comes, who will both bring to light the hidden things of darkness and reveal the counsels of the hearts. (1 Cor. 4:5)

Some of this may perhaps be granted by the adherent of Openness theism. While some who hold this view maintain that God does not even necessarily know everything that happens in the *present*, the real problems from their perspective are caused by God's knowledge of the future. Consequently, some have simply denied God's knowledge of *future* free actions by His creatures.

We must begin with the realization that the debate between Calvinists and Arminians does not concern God's exhaustive foreknowledge. Again, the debate over free will theism *is not a debate between Calvinists and Arminians*. Both camps hold to the orthodox doctrine of God that maintains that God knows the end from the beginning. Before the foundation of the world, God saw the last yellow dog ever to walk down some street at the end of the world, and before eternal times God knew the number of hairs on that yellow dog's back.

Since both camps agree on this, the Reformed have sometimes used this common ground to press their Arminian brothers on the issue of "a predetermined future," which *is* the debate between them. Doesn't exhaustively true foreknowledge on God's part require that the future is set—*settled*—before any of us are born? Some who hold to the doctrine of "free will" have accepted the power of this argument, and have consequently swallowed the conclusion. "Very well, then, if divine foreknowledge destroys free will, then we must deny divine foreknowledge because we simply must keep free will." To their very great credit, evangelical Arminians have stayed faithful to the Scripture at this point, despite the force of the argument.

The adherent of Openness theism may reply that he is simply being logically consistent in a way that the Arminian is not. He is willing to say what necessarily follows from an assertion of free will, and according to him the Arminian is not willing. But this particular theological debate, like all theological debates, cannot be isolated from the other truths taught throughout all Scripture. When *all* of Scripture is taken into account, the Arminian is far more logically consistent in his theology than is the advocate of free will theism. A man in the grip of an idea might be able to say he is far more consistent *with that one particular idea* than others are, but it is a vain boast. Who wants to set one thing that God has revealed about Himself against everything else He has revealed about Himself, and then boast that his logical deductions are "more consistent"? In some narrow sense, they may be, but if the premises for biblical theology are *all of Scripture,* then this lonely consistency is overthrown by all the radical inconsistency and irrationality elsewhere.

So what does the Bible teach about God's *foreknowledge?* "Known to God from eternity are all His works" (Acts 15:18). We must begin by noting that God does not have the same relation to *time* that we have.

> For thus says the High and Lofty One *who inhabits eternity,* whose name is Holy: I dwell in the high and holy place, with him who has a contrite and humble spirit, to revive the spirit of the humble, and to revive the heart of the contrite ones. (Is. 57:15)

A literal rendering of the Septuagint at this place reads, "Thus says the Lord Most High, the One in the highest inhabiting forever." *Forever* is not used here as an adverb, telling us how long the Lord lives. *Forever* is functioning as a noun; *forever is God's house.* So this is saying much more than that God lives for a long time. Eternity is His *dwelling* place. His home is timeless eternity.

> Before the mountains were brought forth, or ever You had formed the earth and the world, even from everlasting to everlasting, You *are* God. (Ps. 90:2)

The reader should be careful to notice the present tense. It is similar to the crucial use of the present tense in Christ's famous answer, "Before Abraham was, I *am*." This is a claim to Deity, a claim based upon His timelessness. He did not say, "Before Abraham was, I *was* too." From everlasting to everlasting, God *is* God. From everlasting, God is God, and to everlasting, God is God. We are not merely told that from everlasting, God *was* God, and to everlasting, God *will be* God.

Because God inhabits eternity, we should not be surprised that His foreknowledge of all future events is as exhaustive as His knowledge of all present and past events.

This is how we may account for the presence of prophecy throughout the Scriptures. When He prophesies in the Bible, God speaks of far more than His own actions—constantly He predicts the actions of others. This is remarkable, and distinguishes our God from all idols.

> Show the things that are to come hereafter, that we may know that you are gods; yes, do good or do evil, that we may be dismayed and see it together. Indeed you are nothing, and your work is nothing. (Is. 41:23–24)

A few moments' thought will reveal countless examples of free actions declared as done long before they were done by the Lord—the decree of Cyrus, the denial of Peter, the betrayal of Judas, the amount of silver used to betray the Lord, the military campaigns of Alexander the Great; the reader may supply hundreds of other examples.

In addition, it is astonishing how many passages talk about the gospel itself in relation to what happened before the world was made. A good example to begin with is 2 Timothy 1:8–10a:

> Therefore do not be ashamed of the testimony of our Lord, nor of me His prisoner, but share with me in the sufferings for the gospel according to the power of God, who has saved us and called us with a holy calling, not according to our works, but according to His own purpose and grace *which was given to us in Christ Jesus before time began*, but has now been revealed by the appearing of our Savior Jesus Christ, who has

abolished death and brought life and immortality to light through the gospel. (2 Tim. 1:8–10)

Grace was extended to sinners in the mind and purpose of God before time began—before sin began. This cannot be reconciled with human wisdom, but it can be reconciled with the teaching of Paul. It *is* the teaching of Paul.

> Paul, a bondservant of God and an apostle of Jesus Christ, according to the faith of God's elect and the acknowledgment of the truth which accords with godliness, in hope of eternal life which God, who cannot lie, promised *before time began,* but has in due time manifested His word through preaching, which was committed to me according to the commandment of God our Savior. (Tit. 1: 1–3)

God promised eternal life through the preaching of the gospel before the beginning of time. The Greek here is clear. The phrase is *pro chronon aionion*—before eternal times. If eternal life was promised before eternal times, and therefore before the beginning of sin, and the preaching of the gospel was the manifestation of this promise, then what does that do to free will theism? More to the point, what does free will theism do to such scriptural statements of the gospel?

According to the Openness view, the gospel is something which God decided to do in history in response to the choices of man. One advocate of the position has said that "history is the combined result of what God and his creatures decide to do." This clearly includes the history of sin and redemption. The Bible says differently, and does so in the plainest possible terms. The gospel of Openness is a temporal response of God's—trouble-shooting the creation—and is not the fulfillment of any pre-temporal promise. But the foundation of our confidence in the gospel is found in the fact that God keeps His Word; He fulfills His promises. Gospel preaching is described by Paul as a manifestation of this pre-temporal promise.

In due time, when the time was right, God manifested His word through preaching. This manifestation is of a promise made before time, made by the God who cannot lie. Paul gives us a wonderful assurance here, and free-will theism, if believed, takes that assurance away. The promise is therefore not the same thing Paul is talking about in Titus; the two gospels are not based on the same purpose or promise.

Peter teaches us about our redemption with the precious blood of Christ—the heart of the gospel, certainly—and he says this about Christ, the sacrificial Lamb.

> He indeed was foreordained before the foundation of the world, but was manifest in these last times for you. (1 Pet. 1:20)

We have here the same concept as in our Titus passage. Something was settled before the world began, and was then revealed later on in the course of history. That something was the cross—the gospel. In this passage it is immaterial (for our discussion) how the word *proegnosmenou* is translated—whether as "foreordained," "foreknown," or "chosen." I believe the NKJV is correct here, but whatever the case, this redemptive transaction, whatever it was, was made before the world began. But an adherent of Openness theology must deny this.

This pre-creation planning of salvation is also clear in Ephesians 1. My application of this passage here does not presuppose a Reformed understanding of it; it doesn't matter for our discussion whether the chosen here are the elect, as Calvinism holds, or foreknown believers, as an Arminian would hold. The point is that the salvation of some sinners was either ordained or foreknown before the foundation of the world.

> just as He chose us in Him before the foundation of the world, that we should be holy and without blame before Him in love. (Eph. 1:4)

If words have meaning, then somebody somehow was chosen in Christ to holiness and blamelessness *before the world was made*. But if anyone was chosen for salvation or known as receiving salvation before the world was made, then that means that such persons are genuine objects of God's knowledge (as the Arminian holds) or genuine objects of God's redemptive love (as the Reformed hold). In either case, God's knowledge of the future is clearly seen. God knew that sin was going to occur, and He created the world anyway—having already planned the salvation of sinners.

The use of the phrase "if words have meaning" is very important here. It is ironic that people can hold reason in very high esteem and say that it is competent to investigate the depths of the wisdom and knowledge of God, as well as the nature of time and eternity, and yet when it comes to reason's legitimate job—determining what the words are actually saying—then such reason falls to the ground. As the prophet says somewhere, if a man can't run with men, how will he compete with horses? If human reason can't even diagram the above sentence—"He chose us in Him before the foundation of the world"—then how can it hope to reconcile divine sovereignty and human "sovereignty"?

If we want to speak biblically, then we must assert that the first job of reason is to understand what the text, on its own, is saying. Suppose someone rejects the teaching of the Bible on God's omniscience, but not because of any grammatical or exegetical reason. Suppose he rejects it because it contradicts something that his "reason" insists on keeping. Who then is his Lord? Reason, or Christ? And who is the servant? Reason, or Christ? And to press it back to the wall, if he doesn't have Christ, then how long will he have reason?

Returning to the Scripture, we are confronted with the issue of why some refuse the gospel. Why do some perish? The Bible affirms both the responsibility and reprobation of a certain class of sinner in one breath.

> They stumble, being disobedient to the word, to which they also were appointed. (1 Pet. 2:8)

These sinners stumble (again, it doesn't matter for our discussion *why* they were appointed to this beforehand), and their stumbling is defined as disobedience to the Word—the gospel. But this was a disobedience to which they were appointed. The Bible says (again, if words have meaning) that certain people were appointed to disobey the Word. Now what is the role of reason here? Should reason remain quietly in her seat, taking notes? Or should she stand on her seat and rail against the Word of God? What is the *reasonable* thing for her to do? Reason is only being reasonable when she submits quietly to the revealed will of God.

We see the same sort of thing in John 12:37–40.

> But although He had done so many signs before them, they did not believe in Him, that the word of Isaiah the prophet might be fulfilled, which he spoke: "Lord, who has believed our report? And to whom has the arm of the Lord been revealed?" Therefore they could not believe, because Isaiah said again: "He has blinded their eyes and hardened their hearts, lest they should see with their eyes, lest they should understand with their hearts and turn, so that I should heal them."

Many such texts could be multiplied and examined in turn, but that is not the problem. As we discussed in the first section, it is the approach to *all* texts that is the problem. Texts such as this, taken at face value, offend the tenets of human wisdom. God has promised us a way of escape from our temptations; He has promised no way of escape from the truth. We ought not be uncertain in our handling of Scripture; we ought not to discuss "possibilities" in the Scripture, working with "maybe this" and "maybe that." That is not how the Word of God comes to us.

YEAH, BUT...

The teaching of the Bible is so plain that some may wonder why there is any debate at all. How can the free will theism position be maintained by anyone? Thorough Bible readers could probably answer the question quite readily. Numerous passages do exist that appear at first glance to cast the doctrine of exhaustive omniscience into question. Such passages have to be addressed as honestly as the passages we have already discussed that set forth the eternality of God. *All* Scripture is profitable.

For example, in Genesis 18, the Bible refers to the Lord coming down to find out if the inhabitants of Sodom were as bad as He had heard. How can this be held together with the teaching of the passages we listed earlier?

> And the LORD said, "Because the outcry against Sodom and Gomorrah is great, and because their sin is very grave, I will go down now and see whether they have done altogether according to the outcry against it that has come to Me; and if not, I will know." (Gen. 18:20–21)

In both Old and New Testaments, we see examples of the invisible, transcendent God focusing Himself in a visible image. In the New Testament we see Christ, the visible image of the invisible God (Col. 1:15), incarnated as a human being. In the Old Testament such pre-incarnate appearances of God are called *theophanies*. Now it is a logical mistake of the first order to take what is predicated of God as manifested in such theophanies and apply it to God in His transcendence.

If we neglect the passages that talk about God's transcendence, His omnipresence, and so forth, we could conclude from this passage that God is in fact limited in what He knows. But consider two problems with this. First, this requires that we neglect the plain teaching of many other passages on the nature of God, passages we have already considered. We must remember all that the Bible says on the subject—*tota et sola Scriptura*.

Second, this view gives a more limited God than anyone wants. Not only do we have a God who is limited in knowledge, but we also have a God who has to walk around if He wants to get somewhere (Gen. 18:2–3), who, when walking, gets His feet dirty (Gen. 18:4), who not surprisingly gets tired (Gen. 18:4), who also gets hungry (Gen. 18:5, 8), and who can be brought to a stalemate in a wrestling match (Gen. 32:24–30). In wrestling with the Angel of the Lord, Jacob claimed to have seen God face to face (Gen. 32:30); Hosea makes it clear that he had seen God (Hos. 12:3–4). The Angel of the Lord is frequently represented in the Old Testament as a theophany—an appearance of God. Both Hagar and the father of Samson consider it in this way (Gen. 16:11–13; Judg. 13:22). Such references and theophanies present to us at face value a god much more limited than anyone is currently presenting. Consequently, we do not really need to refute a position and method that *no one really embraces*.

The objection may come back that such passages simply give us a God who *can* walk, not a God who *needs* to walk. But remember the methodology employed by the advocate of free will theism. If Scripture uses language saying that God searches, an inference is drawn that God is ignorant and needs to search in order for the searching to be "genuine." So, employing the method, why can we not say that if Scripture shows God walking, we must conclude that He needed to walk in order to get wherever He was going?

Two basic options are open to us. We can either recognize that all of Scripture is consistent, and that an infinite God condescends to appear, from time to time, to finite men in a finite form, or we wind up with an Olympian Zeus—a god who sleeps, finds things out, gets hungry, and, if we put up with any more advances in "progressive" evangelical theology, has sexual relations as it pleases him. Of course, right *now* such a thought appalls everyone. But *why?*

If we remember the passages about God's majesty and transcendence, then we take all such passages as face-value descriptions of a theophany, i.e., what happens when God takes on a visible, limited form in order to deal with men. If Scripture can be trusted, this angel of the Lord, this theophany, walks, speaks, knows, does not know, changes direction, wrestles, etc. In a comparable way, our Lord after the Incarnation slept, ate, preached, got tired, did not know certain things, and so forth. All this can be affirmed at face value without abandoning the biblical view of the nature of the transcendent God. In other words, this is not a situation where we must take one set of verses or the other. This is a choice between taking all of the verses, as opposed to taking just some of the verses.

If we do not do this, we soon find ourselves affirming the biblically absurd—in other words, appealing to such examples proves far too much. Such readings of Scripture are not consistently followed by any-one. For example, do we really want to say (any of us?) that God can be defeated by a man in a wrestling match?

> Then Jacob was left alone; and a Man wrestled with him until the breaking of day. Now when He saw that He did not prevail against him, He touched the socket of his hip; and the socket of Jacob's hip was out of joint as He wrestled with him. And He said, "Let Me go, for the day breaks." But he said, "I will not let You go unless You bless me!" So He said to him, "What is your name?" He said, "Jacob." And He said, "Your name shall no longer be called Jacob, but Israel; for you have struggled with God and with men, and have prevailed." Then Jacob asked, saying, "Tell me Your name, I pray." And He said, "Why is it that you ask about My name?" And He blessed him there. And Jacob called the name of the place Peniel: "For I have seen God face to face, and my life is preserved." (Gen. 32:24–30)

This passage gives us a good example of how such theophanies are to be treated in the light of all Scripture. When Nebuchadnezzar points out that no one can restrain God's hand, or say to Him, "What have you done?" he is not expecting to be contradicted with the re-sponse that Jacob knew how to do it.

So in Genesis 32, we do have a statement that God was seen face to face. But this is not all; we also have the plain statement that He was wrestled to a stalemate by a mortal. Now either God is a lot weaker than *anyone* thinks, or He manifested Himself in this way for a pur-pose. When the infinite God "focused Himself down" into a finite point, it was in order that certain men could deal with Him; it was not to mislead them with regard to His infinitude. This is very similiar to the Sodom situation.

Do we really want to say that God needs food in the same way that we do, and that He has to walk down to the store to get it? Remember that on the way to the destruction of Sodom, the Lord came to Abraham *on foot*, and Abraham fed Him *beef*. Does anyone really think the angels and the Lord were talking on the road about who forgot to pack the lunch?

> "Please let a little water be brought, and wash your feet, and rest yourselves under the tree. And I will bring a morsel of bread, that you may refresh your hearts. After that you may pass by, inasmuch as you have come to your servant." They said, "Do as you have said." So Abraham hurried into the tent to Sarah and said, "Quickly, make ready three measures of fine meal; knead it and make cakes." And Abraham ran to the herd, took a tender and good calf, gave it to a young man, and he hastened to prepare it. So he took butter and milk and the calf which he had prepared, and set it before them; and he stood by them under the tree as they ate. (Gen. 18:4–8)

A similar objection to a biblical understanding of God's omniscience is derived from what the Bible says about Christ in the Incarnation. "And Jesus said, 'Who touched Me?'" (Lk. 8:45). Because Christ is fully God, and because the gospels make clear that Christ did not know certain things, does it not follow that exhaustive omniscience is not a necessary characteristic of Deity?

These objections to God's omniscience on the basis of the Incarnation really are in a class of their own. The wondrous fact that *God* was manifested in the flesh (1 Tim. 3:16), or, put another way, that the Logos became flesh and dwelt among us (Jn. 1:14), has been raw material for heretical speculations from the very beginning of the Christian era. Some denied the Incarnation altogether and said that Christ was simply *godlike*. Others said that Christ's soul was divine and His body was human. In other words, God put on a man suit the way a man might put on a gorilla suit. Simply put, the errors were plentiful. At the Council of Chalcedon, the Church successfully excluded all such vain and fruitless speculations. Christ is fully God because the Bible says so, and fully man because the Bible says so, and one person because the Bible says so. He has two natures (divine and human) but is only one person. These fences needed to be put up because proud reason wants to ask how Christ in His humanity could *not* know certain things, and yet in His Deity know everything. The answer is that we do not know. The Incarnation is a true mystery of godliness. Nevertheless, without detailed explanation, Scripture does set the boundaries of what we must affirm—Christ is fully God, fully man, and one person.

Now that which may be predicated of one nature cannot be predicated of the other. That which is true of either nature *can* properly be predicated of the person, but not of the other nature. The importance of this distinction has often been lost. Those who want to say that God in His transcendence does not know certain things because God enfleshed in His humanity did not know certain things have adopted a grievous methodology that cannot be limited to questions of knowledge. If Jesus was God, and Jesus was only five feet ten inches tall, does that make being five feet ten inches tall one of the new attributes of Deity? Or take another pestilent form of this logical error—if Jesus was God, and Mary was the mother of Jesus, then this makes Mary the mother of God.

The Council of Chalcedon guarded their statement against this fundamental logical error when they said, "He was born of Mary the virgin, who is Godbearer *according to His humanity*." In subsequent generations superstitious believers have grabbed the word Godbearer and ignored the critical qualification that Chalcedon placed upon it. In the teaching and methodology of Openness theology, we are now confronted with the same kind of thinking that allows people to think of Mary as the mother of Deity. "Because Jesus is God, and He had a mother, having a mother is one of the new attributes of Deity."

Again, it is ironic that those most prone to making such simple logical mistakes are the same "rationalists" who insist that human reason is capable of plumbing the depths of the immensities of the wisdom of God. In the Incarnation, the Bible reveals that God was manifested in the flesh. *This does not make humanity and Deity synonyms.* So *who* has been His counselor? No man is able to advise Him, and this certainly includes those among us who cannot maintain the distinctions between the most fundamental categories—categories like *whale* and *toaster oven*, or to use a more extreme example, *God* and *man*.

Another class of scriptural objections to the biblical doctrine is a little different. This type of objection looks at expressions used of God in Scripture and reasons from them to a doctrine of limited knowledge on God's part.

"Would not God *search* this out? For He knows the secrets of the heart" (Ps. 44:21). The argument goes that since God has to *search*, He must not have known what He was searching for beforehand. This verse gives a good insight into the use of words such as *search* when used of God in the Bible in such activities as examining the heart. His searching here is described as being based upon His present knowledge of the secrets of the heart. The psalmist says, "For He *knows*." We have the same kind of thing in Psalm 139.

Search me, O God, and know my heart; Try me, and know my anxieties. (Ps. 139:23)

This invitation to God to search and examine is a perfectly natural prayer of humility. David was not asking God to come to him in order to find out things that God didn't know before. This can be seen by what he affirms elsewhere in this particular psalm. The invitation to "search" his heart was *preceded* by a number of important assertions.

David says that God had *already* searched and known him (v. 1); that God knew when he stood up and sat down (v. 2); that God understood his thoughts from afar (v. 2); that God knew his path, his rest, and all his ways (v. 3); that God surrounded him, and had His hand on him (v. 5); that God's knowledge of him was incomprehensible (v. 6); that God's Spirit, God's presence, was everywhere—whether in heaven or in Sheol (v. 8); and that God knew how many days David would live before he had lived one day (v. 16). In light of all this, David's statement must be taken as a natural prayer of humility. "God, I want to be searched, in order that I may be led in the way everlasting." God uses such language as well; when He does, He is stooping to our level in order to reveal Himself to us. The use of words such as "search" is a figure of speech and not to be taken as teaching us that God is a good learner.

Yet another objection to God's omniscience could be taken from certain expressions the Bible uses when speaking of God, or when God Himself is speaking.

And they built the high places of Baal which are in the Valley of the Son of Hinnom, to cause their sons and their daughters to pass through the fire to Molech, which I did not command them, *nor did it come into My mind* that they should do this abomination, to cause Judah to sin. (Jer. 32:35; cf. 19:5)

In order to make the point, free will theists must claim God was completely blindsided by the disobedience of the Israelites. This understanding means not only that God does not exhaustively foresee the future but also that He is not very good at extrapolating future human behavior from present circumstances either. Consider: the Israelites were occupying a land populated with pagans who did abominable things, including the practice of sacrificing their children in the fire of Molech. God repeatedly warned them not to do what the Canaanites were doing, not to imitate their behavior, and it would seem that this abomination would have been included in their temptations. A reasonably intelligent *human* analyst should have been able to foresee that this would be a problem.

But we do not have to rest on such a conjecture. God had warned them clearly before the people ever entered the land.

> And you shall not let any of your descendants pass through the fire to Molech, nor shall you profane the name of your God: I am the LORD. (Lev. 18:21; cf. Deut. 18:10)

God warned them of this possible corruption when they were in the wilderness, but by the time of Jeremiah, He had forgotten what He had said? Divine forgetfulness would be bad enough, but remember that these warnings from God were already written down in Scripture. This means that if God forgot them, He knew His revelation less thoroughly than He expected the Israelites to know it. God is then represented as saying, "Do what I say, not what I do" (Deut. 28:58–59).

The idea that God meant to communicate through Jeremiah that He had never anticipated the possibility of this abomination is excluded by the plain statements of Scripture, and is of course ludicrous on the face of it. But such expressions, both here and throughout Scripture, may *sound like* God never thought of something.

How are we to understand such expressions then? Of course they are a figure of speech called *anthropopatheia*—God is condescending to communicate with *us*, after all, and He uses expressions which must not be taken literally. They are used because this is the way our minds work. To use Calvin's homely phrase, God sometimes lisps to us. We guard against the abuse of this explanation (i.e., explaining *any* part of Scripture away as a "figure of speech") through a careful and thoughtful reading of Scripture. The fact is that God has given us His Word, which contains figures of speech as well as straightforward prosaic statements. The right role of reason is to submissively study His Word so that we might learn to distinguish the two.

In the case given above from Jeremiah, the expression simply means that God never contemplated *commanding* this atrocity of the Israelites. He could and would not contemplate such a thing, for He is immutably holy. He cannot be tempted, and He does not tempt (Jas. 1:13). Instead of saying simply, "I did not command this thing," He says far more forcefully, "It never even entered my head to command this thing."

To take such expressions literally would flatly contradict what the Bible teaches us in straightforward didactic passages about the nature of God, and in addition would lead to a host of problems for *everyone's* theology. For example, do we really want to say that God has a face because the psalmist says that He hides His face? (Ps. 13:1.) Or that God has eyelids? (Ps. 11:4.) Did God literally part the Red Sea through a blast from His nostrils? (Exod. 15:8.) Is His tongue a devouring fire? (Is. 30:27.) Is His power a literal arm? (Is. 53:1.) Does God have *intestines?* (Is. 63:15.)

> Look down from heaven, and see from Your habitation, holy and glorious. Where are Your zeal and Your strength, the yearning of Your heart and Your mercies toward me? Are they restrained? (Is. 63:15)

The phrase "yearning of Your heart" here is literally a reference to bowels. All these examples of anthropomorphism and anthropopatheia are figures of *metonomy*, where one thing is substituted for another. Because humans feel a sensation in their bowels when they are deeply affected, they by metonomy may use a reference to the sensation for the feeling itself. God even describes Himself in descriptions taken from animals. He roars or bellows (Jer. 25:30); He has wings and feathers (Ps. 91:4). *Really?*

Of course these are all figures of speech and not meant to hide or confuse; they are given to us by God in order to communicate with us. God's face refers to His presence, His eyes to His omniscience, His arm to His power, His wings to His protection, and so forth. God speaks of Himself in this way, and so should we. We should echo the language of Scripture in all these places, but we must always remember what we are doing. We are speaking of the invisible Father analogically.

The same is true when we encounter figures that relate to God's knowl-edge—for example, those figures which represent God as repenting or relenting (Gen. 6:6; Exod. 32:12, 14), remembering (Gen. 9:15–16; Exod. 6:5), or forgetting (Ps. 9:18; Ps. 13:1; Jer. 23:39). "Then God re-membered Noah" (Gen. 8:1). Does God smack His forehead in this passage? "Oh, yeah! *Noah!*" Or in Exodus 6:5: "Man, that was close! I almost forgot. The *covenant!*" The answer for anyone who under-stands how human languages work is, "Of course not." And again, if human reason cannot comprehend *human* figures of speech, then how will it do with time and eternity?

It is important to note that while we are dealing with figures of speech in poetic and prophetic passages, we also have necessary figures of speech in the historical passages when an infinite God fo-cuses Himself at a finite point in order to interact with men. When God appears at one place He is not proclaiming Himself absent from other places—even if He declares Himself present here in some em-phatic way. When God relents and changes a course of action, He is not being fickle the way a man would be. What would He change it *from?* Is the change from the way it looked to *us* to be going, or is the change from what *He* had determined and planned? The Bible does not say that everything works out "according to the purpose of Him who works all things according to the counsel of His will, until further notice, or until someone has a better idea" (Eph. 7:28).

Another objection to the orthodox doctrine of God requires a different kind of response (i.e., an extra-biblical reponse) since it is a claim about the process and development of doctrine over the course of church history. The claim is often made that classical theism is really a post-Catholic phenomenon. The idea is that classical theism was formulated and adopted by the church in the patristic and medieval period, and that the Reformers unfortunately failed to jettison this holdover from medieval scholasticism. If we were like the early Christians, the argument goes, we would be post-pagan, and not so post-Catholic. "We must not allow the artificial categories of scholastic theology of the Middle Ages to bind our study of the Word of God."

As Peter Leithart has shown in his essay, such an argument does have some legitimate applications (the Church *has* picked up some barnacles here and there). But the central problem with this claim concerning the omniscience of God is that it is just a straightforward mistake, with nothing confusing about it.

The preacher of Ecclesiastes says nothing is new under the sun (Eccl. 1:10). The human race can safely say, when it comes to the various options in theology, that we have been there and done that, usually several times. The ancient unbelieving world *was* populated with numerous finite deities. While the Homeric Zeus was powerful, his power had limits; the Olympians were residents together with the rest of us in the universe. But this kind of "theology" was held largely by the uneducated and superstitious. Among the educated Greeks, various philosophical options emerged, Stoicism among them. The Stoics were pantheists, which meant they identified the universe with God, which, while it remained idolatrous, exhibits a much loftier understanding of the mysteries confronting us in the creation. This loftier paganism is occasionally put to use in the pages of the New Testament, with one example mentioned earlier that relates to the point under discussion. The quotation says, "For we are also His offspring." The quotation may be from the poet Aratus, or the hymn-writer Cleanthes. In either case, Paul applies this pagan observation in this way: "in Him we live and move and have our being." In other words, every creature lives in the *environment* of God. This was written before the rise of medieval scholasticism.

Among the covenant people of God, the Jews, we find a very high view of exhaustive omniscience. Of course we have already seen this understanding reflected in the Scripture passages we have already discussed, but for those who need the point reinforced, we can easily find it elsewhere as well. For example, in the noncanonical Apocrypha we find statements such as these:

> Such a man only feareth the eyes of men, and knoweth not that the eyes of the Lord are ten thousand times brighter than the sun, beholding all the ways of men, and considering the most secret parts. *He knew all things ere ever they were created;* so also after they were perfected he looked upon them all. (Sirach 23:19–20; KJV)

In other words, God knew everything before anything was created.

> All wisdom cometh from the Lord, and is with him for ever. *Who can number* the sand of the sea, and the drops of rain, and *the days of eternity?*

Who can find out the height of heaven, and the breadth of the earth, and the deep, and wisdom? Wisdom hath been created before all things, and the understanding of prudence from everlasting. (Sirach 1:1–4; KJV)

Who can number the days of eternity? The answer is the God and Father of our Lord Jesus Christ. And no, eternity does not have literal "days."

For the Spirit of the Lord *filleth the world*: and that which containeth all things hath knowledge of the voice. (Wisdom of Solomon 1:7; KJV)

We have already discussed Jeremiah's doctrine that God fills heaven and earth. No place excludes Him. Or, as this passage from 2 Esdras puts it, His Spirit fills the universe. He is obviously ignorant of nothing in that universe.

Yea, and the Spirit of Almighty God, which made all things, and searcheth out all hidden things in the secrets of the earth, surely he knoweth your inventions, and what ye think in your hearts, even them that sin, and would hide their sin. Therefore hath the Lord exactly searched out all your works, and he will put you all to shame. (2 Esdras 16:62–64; KJV)

We see here the moral implications of the exhaustive omniscience of God. The fact that *God knows* is a matter of concern to those who want room in their hearts to hide their sin. And it ought to be.

Then Susanna cried out with a loud voice, and said, "O everlasting God, that knowest the secrets, *and knowest all things before they be*." (Susanna 42; KJV)

Susanna knew far better than our modern "rationalistic" explainers. Before anything comes to pass, God knew it. If it comes to pass, then God knew it beforehand. This has been the simple faith of true believers *for millennia*. Susanna had not been reading Thomas Aquinas. Now if God knows all things before they came to be, as Susanna believed, this means necessarily that the knowledge of God is *immutable*. His knowledge does not grow as He interacts with the busy world.

Of course the point being made by such citations is not that such statements are as authoritive as Scripture, but simply to show that this kind of thinking was taken for granted among followers of the true God long before the first medieval scholastic ever "muddied" the theological waters. Put another way, the orthodox understanding of God's omniscience is historically *ancient* and can be demonstrated as such.

The point is not to be unnecessarily insulting, but the idol of rationalism does need to be laughed at. Those who vaunt the powers of reason have far too much trouble when it comes to one of the tasks that reason *can* perform, such as diagramming sentences. So the accusation that those who are faithful to the biblical teaching on this issue are trapped by patristic or medieval categories may be effective as a debating point. But it will only remain effective until those who have been swayed by it discover how false it is.

Relevance to the Gospel

As Scripture presents it, the gospel begins with our need for the gospel. As sinners we are united in a deep covenant with Adam; we are united with Adam in his disobedience and death, and we have no individual escape. We were plunged into sin by means of a corporate head, so we must be removed from sin the same way. But we need to realize more than just the fact that we are "in sin." We are in sin and under the wrath of a holy God: Adam's sin determined what we are. But how does a holy God respond to what we are? His anger is hot against us—even Christians by nature were under His wrath before the intervention of His grace. Nothing in our nature or character distinguished us from those who are not saved.

So the gospel comes to us while we were in this condition—united with Adam and under the wrath of God. For our salvation, Scripture calls us to look to the *person* and *work* of our Lord Jesus Christ. With regard to the first, our Savior serves as a bridge between God and man and is Himself both God and man. With regard to the second, our Savior, the God/Man, died on the cross to secure the forgiveness of all His people, and He rose again from the dead to secure their justification. To all of this, the response required of the sinner is that of repentance and belief. But lest anyone boast, even these are the gift of God, given by Him as the instrument of salvation and used to build upon the ground of our salvation, which is, again, the person and work of our Lord.

Now our purpose here is to concentrate on one aspect of this. The gospel can be overthrown when we tinker with any aspect of it, but in our day one of the more common (and undetected) ways of assaulting the gospel is through the attempt to put certain attributes of God "on the table" for debate amongst Christians.

"Surely we can all be Christians together, and disagree over how much God knows?" The answer is *no* and is directly related to our re-hearsal of the gospel above. The Bible repeatedly and emphatically connects our salvation through the gospel to a proper understanding of *who Jesus is*. "Who is a liar but he who denies that Jesus is the Christ? He is antichrist who denies the Father and the Son" (1 Jn. 2:22). "Whoever believes that Jesus is the Christ is born of God, and every-one who loves Him who begot also loves him who is begotten of Him" (1 Jn. 5:1). In order to be considered "born of God," a man must affirm that Jesus is the Christ. But what does this title—*Christ*—involve? John does not mean that anyone who uses the word "Christ" is auto-matically saved. This would include virtually every cultic group in the history of the church. He refers to a proper *confession* of Christ, a con-fession that must be defined biblically.

In Christ, the mystery of godliness was manifested. "And without controversy great is the mystery of godliness: *God* was *manifested* in the flesh, justified in the Spirit, seen by angels, preached among the Gen-tiles, believed on in the world, received up in glory" (1 Tim. 3:16). "And you know that He was *manifested* to take away our sins, and in Him there is no sin" (1 Jn. 3:5). "He who sins is of the devil, for the devil has sinned from the beginning. For this purpose the Son of God was *man-ifested*, that He might destroy the works of the devil" (1 Jn. 3:8). Our salvation was a manifestation. This necessitates the obvious ques-tion—manifestation of what? The answer of Scripture is clear—in Christ *God* was manifested in the flesh for our salvation. The finitude of Christ's humanity was "added" to His Deity, and was not an "in-finite subtraction" from it.

"In this the love of God was manifested toward us, that God has sent His only begotten Son into the world, that we might live through Him" (1 Jn. 4:9). Christ is the "only begotten" Son of the Father. This refers to the unique essential relationship between the Father and the Son.

Such questions surrounding the Deity and Incarnation of Christ may initially seem arcane and impractical to some. Evangelical Christians instinctively understand the importance of Christ's death on the cross, i.e., they understand the importance of His *work*. But a proper understanding of His *person* is equally important. Consider the Bible's very blunt teaching on this; our salvation rests upon an accurate confession of Christ's *identity*.

"Whoever confesses that Jesus *is* the Son of God, God abides in him, and he in God" (1 Jn. 4:15). "Who is he who overcomes the world, but he who believes that Jesus *is* the Son of God?" (1 Jn. 5:5). "And we know that the Son of God has come and has given us an understanding, that we may know Him who is true; and we are in Him who is true, in His Son Jesus Christ. *This is the true God and eternal life.* Little children, keep yourselves from idols. Amen" (1 Jn. 5:20–21). Anything less than this confession is an idol of some sort or other. And we know that idols do not save. The man who trusts in them will be brought to shame.

As Christians we confess that God became *man*. The opportunities for clever men to steal our inheritance at this point are obvious.

> For many deceivers have gone out into the world who do not confess Jesus Christ as coming in the flesh. This is a deceiver and an antichrist. Look to yourselves, that we do not lose those things we worked for, but that we may receive a full reward. Whoever transgresses and does not abide in the doctrine of Christ does not have God. He who abides in the doctrine of Christ has both the Father and the Son. (2 Jn. 7–9; 1 Jn. 4:2–3)

The Bible teaches us, in the strongest possible terms, that our salvation depends upon a faithful continuance in *the doctrine of who Christ is*.

As Christians we believe in the name of Jesus. "And this is His commandment: that we should believe on the *name* of His Son Jesus Christ and love one another, as He gave us commandment" (1 Jn. 3:23). "He who has the Son has life; he who does not have the Son of God does not have life . . . and that you may continue to believe in the *name* of the Son of God" (1 Jn. 5:13). In the world of the New Testament, a name was a much greater thing than a mere label. Believing in the name of Christ is inseparable from believing in His true *identity*.

And believing in the name of Jesus was essential to salvation. This matter is clearly related to the gospel.

So this is how one's view of God's omniscience affects the gospel and either upholds it or overthrows it. We have seen it is necessary to affirm that Jesus is God in order to be considered born of God. Now how would this affirmation be required of us with regard to Christ, but not with regard to *God?* We do not want to be found in the curious position of maintaining that in order to be saved we must affirm the full Deity of Jesus Christ, but that it is not necessary to affirm the full Deity of God. If omniscience is an essential attribute of Deity, as has been shown earlier, then a denial of it is a denial of Deity. This is what we are discussing when we address the attributes of God—the identity of God, the *Godness* of God. When Paul rebukes the Corinthians because they were being led astray, he recognizes that false teachers still use the *name* Jesus.

> But I fear, lest somehow, as the serpent deceived Eve by his craftiness, so your minds may be corrupted from the simplicity that is in Christ. For if he who comes preaches another Jesus whom we have not preached, or if you receive a different spirit which you have not received, or a different gospel which you have not accepted—you may well put up with it! (2 Cor. 11:3–4)

"Another" Jesus is identifiable only by the attributes which are predicated of him. If someone were to claim that he knew a Henry Smith, someone else might say, "Oh, I know him too!" But when they get to talking, they discover that one of the Smiths is over six feet tall, and the other is barely over five. One is three hundred pounds, and the other is one-hundred fifty pounds. It would not be long before they decided they were talking about different people with the same name. They decided this on the basis of the differences between their *attributes.*

We learned earlier that a denial of the Son is tantamount to a denial of the Father. The road is a two-way street; a denial of the Father is a roundabout way of denying the Son.

This difference is analogous to the difference that Christians have with the Mormons. The LDS use the name *Jesus Christ* but have a different definition of His person, attributes, and character. Christians would therefore say that we are not talking about the same Jesus as they are, even though Christians and Mormons would both refer to all of the same events in His life, death, and resurrection, and would do so from the same New Testament. Mormons would want to say they are referring to Jesus of *Nazareth*, not Jesus from Guatemala. But this does not matter. They deny certain essential attributes that Scripture attributes to Christ, and so they are following an idol of their own imaginations. The fact that they place a biblical name on this idol is immaterial. When the Israelites worshipped the golden calf that had brought them up "out of the land of Egypt" they were still worshipping an idol—even though they *had* been brought up out of the land of Egypt. In a similar way, our concern is that this new definition of omniscience strips God of His Deity. That being so, we are not talking about the same Person, and when Christ is affirmed as being God, the affirmation is worthless. The Father has already been denied. How can we retain the Son?

We can see that the teaching of Openness theism is therefore an assault on the gospel. The gospel is not an abstraction, suspended in space. We must define the gospel through how it appears in Scripture—contextually and exegetically. Our information about the content of the gospel, its relation to connected truths, and the biblical way to understand and obey it must come from the Scriptures. We have done this. We have seen how the Bible describes God, and we have seen that the Bible connects a proper confession of the Deity of Christ to salvation. We must conclude the gospel rests upon a certain understanding of God, and that this understanding is *not* optional, or up for discussion.

> He saw that there was *no man*, and wondered that there was no intercessor; therefore *His own arm brought salvation* for Him; and His own righteousness, it sustained Him. (Is. 59:16)

In order to be saved, we must know the Lord, and we must know Him as He has revealed Himself. This means that salvation cannot be understood outside the confines of what we call classical theism. "Great is our Lord, and mighty in power; His understanding is infinite" (Ps. 147:5). Put very simply, this means that the God who saves knows everything. If He does not know everything, including the future, He is not God as He has revealed Himself, the God who saves.

We must not trifle with God. God is not restricted in what He is able to do. Nothing outside His own good purposes, His own nature and character, restricts Him in any way. "Indeed these are the mere edges of His ways, and how small a whisper we hear of Him! But the thunder of His power who can understand?" (Job 26:14). No one understands the majesty of our God, least of all our modern theologians who deeply want a kinder, gentler god. Well, they can have him.

FINAL APPLICATIONS

Even after all this, some might still want to ask what practical difference the doctrine of omniscience makes. Why is this important? Ideas have consequences and destinations, and these ideas of free will theism are extremely dangerous in their day-to-day practical implications, and not just dangerous with regard to eternity. Some Christians are suspicious of "all this doctrine" but understand the importance of practical Christian obedience. While this suspicion is not scriptural, the emphasis upon practical holiness *is* biblical.

So what are some of the possible practical ramifications? The point is not that every advocate of free will theism teaches these things which follow; the point is rather that such teaching will have these effects, whether intended or not.

The Bible says this doctrine that "God does not know" creates the temptation to tolerate secret sin, and it appeals to those who want room for secret sin. Open disobedience may be checked because of the eye of man, but secret sins are no longer resisted because of the eye of God. For example, there soon comes a temptation to indulge in evil thoughts. If God does not know my thoughts, and may never know them, then to whom am I accountable? In time this leads to a tolerance of open sin, including the sin of denying the teaching of the Bible—which we have already addressed.

> Yet they say, "The LORD does not see, nor does the God of Jacob understand." Understand, you senseless among the people; and you fools, when will you be wise? He who planted the ear, shall He not hear? He who formed the eye, shall He not see? He who instructs the nations, shall He not correct, He who teaches man knowledge? The LORD knows the thoughts of man, that they are futile. (Ps. 94:7–11)

Related to this, the doctrine of free will theism creates the temptation to confess sin *partially*. If a man is in the habit of thinking about what God does *not* know, the opportunities for self-deception are great. But any attempts to confess sin dishonestly are practical denials of God's omniscience, even among those who affirm the doctrine with their lips. We should not be surprised that theological denials of His omniscience give additional room for this sin to hide.

An advocate of free will theism might respond that he could with perfect consistency maintain that God will in fact discover every sin, and that God will in fact judge every motive. Perfect justice will be fulfilled on the Last Day. While of course this position is more admirable than insisting that God will *not* discover which things slipped through the cracks on the Day of Judgment, an important thing must still be noted about such an assertion. It is a radical "shrinking back" from the exegetical method embraced by this entire school of thought. Earlier we saw the method insist that words like *search* must mean the same thing when applied to God as when they are applied to men. God must be ignorant then in order truly to search. Words like *remember* and *sorrow* are applied in the same way.

And the LORD was *sorry that He had made* man on the earth, and He was grieved in His heart. (Gen. 6:6)

Now when I am sorry about something I have done, it is because I have either sinned or screwed up. I have either disobeyed or made a mistake. *So why do we not employ the method here?* Why shrink back now? If God can err in *making* men, as Genesis plainly states, then what principle prevents Him from erring while judging them? If an immutable, unchanging, inerrant God tells me that He will bring every motive and idle word into perfect judgment, then I had better listen up. But if I am told the same thing by a mutable, changing god who sometimes forgets, and other times backtracks, and at other times admits that *he did the wrong thing*, then how do I know that a perfect judgment will come to pass? If we worship an interactive god who sometimes says, "Oops," then how on earth can we consistently stand on his promises? The best we can be certain of is that he will try to judge rightly. If he remembers.

Thinking that God is limited in His knowledge also creates the temptation to worship God formally and externally. "Nevertheless they flattered Him with their mouth, and they lied to Him with their tongue" (Ps. 78:36). Where does this sin of hypocrisy come from, if not from deficient views of what God *knows*? When someone lies to God, he has to believe, at some level of his being, that God *can* be lied to. But God can only be deceived if He is limited in His knowledge.

An exhaustively omniscient God is beyond deception, and meditating upon this fact is always good for the soul.

CONCLUSION

Our God is an eternal God. His Spirit is eternal (Heb. 9:14). His glory is eternal (1 Pet. 5:10). As we have seen, this means much more than that He is *old*. Because He is eternal, and not simply long-lived, we may take refuge in Him. "The eternal God is your refuge, and underneath are the everlasting arms" (Deut. 33:27).

Even the pagans were expected to understand this eternal aspect of His nature and character. "For since the creation of the world His invisible attributes are *clearly seen*, being understood by the things that are made, *even His eternal power and Godhead*, so that they are without excuse" (Rom. 1:20). The fact that professing Christians have come to deny in the Scriptures what even the pagans were required to see in the created order is almost beyond comprehension. Much more is required than mere affirmation of the word *eternal*; the word must be used in its biblical sense. And if the pagans were without excuse for what they did, how shall we answer the Lord if we forsake what He has revealed to *us*?

> Now to the King eternal, immortal, invisible, to God who alone is wise, be honor and glory forever and ever. Amen. (1 Tim. 1:17)

GOODNESS

IO

Pastoral Implications of Open Theism

Thomas K. Ascol

In many respects Open theism is a perfect theological fit for the contemporary American *zeitgeist*. In an age where empathy trumps truthfulness we are more comforted by someone who feels our pain than by someone who speaks honestly, unequivocally, and consistently. Disappoint us if you will, fail to keep your promises if you must, but do not cease to reassure us that you really feel for us. The God of Open theism perfectly fits this criterion.

Greg Boyd claims that the differences between the Openness and orthodox views of God are "relatively unimportant," "peripheral," and "minor."[1] Other chapters have thoroughly debunked that notion from biblical, doctrinal, and historical perspectives. Open theism cannot legitimately be classified as a subset of evangelicalism. It is a radically different understanding of reality and therefore of the real God. Its implications for the Christian life are as far-reaching as they are devastating.

Some of these implications are self-consciously held and celebrated by the proponents of Open theism. For instance, Boyd finds it pastorally helpful to be able to counsel a person who has experienced great tragedy that God was as surprised as everyone else at what happened. In Boyd's mind this makes God kinder and gentler and therefore more trustworthy.[2] Other implications are more subtle and may well be renounced by Open theists but, as will be seen, are nevertheless inherent in their system of thought. One cannot possess a forest without owning the trees, no matter how vehemently he might protest to the contrary.

[1] Greg Boyd, *God of the Possible* (Grand Rapids: Baker, 2000), 8, 20, 89.
[2] Ibid., 103–6.

UNDERMINES CONFIDENCE IN SCRIPTURE

Boyd argues that "if we simply accept the plain meaning of Scripture" we will concur with Open theism's claims that sometimes God "regrets how decisions he's made turn out," "questions how aspects of the future will go," "experiences frustration because free agents choose unlikely courses of action," and "genuinely changes his mind about intended courses of action."[3] His optimistic overstatement notwithstanding, the Openness perspective actually calls into question Scripture's "plain meaning" and violates fundamental principles of interpretation. The result is a huge cloud of doubt left hanging over the perspicuity and reliability of Scripture.

A long standing principle of hermeneutics declares that passages which clearly assert a doctrine or principle are to be used to shed light on narrative passages.

> Interpret historic material by didactic material. Historical material is narration, the accounts of what happened in the past. Didactic material is teaching material. It is important for the didactic material to interpret the historical material rather than the other way around.[4]

The importance of this guiding principle can be demonstrated by applying it to the Bible's teaching on the sinfulness of mankind. Romans 3:23 makes a straightforward affirmation of the universality of human sinfulness, "For all have sinned and come short of the glory of God." This didactic passage sheds light on other passages that are narrative or testimonial. For example, the story of Daniel's life might lead one to believe that, because there is no record of any sin he committed, he was a sinless man. If the narrative passages of his life were all that we had then we, at best, could not refute such a claim.

If the principle articulated above is followed, there will be no danger of reaching that conclusion. Though the narrative might suggest that there was no sin in Daniel, the didactic passage assures us that

---

[3] Ibid., 87.

[4] James M. Boice, *Standing on the Rock, Biblical Authority in a Secular Age* (Grand Rapids: Baker Books, 1994), 82. See also Robertson McQuilkin, *Understanding and Applying the Bible* (Chicago: Moody, 1992), 233–34, and R.C. Sproul, *Knowing Scripture* (Downers Grove: InterVarsity Press, 1977), 68–75. Sproul points out the need for particular care in recognizing phenomenological language in biblical narrative.

there was. By giving priority to clearly stated teaching regarding sin and using the light that it sheds on the story of Daniel's life, we will resist making any claims of sinlessness for him.

Open theists turn this principle of interpretation on its head. John Sanders goes to great lengths to establish patterns from narrative passages on divine–human relationships and then uses those patterns to reinterpret clear, didactic Scriptures. The stories of Adam, Noah, Abraham, Gideon, Moses, and David are all cited as examples of God changing his mind, repenting, being disappointed, or caught off guard by what happened.[5] The survey of these stories is set forth as evidence "that God is in a dynamic give–and–take relationship with humans and in which God sometimes does not get what he wants."[6]

Efforts to interpret these texts in the light of didactic passages that assert God's sovereign control over people and events (what Sanders calls "pancausality texts") are charged with "hermeneutical malpractice."[7] Statements like the following are all reinterpreted in light of narrative "evidence" of the Openness of God:

- "O house of Israel, can I not do with you as this potter?" says the LORD. "Look, as the clay is in the potter's hand, so are you in My hand, O house of Israel!" (Jer. 18:6)
- A man's heart plans his way, But the LORD directs his steps. (Prov. 16:9)
- The king's heart is in the hand of the LORD, Like the rivers of water; He turns it wherever He wishes. (Prov. 21:1)
- Who has made man's mouth? Or who makes the mute, the deaf, the seeing, or the blind? Have not I, the LORD? (Exod. 4:11).

Some of the results would be amusing if the stakes involved were not so high.

For instance, Proverbs 16:9 and 21:1 are taken to mean only that "God directs his people's steps (16:9) and guides the king of Israel (21:1) when he seeks God's wisdom." Exodus 4:11 becomes nothing more than "a general statement that such things happen in God's

---

[5] John Sanders, *The God Who Risks, a Theology of Providence* (Downers Grove: InterVarsity Press, 1998), 41–75.
[6] Ibid., 81.
[7] Ibid.

world" and an admission that He takes "full responsibility" for creating such a world where defects are possible.[8]

With its presupposition that God has only limited knowledge of what will happen in the future, Open theism must reconstruct plain statements of Scripture to the contrary. The story of Joseph provides a case in point. At the end of the narrative Joseph makes his famous declaration to his frightened brothers, which reflects his simple and complete confidence in God's sovereign, detailed arrangement of his life. It is his divinely inspired explanation of the events of his life: "But as for you, you meant evil against me; but God meant it for good, in order to bring it about as it is this day, to save many people alive" (Gen. 50:20).

Sanders' interpretation of this verse is dismissive at best. He writes, "I take this to mean that God has brought something good out of their evil actions." He further comments, "Although he [Joseph] acknowledges that they sold him into Egypt, he suggests that everyone look on the bright side—what God has done through this. Their lives and those of the Egyptians have been spared the devastating effects of the famine."[9] From a profound, theological declaration of God's unmitigated providence, Sanders reduces Joseph's words to, "Serendipity!"

Whether intentional or not, the Openness reading of Scripture, if followed consistently, renders direct teachings of the Bible vacuous if not incomprehensible.

UNDERMINES CONFIDENCE IN GOD

The Open theistic vision of God is one which robs believers of comfort and confidence. The traditional understanding of God gives full weight to those biblical declarations that describe Him as "Lord God Almighty... King of the Saints" (Rev. 15:3), Who "rules over the nations" (Ps. 22:28) and "the raging of the sea" (Ps. 89:9), and Who shall "reign forever and ever" (Exod. 15:18; cf. Pss. 93:1, 96:10, 9:1, 99:1, 146:10). Nebuchadnezzar's inspired declaration of God's unhindered, meticulous exercise of His divine providence is no embarrassment to orthodox theism:

[8] Ibid., 84–85.
[9] Ibid., 55.

All the inhabitants of the earth are reputed as nothing;
He does according to His will in the army of heaven
And among the inhabitants of the earth.
No one can restrain His hand
Or say to Him, "What have you done?" (Dan. 4:35)

Open theism dismisses the view of God and providence that these verses naturally portray because it does not "fit" with the "biblical story" as they see it.[10] Instead of recognizing God as the unrivaled Ruler of the universe, free will theists want to portray Him as the "cosmic Gambler." This view of God is supposed to engender comfort and hope on the part of believers, but in fact it destroys the very foundation which the Bible establishes for trusting God.

Sanders is quite plain in expressing his desire to replace God as King with God as "risk taker."[11] God took a chance in creating a world He populated with creatures who are endowed with libertarian free wills. He did so in an effort to accomplish "the divine project," which "involves the creation of significant others who are ontologically distinct from himself and upon whom he showers his caring love in the expectation that they will respond in love."[12] This risk, Sanders argues, had a "great chance of success and little possibility of failure;" in fact, "although sin was possible—given this sort of world—it simply was not plausible in view of the good environment God established and the love he bestowed."[13]

But any honest reading of history or Scripture demonstrates that the "divine project," as Sanders defines it, is a colossal failure. Jesus said that only a "few" will enter the narrow gate and walk the narrow path of loving God (Mt. 7:13–14), and missiological analyses of Christian history certainly confirm His announcement. If the sin and degradation of the world are the result of a highly implausible disruption in God's low-risk creative venture, how can anyone be expected to trust Him for future "projects?"

Open theism reduces God to a cosmic gambler—and not a very successful one at that. He created billions of image bearers, gambling that they would choose to love and trust Him. This was to have been

[10] Ibid., 228.
[11] Ibid., 11. See Boyd, *God of the Possible*, 57–58.
[12] Sanders, *Risks*, 169.
[13] Ibid., 172.

178 BOUND ONLY ONCE

an "almost sure thing" because of His love and provision. But, in terms of sheer quantitative analysis, His gamble hardly paid off. From creation to the present the Openness God has continued to take risks, only to experience repeated failures. Both the Bible and history are filled with accounts of people and "projects" that He counted on in vain.[14]

How can such a God be trusted? If that which He has intended to do has so catastrophically and repeatedly failed to come to pass, why depend on Him to fulfill any of His promises, no matter how well-intentioned they may be? I would sooner risk my family's finances on a lottery ticket than my soul to a gambler with such a poor track record.

Boyd does not see this problem and, in fact, argues that the Openness view of God makes Him more trustworthy than the classical view. Instead of seeing God as meticulously ruling and overruling all of the affairs of life for good and holy purposes, Boyd chooses to think of God's exercise of providence as being like a child's "Choose Your Own Adventure" story, in which the author creates a number of possible plots that the reader can progressively select as he or she progresses through the book. In a similar way "the God of the possible is the author of the whole story line of creation and the one who offers possible alternatives to his human and angelic creations," thus leaving "plenty of room for individuals to exercise free will."[15]

A God who exhaustively knows the future or who ordains it is not worthy of trust, Boyd says, because that bad thing that He knows will happen to you in two days must infallibly happen, no matter what you do or do not do. He complains,

> How does believing this help you "trust God"? What are you really trusting God for? To simply know from all eternity that this terrible event is going to happen to you: What security is there in that: How does this belief help you in the least?[16]

Far better, Boyd contends, to have a God who knows this thing not as an inevitability but as merely one of many possibilities that might befall you in two days. In this case, God works to encourage you to create

---

[14] See, for example, ibid., 71–72 and Boyd, *God of the Possible*, 55–56.
[15] Boyd, *God of the Possible*, 43.
[16] Ibid., 151.

a future which avoids that bad possibility—especially if "you are a person who frequently talks and listens to God" and "have family and friends who pray for you on a consistent basis." In such cases God "can be trusted to inspire [you] to avoid certain future possibilities he sees coming."[17]

Of course, what Boyd fails to address is why anyone should be willing to trust the promptings of a God whose best intentions have been thwarted time and again throughout history. Indeed, an episode out of his own pastoral experience stands in protest against his theory. He tells the story of "Suzanne," a young woman who was "raised in a wonderful Christian home," had been a "passionate, godly disciple of Jesus Christ" from her youth, and had a near lifelong desire to be a missionary to Taiwan.[18] She prayed daily for her future husband that he would share her vision for Taiwan, "remain faithful to the Lord and remain pure in heart." She met and courted such a man for more than three years during college. After months of prayer, fasting, and consulting with their parents, pastor, and friends, everyone agreed that "this marriage was indeed God's will." Suzanne herself received a special confirmation of this while in prayer one day.

Shortly after her marriage, while in missionary school, Suzanne's husband began a pattern of adultery and abuse and refused to be helped or to repent. When he filed for divorce she was left pregnant, "angry," "emotionally destroyed and spiritually bankrupt." In order to help her deal with the devastation of her ordeal, Boyd offered her "an alternative way of understanding the situation." He writes, "I suggested to her that God felt as much regret over the confirmation he had given Suzanne as he did about his decision to make Saul king of Israel (1 Sam. 15:11, 35; see also Gen. 6:5–6)."[19] But why didn't God work in Suzanne to encourage her to create a future that avoided this possibility? Surely she fits Boyd's profile of the type of person who can trust the open God to do just that.

How can God be "trusted to inspire" His children to take certain decisions when He Himself is as fallible as we are because He does not exhaustively know the future? It is hard to see how this view does not reduce God to the level of a television meteorologist—one who,

---

[17] Ibid., 152.

[18] The details of this story, from which the quotes of this paragraph are taken, can be found in ibid., 103–6.

[19] Ibid., 105.

because He is an expert in His field, has access to information that is not readily available to others, is in a better position than most to make educated guesses about the future. The question remains, "Why should we trust such a God?"

It is one thing to base your picnic plans on a weatherman's forecast. If unexpected rain ruins your day you may be disappointed and even frustrated with him and his predictions, but you recognize that he is only making an educated guess about meteorological patterns. You don't expect him to be infallible. But we have much higher expectations of God. If He inspires us to actions that He later regrets, then He is ultimately untrustworthy.

The classical view of God will never lead to that conclusion. If, contrary to Open theism, God knows the end from the beginning (Is. 46:10) and thinks and works in ways that are much higher than our ways (Is. 55:8–9), then we can trust Him to work all things—including inexplicably bad things—together for our good (Rom. 8:28). Remove God's sovereign control over life and His complete knowledge of the future and the very foundation for trusting Him begins to crumble.

Undermines Faith in Christ

Open theism's revisioning of the nature of the future and of God erodes the very heart of the Christian faith by undermining faith in Jesus Christ. No doubt this is one of the unintended implications of Openness proponents—and one that they would strongly renounce. But when God's limited foreknowledge is applied to the incarnation and crucifixion, the credibility of Christ and the biblical witness to Christ are compromised.

In the Openness scheme Jesus did not—could not—know beforehand that He would be called to die for sinners. Sanders unashamedly reconstructs the events leading up to and surrounding Christ's death to portray both Father and Son deciding only at the last minute that Jesus had to die. "Although Scripture attests that the incarnation was planned from the creation of the world, this is not so with the cross. The path of the cross comes about only through God's interaction with humans in history." Not until the agonizing prayer in Gethsemane do "Father and Son . . . both come to understand that there is no other way." Even after this new discovery comes to God, the question still hangs over Jesus, "Will this gambit work?"[20]

Jesus' predictions of His betrayal, death, and resurrection are disregarded as general observations of future possibilities rather than, as He intended, evidencing that He is the Messiah. Boyd believes that "Scripture makes the most sense when we understand Jesus' predictions about Judas's betrayal" as a well-informed prediction based on good insight into Judas's character.[21] In Boyd's view, God planned the basic outline of Jesus' death. Then, when he observed Judas turning himself into a "son of perdition," all God had to do was figure out "how he might strategically weave the wicked character" of Judas into the divine plan.[22]

But this construction is evidently still too deterministic for Sanders. Jesus, he argues, did not really know that Judas would betray Him. Even when He told Judas, "What you do, do quickly" (Jn. 13:27), a huge risk was involved, "since there is no guarantee which way Judas will decide."[23] The foretelling of Peter's denial is treated similarly. Sanders finds it preferable to view Jesus' prediction as an educated guess that in no way suggests He knew with certainty what would happen before it happened. None of Jesus' prophecies concerning His death and resurrection "require exhaustive foreknowledge." In Sanders' mind the cross was not planned before creation, and Jesus Himself did not certainly know beforehand what events would lead up to and surround His arrest and execution.[24] Things could have gone quite differently, and according to Open theism, it would not have made one bit of difference in the life and ministry of Jesus or in our own esteem of Him.

Jesus, however, viewed the matter quite differently. In the upper room discourse He specifically links His predictions to His deity and to His disciples' belief in His deity. When washing His disciples' feet

[20] Sanders, Risks, 100–01. He writes, "My own view is that the incarnation was always planned, for God intended to bring us into the joy and glory shared among the triune Godhead (Jn. 17:22–24). Human sin, however, threw up a barrier to the divine project, and God's planned incarnation had to be adapted in order to overcome it." Ibid., 103.

[21] Boyd, God of the Possible, 37.

[22] Ibid., 38.

[23] Sanders, Risks, 99.

[24] Ibid., 134–36.

He said, "You are not all clean" (Jn. 13:11), in an obvious reference to Judas. He alluded to Judas again a few verses later by identifying him with an Old Testament prophecy: "I do not speak concerning all of you. I know whom I have chosen; but that the Scripture may be fulfilled, 'He who eats bread with Me has lifted up his heel against Me'" (Jn. 13:18). Three verses later Jesus pointedly declares, "Most assuredly, I say to you, one of you will betray Me" (v. 21). Finally He singles out Judas as the betrayer by passing a piece of bread to him (v. 26).

In the midst of these clear expressions of foreknowledge, Jesus explains to the disciples why He is telling them these things: "Now I tell you before it comes, that when it does come to pass, you may believe that I am He" (Jn. 13:19). The "He" is supplied by translators. Literally what Jesus says is "that you may believe that I am [ego eimi]." He connects His foreknowledge of events, and His announcing of them, to His deity and to the disciples' recognition of it. It obviously mattered to Jesus that He be understood as foretelling with certainty what was going to happen to Him. His foreknowledge is foundational to the disciples' belief in His deity.

Diminish Jesus' foreknowledge and you bring His deity into question and thereby undermine the faith of those whom He calls to trust Him. Yet, this is precisely the effect of Open theism. We are asked to keep trusting a Christ who was prone to mistakes because He could not know the future exhaustively. As John Piper has commented on this passage, Jesus' foreknowledge "was an essential aspect of his glory as the incarnate Word, the Son of God. The denial of this foreknowledge is, I believe John would say, an assault on the deity of Christ."[25]

UNDERMINES PRAYER

Proponents of Open theism regard the "status of petitionary prayer within this model to be one of its most attractive features."[26] Prayer is seen as a means of influencing God to the degree of moving Him to

[25] John Piper, "Why the Glory of God is at Stake in the 'Foreknowledge' Debate," *Modern Reformation* (September/October 1999), 42.

[26] David Bassinger, "Practical Implications," in *The Openness of God*, by Clark Pinnock et al. (Downers Grove: InterVarsity Press), 162. Boyd writes, "I do not see that any view of God captures the power and urgency of prayer as adequately as the Open view does, and, because the heart is influenced by the mind, I do not see that any view can inspire passionate and urgent prayer as powerfully as the Open view can" (*God of the Possible*, 98).

reverse His own plans. Conversely, God is so dependent on prayer that at times, because of the failure of people to pray, He abandons plans that He would prefer to carry out.[27]

One's understanding of providence necessarily impacts his view of prayer. What God can do or has chosen to do in His relationship to the world governs the ways that we invoke His help for specific needs. The Openness view of reality eliminates the specific control that God exercises over creatures. Because the future is not "real" and therefore cannot be known by God, and because people have libertarian freedom, God is dependent on people to help Him create the future. When God is viewed as having this kind of contingency in relation to His creation, petitionary prayer is ultimately undermined in the life of the believer.

This may not be immediately apparent. In fact, Open theism may initially appear to have the exact opposite effect. Boyd argues that his view is a great motivation for prayer because in it God can be significantly affected and influenced by us. Many biblical examples are cited by Open theists as proof that prayer does indeed bring about a change in God's mind. Abraham (Gen. 18:22–33), Jacob (Gen. 32), Moses (Exod. 32:14, 33:1–2, 14; Deut. 9:13–29), Hezekiah (2 Kgs. 20:1–6), and Amos (Amos 7:1–6) are all regarded as having altered God's intentions through their petitions.[28] Prayer is seen as the creature's way of exercising "spiritual say-so," which God decided to share by making personal beings.[29] Because prayer can change God's plans, people should be excited about getting in on the effort to do just that in order to create a future that conforms to their own desires.

God's stated repentance and His response to prayers that plead for something different from that which has been previously announced are hermeneutical conundrums that challenge biblical interpreters of every persuasion. Open theists profess to solve the problems (and to stake out the exegetical high ground in doing so) by taking such passages "literally."[30] Traditionalists, we are led to believe, simply skirt around these passages, thereby robbing people of real incentive to pray passionately.

Reformed commentators and others throughout history have

[27] Boyd, *Possible*, 97; Sanders, *Risks*, 273–74.
[28] Boyd, *God of the Possible*, 82–85; Sanders, *Risks*, 53–54; 63–66.
[29] Boyd, *God of the Possible*, 96–97.
[30] Ibid., 84.

addressed these challenges without giving up the classical view of God.[31] There can be no doubt that the prayer lives of the biblical characters cited were characterized by passion, fervency, and effectiveness. It does not follow, however, that these qualities were born of an Open view of God. Furthermore, when these examples are considered in their broader context, they set forth a view of reality (and therefore, God) that is radically different from that of Open theism. The vision of God and His world that emerges can and should invigorate heart-felt prayer in ways that the Openness view cannot.

Consider the case of Hezekiah. Isaiah is sent by God to tell the sick king, "Set your house in order, for you shall die, and not live" (2 Kgs. 20:1). After Hezekiah prays with bitter tears, God, in response to the prayer, promises him an additional fifteen years of life. Boyd sees this account, which was determinative in his own theological pilgrimage, as demanding an Openness view of God.

> Now, if we accept the classical view of foreknowledge and suppose that the Lord was certain that he would *not* let Hezekiah die, wasn't he being duplicitous when he initially told Hezekiah that he would not recover? And if we suppose that the Lord was certain all along that Hezekiah would, in fact, live fifteen years after this episode, wasn't it misleading for God to tell him that he was *adding* fifteen years to his life?[32]

Boyd cannot escape his own criticism because the Openness view must also deal with the fact that God said something was going to happen which did not happen. The Open theist concludes that God spoke out of ignorance because He did not know Hezekiah would pray with such passion and fervency as to change the divine plan. Since God did not know, there is no moral dilemma in His reversal of His announced plans. The classical theist concludes that God's threat carried an implicit exception and that He did know that Hezekiah would repent and pray. Thus, God intended all along to extend the king's life fifteen years and to do it in response to prayer.[33]

---

[31] Besides standard, time-tested writers like John Calvin, John Gill, and Matthew Henry, many contemporary expositors have convincingly addressed the exegetical questions raised by Open theists. One of the most thoughtful of the latter is John Piper, who has published several articles on the web site of the Baptist General Conference. See his *Answering Greg Boyd's Openness of God Texts*, 11 May 1998, and *The Enormous Ignorance of God: When God Doesn't Know the Future Choices of Man*, 2 Dec. 1997, available at http://www.bgc.bethel.edu/4know/pessays.htm

[32] Boyd, *God of the Possible*, 82.

[33] See Piper, *Answering Greg Boyd's Openness of God Texts*.

The classical view is supported by the broader context of this story. When Hezekiah died, his son Manasseh, who was twelve years old, became king in his place (2 Kgs. 20:21, 21:1). What this means is that Manasseh was born during the fifteen-year extension of Hezekiah's life. Sanders says that if Hezekiah had not prayed to God, "biblical history would have been different."[34] But that is a woefully inadequate understatement. Had Hezekiah died when Isaiah first spoke to him, he would have left no heir to the throne and the promise that God made to David three hundred years earlier would have been broken. The Lord had promised David, "You shall not lack a man on the throne of Israel" (1 Kgs. 2:4), which "simply affirms that the posterity of David was not to be cut off, so as to leave no offshoot which could take possession of the throne."[35]

If, as Boyd and his colleagues contend, God was truly ignorant of the timing of Hezekiah's death when He sent Isaiah to him, then we are left with insurmountable doubts about the Lord's faithfulness. Had Hezekiah died before his son Manasseh was born, God's Word would have failed. And if God cannot be trusted to do what He says, why ask Him to do anything at all? This blasphemous thought, which emerges (no doubt unintentionally) from Open theism's view of God will quench any desire to pray with passion and fervency.

This problem is compounded if God is viewed as having created a world in which people have the power to do things He never intended to happen. Any specific intervention by God to interfere directly with a person's chosen course would be a violation both of the individual's personhood and of the "rules of the game God sovereignly established" in creating people with libertarian freedom.[36] How could someone pray passionately for God to restrain evil people or protect His own people if He genuinely believes that the rules by which God is bound prohibit Him from ever removing the potential to choose evil

---

[34] Sanders, *Risks*, 271.

[35] C.F. Keil and C. Delitzsch, *Commentary on the Old Testament*, volume 3; translated by James Martin (Grand Rapids: Eerdmanns, 1986), 28.

[36] Sanders, *Risks*, 222; cf. 194–95. David Bassinger tries to hedge his openness bet at this point. He admits that God "can unilaterally intervene in earthly affairs" but quickly adds that "a key assumption in the Open model is that God so values the inherent integrity of significant human freedom—the ability of individuals to maintain control over the significant aspects of their lives—that he will not *as a general rule* force his created moral agents to perform actions that they do not freely desire to perform or manipulate the natural environment in such a way that their freedom of choice is destroyed" (*Openness*, 160–61, emphasis added).

from a person? Would not such prayer be asking God to do what He has committed Himself not to do?

The examples of fervent prayers that we have in the Bible are not the least bit inhibited in these ways because they are not at all based on an Open view of God. When Daniel prayed for the restoration of Judah, he was motivated by his recent discovery of God's promises to do just that (Dan. 9:1–19). When Zerah led a million Ethiopian soldiers against Judah, Asa prayed, "O LORD, You are our God; do not let man prevail against You!" (2 Chr. 14:11). There is not the slightest hint of concern about any violation of Zerah's free will. A similar lack of concern is found in one of Hezekiah's earlier prayers against the Assyrian commander, Rabshakeh: "Now therefore, O LORD, our God, I pray, save us from his hand, that all the kingdoms of the earth may know that You are the LORD God, You alone" (2 Kgs. 19:19).

Such examples could be multiplied many times over. The Bible is filled with prayers that exude great confidence in God to do all that He has promised He will do and bold petitions for God to specifically and directly intervene by causing people to change their intended course of action. Confidence in God's unmitigated sovereignty coupled with a clear-headed awareness of our own personal responsibility provides a much stronger foundation for passionate prayer than the one offered by Open theism.[37]

UNDERMINES CONFIDENT LIVING

The Openness view rejects the idea that a person can be genuinely free if his actions are in any way determined by God. By defining freedom in libertarian terms, Open theists exclude all thought of God's precise control over the world. This stems from an unwillingness to recognize a distinction between God's revealed will and His decreed will. Sanders gratuitously dismisses this distinction as "another example of the attempt to discover a God beyond the God of Scripture on the basis of a human ideal."[38] But Scripture gives ample reason to think in these terms: "The secret things belong to the LORD our God, but those things which are revealed belong to us and to our children

---

[37] An excellent resource for comparing the Openness view of providence and prayer with other models is Terrance Tiessen, *Providence and Prayer, How Does God Work in the World?* (Downers Grove: InterVarsity Press, 2000).

[38] Sanders, *Risks*, 331, fn. 5.

forever, that we may do all the words of this law" (Deut. 29:29). If one does not distinguish between God's secret will and His revealed will, then the biblical claims regarding God's designs, intentions, and desires become terribly confusing.[39]

If God is not in control, then who is? No one, according to free will theists. In their scheme the world is at the collective mercy of libertarian human wills, libertarian free angelic wills and God. Of course, neither people nor angels have as much power as God, but neither does God have complete control over them.[40] One of the most devastating implications of this is the existence of gratuitous evil in the world. Sanders admits that "at least some evil is pointless" and "God does not have a specific divine purpose for each and every occurrence of evil."[41] Boyd also concedes this point: "It is true that according to the Open view things can happen in our lives that God didn't plan or even foreknow with certainty (though he always foreknew they were possible). This means that in the Open view things can happen to us that have no overarching divine purpose."[42]

This thought, which is rightfully disconcerting for those who have come to see God's unmitigated sovereignty taught in Scripture, is applauded by Open theists as a significant theodicy. Boyd believes that "it offers the most plausible way out of the dilemma of assuming God has a purpose for allowing particular evils."[43] Bassinger is even more enthusiastic:

> Moreover, viewing evil in this manner has practical significance. For instance, it means that we, unlike proponents of specific sovereignty, need not assume that some divine purpose exists for each evil that we encounter. We need not, for example, assume when someone dies that God "took him home" for some reason, or that the horrors many experience in this world in some mysterious way fit into God's perfect

---

[39] Theologians have made this distinction in various ways throughout history. For a very helpful treatment of the issue from a biblical–theological perspective, see John Piper, "Are There Two Wills in God? Divine Election and God's Desire for All to Be Saved," in *The Grace of God, the Bondage of the Will*, eds. Thomas R. Schreiner and Bruce A. Ware (Grand Rapids: Baker, 1995), 2 vols. 1:107–31.

[40] Boyd, *God of the Possible*, 153; Tiessen, 100–2. Boyd has called attention to the demonic realm of influence from the Openness viewpoint in his *God at War: The Bible and Spiritual Conflict* (Downers Grove: InterVarsity Press, 1997).

[41] Sanders, *Risks*, 261–62.

[42] Boyd, *God of the Possible*, 153.

[43] Ibid., 99.

plan. We can justifiably assume, rather, that God is often as disappointed as are we that someone's earthly existence has ended at an early age or that someone is experiencing severe depression or that someone is being tortured.[44]

He continues,

> From our perspective, to view specific tragedies in this world as the result of a system over which God has chosen not to exercise complete control is more appealing than to view such events as the outworking of some specific, preordained divine plan.[45]

This perspective fails to deal adequately with the death of Jesus. The paradigm by which all evil in the world must be judged is that which took place at the cross. In the crucifixion we are forced to recognize the two different ways of willing in God. We find ground for hopeful and confident living in a fallen world. The death of Jesus Christ is the greatest miscarriage of justice which the world has ever witnessed. The only innocent man who has ever lived was crucified as a common criminal. Yet, how does the Bible require us to think about the cross? Was it God's will? Or was it a violation of His will? The Open Theist must choose between these two questions, because they refuse to see any distinction in the ways that God wills things. The classical theist sees the cross as the fulfillment of God's decreed will (which He purposed from eternity) and a violation of His revealed will (namely, the commandment not to murder).

The early apostles did not view the death of Jesus from an Open theistic point of view. At Pentecost, Peter preached Christ as, "Him, being delivered by the determined counsel and foreknowledge of God, you have taken by lawless hands, have crucified, and put to death" (Acts 2:23). "Determined counsel and foreknowledge of God" means it was God's (decreed) will. "Lawless hands" means it was contrary to God's (revealed) will. This same perspective is found in the disciples' prayer recorded in Acts 4:24–30. It is difficult to understand, in the light of this apostolic viewpoint, why Boyd is driven to help us "rid ourselves of any lingering suspicion that evil somehow fits into the eternal purposes of God."[46]

---

[44] Bassinger, "Implications," 170.
[45] Ibid., 171.
[46] Boyd, God of the Possible, 102.

If the greatest evil in all the world, though a clear violation of God's revealed will, was definitely decreed by God for the good of His people, then why would we not believe that in a similar way all lesser evils in the world, though contrary to God's commandments, nevertheless fall within His good, wise, and sovereign will for those who love Him and are called according to His purpose? Such a view of God's ways with us in no way diminishes the tragedy of evil and suffering. But it does give us reason to live with joy and hope in the midst of suffering. For though the pain which a child of God endures may seem pointless, it cannot be. No suffering by believers in this world is ever wasted. Joseph, Job, Stephen, Paul, and any other believer who, like their Lord, experience evil in this world may take hope and be confident that God is working out His good and wise purposes through their sufferings.[47]

The opening question and answer in the Heidelberg Catechism summarizes this hopeful vision of the Christian life in a wonderful way. The question is, "What is your only comfort in life and in death?" to which the following answer is given.

> That I am not my own, but belong—body and soul, in life and in death—to my faithful Savior Jesus Christ. He has fully paid for all my sins with His precious blood, and has set me free from the tyranny of the devil. He also watches over me in such a way that not a hair can fall from my head without the will of my Father in heaven; in fact, all things must work together for my salvation. Because I belong to Him, Christ, by His Holy Spirit, assures me of eternal life and makes me wholeheartedly willing and ready from now on to live for him.

No Open theist will ever know such comfort.

Conclusion

The devotional house in which one lives will be largely determined by the doctrinal foundation on which he builds. The vibrant, joyful life of faith that marked the New Testament church was rooted in a steadfast commitment to the "apostles' doctrine" (Acts 2:42). The Apostle

---

[47] Piper has a good, brief essay on this point entitled, *Pastoral Implications of Greg Boyd's View in Dealing with Suffering*, 8 April 1998, available at http://www.bgc.bethel.edu/4know/pessays.htm

Paul regularly structured his arguments in his letters to the early churches so that his imperatives rested upon his indicatives. First he laid a doctrinal foundation (for example, in Rom. 1—11 and Eph. 1—3), then he exhorted his readers to live up to that which they believed (as in Rom. 12—16 and Eph. 4—6). Right believing leads to right living.

It is hard to understand, then, the almost nonchalant attitude of Boyd when he writes, "Next to the central doctrines of the Christian faith, the issue of whether the future is exhaustively settled or partially Open is relatively unimportant. It is certainly not a doctrine Christians should ever divide over."[48] Contrary to the way Boyd makes it sound, Open theism is not simply a philosopher's debate. Redefine reality and the God of reality changes with it. What is at stake is the very doctrine of God, and with that, every aspect of the Christian life.

As A.W. Tozer noted in the middle of the last century, "The gravest question before the Church is always God Himself, and the most portentous fact about any man is not what he at a given time may say or do, but what he in his deep heart conceives God to be like." He goes on to observe, "Were we able to extract from any man a complete answer to the question, 'What comes into your mind when you think about God?' we might predict with certainty the spiritual future of that man."[49] Open theism's redefinition of God bodes ill for those who embrace it. If our vision of God is diminished, vital godliness is sure to shrink with it.

[48] Boyd, God of the Possible, 8.
[49] A.W. Tozer, The Knowledge of the Holy (San Francisco: Harper and Row, 1961), 1.

II

Moses' Bush or Procrustes' Bed

Steve M. Schlissel

Procrustes was the mythological giant of Attica. "He placed all who fell into his hands upon an iron bed. If they were longer than the bed he cut off the redundant part; if shorter, he stretched them till they fitted it."[1] The history of fallen man could be characterized as one long attempt to force God Almighty into a Procrustean bed. We want God to fit our expectations, to comply with our demands, to submit to our definitions. This was the case in the Garden, the case at Mount Sinai, and the case at the Incarnation. "If God wants a part in this world," says Adam and his true sons, "He'll take it on our terms."

In the Garden, God's loving prohibition was dismissed as harshly restrictive. God had offered only one reason not to eat the fruit; Eve found three reasons to eat. Three against one. And in the bargain she bought into a redefinition wherein God was evil and the serpent was good. "He wants to keep me from being all I can be. He's afraid, He's petty, stingy, and jealous." It's truly amazing that God let our first parents live to be redeemed.

At Sinai, my forefathers wanted to shake off the sand between their toes and get moving. If God wanted to accompany them, He'd have to do so on their terms. So they cast themselves a golden idol in the shape of a calf, set up an altar to it, bowed down to it, offered sacrifices to it, and proclaimed, "This is your god, O Israel, who brought you out of Egypt." It's truly amazing that God allowed Moses to persuade Him not to destroy them.

When God became a man, He came unto His own, but His own would not receive Him. They had their own ideas about God, right

---

[1] *Benét's Reader's Encyclopedia* (New York: Harper & Row, 1987).

and wrong, good and evil, and about what the kingdom of God ought
to look like, and who ought to be in it. When they heard God's ideas
spoken by His only begotten Son, they decided, "He must go." They
killed Him. It's truly amazing that the world was permitted to continue, but it did so only in virtue of Jesus' prayer: "Father, forgive
them, for they know not what they do."

And today, it seems, we still don't get it. We still miss the point of
God's encounter with Moses at the burning bush. Moses had asked,
"Suppose I go to the Israelites and say to them, 'The God of your
fathers has sent me to you,' and they ask me, 'What is his name?' Then
what shall I tell them?" God replied "I AM WHO I AM. This is what
you are to say to the Israelites: 'I AM has sent me to you.'" This was
more than a reminder of God's immutability, though it certainly was
that. It was the Divine insistence that God alone may identify God.
God alone knows who He is. Our part is to shut up and listen.

This last sentence is not in the least crude. It is essentially what we
are told in Romans 9, as Paul walks us through a course in God's sovereignty. As if disputing with the advocates of the so-called Openness
of God, Paul argues, "You will say to me then, 'Why does He still find
fault? For who has resisted His will?'" His answer? "Shut your mouth.
You've gone too far for a mere creature." To wit, "But indeed, O man,
who are you to reply against God? Will the thing formed say to him
who formed it, 'Why have you made me like this?'" The sovereign God
cannot be ontologically identified by man, nor can He be economically
judged by man. It is man in the dock and God will not trade places,
save in the cross of Christ.

Yet we have noted that the history of man, both without and within
the covenant, is characterized by the seemingly irrepressible desire to
rework God into his own image, to bind Him, as it were, into Procrustes' bed and then . . . flatten here, cut there. The most recent attempt has been to shear God of His foreknowledge in order to make
room for our "free will."

This leads us to three considerations: (1) The Openness of God error arises not only from wrong thinking, but perhaps even more from
a wrong methodology. Herman Bavinck, perhaps the greatest theologian of the twentieth century, could have saved this error's proponents
a lot of time if they had written less and listened more. (2) The Openness of God, though recently appearing in Christian circles, is not a
new teaching. (3) The Openness of God will probably gain a wide and

sympathetic hearing because it resonates perfectly with the world's current clamoring for a more man-centered deity, particularly an androgynous one. The consequences of this doctrine being embraced, however, will be an acceleration of the societal breakdown we have been experiencing and the death of hope. Free cultures cannot be built on tentative deities. Tentative deities will always be recruited into the service of tyrannical states.

Don't Speak Until You're Spoken To

It is a foolish thing, when speaking about God, to be in a hurry. That is why Dr. Bavinck, in his remarkable book, *The Doctrine of God*, begins by examining God's *incomprehensibility*. It is more than "O man, who are you to reply against God?"—it is, "O man, who are you even to *speak* about God?" The fear of God, according to Bavinck, must be the element that inspires and animates all theological investigation.

When such fear, by God's grace, prepares man to approach properly this most holy subject, he discovers at once that he has difficulty saying anything *solid* about God. If God is incomprehensible, how can unaided man venture to speak of Him at all? And even when man says that God is *infinite, eternal, and unchangeable,* is he not really only saying what God isn't? He *cannot* be measured by space, He is *not* subject to time, He does *not* change.

But how can we predicate even these things of God with confidence? Because God *reveals Himself to man.* God is the initiator. No one can define Him, it is true, but neither can anyone *know Him* unless He first reveals Himself. "Religion and the knowledge of God can have their origin only in revelation. If God does not reveal himself in his creatures, knowledge of him is evidently unattainable."[2]

Yet, even when God does give knowledge of Himself to man,

> the character and the degree of that knowledge is of a peculiar and very limited character. For, though God to a certain extent becomes manifest in the creature, there remains in him an infinite fullness of power and of life which does not become manifest. His knowledge and power are not exhausted in the universe, neither are they effused thereon to their full extent. It is even impossible for God fully to reveal himself to

[2] Herman Bavinck, *The Doctrine of God*, translated by William Hendriksen (Edinburgh: Banner of Truth, 1979), 41.

and in his creatures, for the finite does not grasp the infinite. No one knoweth the Father save the Son, Mt. 11:27; cf. Deut. 29:29. Moreover, that which God reveals of himself in and through creatures is so rich and so deep that it can never be fully known by any human individual. In many respects we do not even understand the universe of created beings, which again and again confronts us with enigmas and mysteries. How then should we be able to understand the revelation of God in all its riches and depth? But by admitting all this we by no means deny God's knowability. God's incomprehensibility, instead of abrogating his knowability, presupposes and affirms the same. The unsearchable riches of the Divine Being constitutes a necessary and important element of our knowledge of God. The fact remains that God is knowable to us in that manner and in that degree in which he reveals himself to us in creation.[3]

And, of course, in His Word.

Later, Bavinck will explain how God *names Himself* in Scripture as a means of making Himself known to us. However, God's names tell us what He is in relation to us; they cannot tell us what He is in Himself.

God's names . . . have this in common; they are all derived from God's revelation; there is not one name which is expressive of the being of God "in itself." The "revealed name" is the basis of all the "names by which we address God."[4]

Knowledge of God as He is in Himself is known to God alone. To have exhaustive knowledge of God in Himself, one must *be God.* "No one knows the thoughts of God except the Spirit of God" (1 Cor 2:11). This presents a "problem" in the pursuit of the knowledge of God that must be recognized and submitted to; failure to acknowledge this "problem" will result in the practice of theology becoming sin and presumptuousness. What is this "problem"? It concerns the language God will use to make Himself known to man. Bavinck's instruction here is absolutely vital, especially as it bears on the alleged Openness of God, because Openness advocates have chosen to build their case relying heavily on one anthropomorphism, viz., God's "repenting," or changing His mind. But Bavinck explains:

[3] Ibid., 41–42.
[4] Ibid., 86

[W]hereas God's revelation in nature and Scripture is definitely directed to man, God uses human language to reveal himself and manifests himself in human forms. It follows that Scripture does not merely contain a few anthropomorphisms; on the contrary, all Scripture is anthropomorphic. From beginning to end Scripture testifies a condescending approach of God to man. The entire revelation of God becomes concentrated in the Logos, who became "flesh." It is as it were one humanization, one incarnation of God. If God were to speak to us in divine language, no one would be able to understand him; but ever since creation, he, in condescending grace, speaks to us and manifests himself to us in human fashion. Hence, all the names with which he allows us to address him are derived from earthly and human relations. Accordingly, in Scripture he is called El, the Mighty One; El-Shaddai, the Powerful One; YHWH, the One who is; moreover he is called Father, Son, Spirit, good, merciful, gracious, righteous, holy, etc., expressions which are based on human relations and are applied to God metaphorically. Even the so-called incommunicable attributes; e.g., immutability, independence, unity, eternity, omnipresence, etc., are derived by Scripture from forms and expressions which pertain to finite existence, and hence are expressed negatively. Thus, eternity must needs be presented to as a negation of time. Scripture never even attempts to describe these divine perfections positively, that is to say; without indicating the relation to finite existence.[5]

I'm going to ask you to forgive and indulge me as I bring to you an extended Bavinck-fest (a long quotation). Dr. Bavinck drives home the point, with a power rarely displayed, that not just some of what we read, but *everything* about God in the Bible, is conveyed in anthropomorphic terms. Let us follow his argument and consider it, for when these truths are embraced, they engender a humility that would keep us from the Openness blunder:

But Scripture is even more emphatic in its anthropomorphism. Whatever pertains to man, whatever pertains to creatures, is applied to God; especially "human organs, members, sensations, affections," etc. God has a soul, Lev. 26:11; Mt. 12:28; and a Spirit, Gen. 1:2; etc. Mention is never made of God's body, although in Christ God assumed a real human body, John 1:14; Col. 2:17; and the church is called the body of Christ, Eph. 1:22; but all the terms expressive of bodily organs are applied to God; mention is made of his countenance, Exod. 33:20, 23; Is. 63:9; Ps. 16:11; Mt. 18:10; Rev. 22:4; his eyes, Ps. 11:4; Heb. 4:13; his

[5] Ibid., 86–87.

eyelids, Ps. 11:4; the apple of his eye, Deut. 32:10; Ps. 17:8; Zech. 2:3; his ears, Ps. 55:1; nose, Deut. 33:10; mouth, Deut. 8:3; lips, Job 11:5; tongue, Is. 30:27; neck, Jer. 18:17; arms, Exod. 15:16; hand, Num. 11:23; right hand, Exod. 15:12; finger, Exod. 8:19; heart, Gen. 6:6; the "yearning of his heart" (A.V.: "sounding of his bowels"), Is. 63:15; cf. Jer. 31:20; Lk. 1:78; his bosom, Ps. 74:11; foot, Is. 66:1. Further, every human emotion is also present in God; e.g., joy, Is. 62:5; rejoicing, Is. 65:19; grief, Ps. 78:40; Is. 63:10; anger, Jer. 7:18, 19; fear, Deut. 32:37; love, in all its variations; e.g., compassion, mercy, grace, longsuffering, etc.; furthermore, zeal and jealousy, Deut. 32:21; grief, Gen. 6:6; hatred, Deut. 16:22; wrath, Ps. 2:5; vengeance, Deut. 32:35.

Further, human actions are ascribed to God, as knowing, Gen. 18:21; trying, Ps. 7:9; thinking, Gen. 50:20; forgetting, 1 Sam. 1:11; remembering, Gen. 8:1; Exod. 2:24; speaking, Gen. 2:16; calling, Rom. 4:17; commanding, Is. 5:6; rebuking, Ps. 18:15; 104:7; answering Ps. 3:4; witnessing, Mal. 2:14; resting, Gen. 2:2; working, John 5:17; seeing, Gen. 1:10; hearing, Exod. 2:24; smelling, Gen. 8:21; tasting, Ps. 11:4, 5; sitting, Ps. 9:7; rising, Ps. 68:1; going, Exod. 34:9; coming, Exod. 25:22; walking, Lev. 26:12; descending, Gen. 11:5; meeting, Exod. 3:18; visiting, Gen. 21:1; passing, Exod. 12:13; casting off, Judg. 6:13; writing, Exod. 34:1; sealing, John 6:27; graving, Is. 49:16; smiting, Is. 11:4; chastening, Deut. 8:5; punishing, Job 5:17; binding up the wounds and healing, Ps. 147:3; cf. Ps. 103:3; Deut. 32:29; killing and making alive, Deut. 32:29; wiping away tears, Is. 25:8; wiping (out), 2 Kings 21:13; washing, Ps. 51:2; anointing, Ps. 2:6; cleansing, Ps. 51:2; decking with ornaments, Ezek. 16:11; clothing (with), Ps. 132:16; crowning, Ps. 8:5; girding with strength, Ps. 18:32; destroying, Gen. 6:7; laying waste (making a waste), Lev. 26:31; killing, Gen. 38:7; plaguing, Gen. 12:17; judging, Ps. 58:11; condemning, Job 10:2; etc. Furthermore, God is often called by names which indicate a certain office, profession, or relation among men. Hence, he is called bridegroom, Is. 61:10; husband, Is. 54:5; father, Deut. 32:6; judge, king, lawgiver, Is. 33:22; man of war, Exod. 15:3; hero, Ps. 78:65; Zeph. 3:17; builder (architect), and maker, Heb. 11:10; husbandman, John 15:1; shepherd, Ps. 23:1; physician, Exod. 15:26; etc., while in connection with these mention is made of his seat, throne, footstool, rod, scepter, weapons, bow, arrow, sword, shield, wagon, banner, book, seal, treasure, inheritance, etc. In order to indicate what God is for his children language derived from the organic and inorganic creation is even applied to God. He is compared to a lion, Is. 31:4; an eagle, Deut. 32:11; a lamb, Is. 53:7; a hen, Mt. 23:37; the sun, Ps. 84:11; the morning star, Rev. 22:16; a light, Ps. 27:1; a torch, Rev. 21:23; a fire, Heb. 12:29; a fountain, Ps. 36:9; the fountain of living waters, Jer. 2:13; food, bread, water, drink, ointment, Is. 55:1; John 4:10; 6:35, 55; a rock, Deut. 32:4; a hiding place, Ps. 119:114; a tower, Prov. 18:10; a refuge, Ps. 9:9; a shadow, Ps. 91:1; 121:5; a shield, Ps. 84:11; a way, John 14:6; a temple, Rev. 21:22; etc.

Scripture calls upon the entire creation, i.e., upon nature in its several spheres and especially upon man, to contribute to the description of the knowledge of God. Anthropomorphism seems to be unlimited. In order to give us an idea of the majesty and exalted character of God, names are derived from every kind of creature, living and lifeless, organic and inorganic. Although in himself God is "anonymous, i.e., without name," nevertheless, in his revelation he is "polyonomous, i.e., possessing many names."[6]

In view of this evidence, it is obviously utterly preposterous to extract *one anthropomorphism* employed by God in Scripture and then seek to make that the base from which we are to work backward, as it were, and upward, into God Himself (!), and then revise Him, fit Him on Procrustes' bed, and use this new god made in our image to solve the problems our puny minds can never wrap themselves around. The advocates of Openness speak when they should be silent. It is a fitting citation Bavinck here brings from Augustine:

"All things can be said of God, but nothing is worthily said of him. Nothing is more wide-spread than this poverty of expression. Thou seekest a fitting name for him; thou canst not find it."[7]

The LORD is in his holy temple: let all the earth [especially those who would "open" God] keep silence before him (Hab. 2:20).

WHERE HAVE I HEARD THIS BEFORE?

It should come as no surprise that theologians from each of the three great religions claiming biblical descent have tried to come to grips with the problem of how divine sovereignty relates to human freedom. Each religion has had proponents who emphasize sovereignty to the negation of human freedom, those who have advocated human freedom to the effective negation of divine sovereignty, and those who have sought to stress both. Interestingly, however, Islam has *tended* to fall into the fatalistic camp in which man's freedom is swallowed up by *kismet*; Judaism has very clearly, for all practical purposes, concerned

---

[6] Ibid., 86–88.
[7] Ibid., 88.

itself primarily with human liberty; but Christianity, particularly reformational Protestantism, has striven to carefully emphasize both
equally.

Each of these "tendencies" lead, in turn, to others. Politically, for
example, consistent Islam tends to be autocratic; Judaism tends to
prefer centralized administrations that were *democratically* elected;
consistent Christianity, as in reformational Protestantism, tends toward republican, representative government. One might say that, ontologically, Islam is rooted in the rule of the one, Judaism in the rule of
the many, and Christianity in the one and the many.

Further, the relationship between divine sovereignty and human
responsibility plays out in each religion's respective approach to people of other religions. Consistent Islam tends to convert by the sword;
Christianity (of the reformational sort) seeks to convert by prayer and
persuasion. Judaism, however, has never had a sustained interest in
converting others: it is a self-absorbed religion. This may help to explain why the greatest post-biblical attainments of Judaism have come
either when she was nursing at the left breast of Islam or the right
breast of Christianity. Though she claims to be the mother of both religions, historically she has been the dependent child.[8]

All of this is just to say that the answer to the question of the relationship between divine sovereignty and human responsibility does
not arise from, nor remain in, a vacuum. It is answered from out of a
system and then further qualifies and defines that system. This is why
we should be concerned about the Openness of God error. Its tendency is toward Judaism, not toward historic Christianity.

We have already acknowledged that Jewish thought on this subject
spans the spectrum. Gersonides (Levi ben Gershom, 1288–1344)
could have co-authored "The Openness of God." He held that "God
does not know beforehand how a man will behave in particular circumstances."[9] The Spanish Jewish philosopher, Hasdai Crescas (d.
1412), is generally regarded as having a "Calvinistic" spirit in approaching this question, preferring to emphasize divine sovereignty
even if it appears to impinge upon human freedom. Maimonedes

---

[8] Even today, Israel may well lay claim to being the most dependent of the techno-
logically advanced nations. Without the Christian West to aid her, I fear she would
disappear in a day.

[9] Lewis Jacobs, *The Jewish Religion: A Companion* (New York: Oxford University
Press, 1995), 186.

(1135–1204), generally regarded as the greatest Jewish thinker in the Middle Ages, affirmed no contradiction between divine sovereignty and human freedom, saying that it is beyond our human ability to comprehend exactly how this is so.

On the popular level, however, there is no dispute concerning which side of the issue concerns the average observant Jew: it is human freedom. "The doctrine of free will . . . is often referred to as one of the basic principles of Judaism. It is consistently assumed that God has taught man what is right and what is wrong and left him to choose between the alternatives and the consequences."[10] Rabbi Akiva said, "All is foreseen, but freedom of choice is given."[11] Rabbi Chanina said, "All is decreed except if (a person) will be bad or good. Everything is in the hands of God except the fear of the Lord."[12]

We can now see that the Openness advocates are indeed going to rendezvous with the rabbis. Rashi, in Berachos 33b and Megilla 25a, asserted that "God decrees the future of every person, whether he is to be tall or short, rich or poor, wise or foolish, white or black. Whether he is to be good or bad does not come from heaven [God]. He [man] is given two paths and he is to choose the good." Saadia Gaon says, "As soon as man makes a choice between alternatives God knows it. In other words, the decision of man precedes God's knowledge of it." Judah Ha-Levi followed Saadia, holding that "the decisions of man precede God's knowledge." Abraham Ibn Daud followed Judah Ha-Levi, believing that "in order to give room to man's will to assert itself freely, He left certain actions undecided in His own mind."[13]

Thus, though Maimonedes rejects this course, it has become the popular "truth" for observant Jews. Free will is "axiomatic in Judaism."[14] And there is a reason for this emphasis on man's freedom in Judaism: Judaism is primarily an ethical religion. The importance of this point as it bears on the question of the current teaching on the Openness of God cannot be overstated.

---

[10] Philip Birnbaum, *Encyclopedia of Jewish Concepts* (New York: Hebrew Publishing Co., 1993), 76.

[11] Cited in *The Encyclopedia Judaica* at the entry, "Providence."

[12] Rabbi Sholom Klass, *Response of Modern Judaism* (New York: The Jewish Press, 1992–5752), 499–500.

[13] Ibid., 503.

[14] Jacobs, *Jewish Religion*, 174.

Judaism is fundamentally an ethical religion, whereas Christianity is fundamentally a redemptive religion. Judaism believes in what it does; Christianity does what it believes. In Judaism, ethics leads to redemption; in Christianity, redemption leads to ethics. In Judaism, man observes God's Law in order to be saved. In Christianity, man is saved in order to observe God's Law. In Judaism, you do good to be redeemed. In Christianity, you do good because you've been redeemed.

These truths bear mightily on the matter now being controverted. For a redemptive religion is concerned with spelling out the truth concerning God's initiatory—even unilateral—work in redeeming, thus leading to a body of dogma to be believed, whereas an ethical religion will bypass dogma (more or less) and dwell upon observance, leading to a body of casuistic minutiae. In a redemptive religion, concern with the problem of God's sovereignty and man's responsibility will tend to be "resolved" with an emphasis on God's sovereignty, but in a religion where man saves himself by right choices, God's sovereignty will be eagerly sacrificed on the altar of man's "freedom."

Thus, the teaching of the Openness of God is, in actuality, not a return to the covenantal religion of the Bible as it claims. It is my opinion that Openness advocates could have contributed to such a return had they been wearing a biblical and historical harness, such as was put on by Bavinck before considering *any* theological question. But their methodology was determined by their presupposition which was, in turn, determined by the objective they wished to achieve: a vindication of human freedom.

That this redefining of God means a redefining of Christianity is very clear. What I hope you can see is the character this change will have. It will change Christianity from a religion that promulgates ethics based on God's redemptive activity to a religion that achieves redemption based on man's ethical activity. While ostensibly seeking to "rescue" God from being responsible for evil, it instead confers upon man the merit of intrinsic and active righteousness.

If reformational Protestantism tended toward one side of the matter under discussion, it was certainly to speak of man being bound and God being free. While cleverly calling their doctrine the Openness of God, the fact is that in their system, it is man who is open and free while God has been bound. This doctrine, if widely accepted, will be the third (and final?) Procrustean attack on Western Christianity.

The War Against the God Who Acts

The question remains one of whether we would be those who humbly remove their sandles and listen to God speaking from the burning bush, or those who would strap Him onto Procrustes' bed. In the latter case we seek to define God, drawing from our limited vocabulary, denying to Him what extends beyond our confines; we then seek to impose our definitions on heaven. In the former case, God retains the sole right to define Himself, is the sole initiator in revealing Himself, and the sole actor in redeeming us. Israel produced no plagues upon Egypt. They stood still and saw the salvation of the Lord.

We want God to stand still and see the salvation of man. We are sinners determined to rob God of His *acts;* we are sinners with "acts to grind."

The first Procrustean act of man was evolutionism, by means of which we cut off the feet upon which a social order could be built. It was not God who created by His act, by fiat: the worlds just happened. Therefore it is not God upon whom a social order must be built.

The second Procrustean act of man was egalitarianism, wherein God's acts of ordering were denied. God was forbidden to arrange man's social order, parts, and whole. We stretched and pulled until all was arranged flat and even upon the bed, with no distinction allowed to rise.

The final Procrustean act of man is introduced in the Openness of God, by which we lop off His head (in our vain minds), denying to Him the right and power to rule everything, at all times, from the beginning to the end of time, to accomplish all His holy will. We will not have God as *the Actor,* determining who shall be with Christ in heaven and who will not. All determinative acts belong to man. Evolution says God couldn't begin creation; egalitarianism says He may not order creation; Openness says He won't complete it.

The way toward the third Procrustean attack has been paved by the doctrine of Openness. In "Gutting the Godhead," a review of *The Openness of God,* Pastor Richard C. Kleug observed:

> The fact that such a thesis would gain a favorable hearing among professing Christians is a frightening indication of widespread doctrinal corruption. Our forefathers—both Calvinist and Arminian—would have been aghast to think that their children would be denying the

foreknowledge of God! [In approaching this book, it is] most instruc-
tive to read the last section first, regarding the practical implications of
the Open View of God. There you will learn that God's guidance may
prove to be wrong, that prayer for God to work in the hearts of others
may be regarded as improper, and that trials do not necessarily have a
purpose. Then go back and see what road the authors took to arrive at
this desert. The "Open God" pictured here no doubt will appeal to
those who seek a Touchy-feely-God-as-therapist, and who above all are
jealous to grant absolute sovereignty to the will of man.

What we are facing as we look at the Openness view is Phase Three
of man's Procrustean procedure. Through Phase One, our embrace of
evolution and our rejection of our Creator, we lost our foundations.
We lost the foundation of work and rest, of marriage and family, of
right and wrong. In failing to follow God's definition of Himself (Almighty Maker of heaven and earth), we lost the ability to define ourselves. Everything was up for grabs and the one who died with the
fullest fists was said to win.

With Phase Two, in which equalitarianism replaced covenant head-
ship, the destruction of the family was insured. Husband and wife
would no longer be a covenanted unit but a pair of warring entities
competing for limited power. By spreading authority equally on the
Procrustean bed, all authority was lost. Only power remained. Might
makes right, and might is sought through political machinations and
statist coercion.

Phase Three seeks to remove whatever remains of the sovereign
God—particularly through removing from society the testimony
borne to Him by reformational churches and individuals. We stand to
lose more than we have heretofore. That is why Pastor Kleug in wisdom bade us look at the end of the book first. "See what you'll be giving up: God's guidance, prayer, meaning." When we leave off hearing
God from the burning bush and instead imagine that we can surgically
alter Him thrice on Procrustes' bed, we lose our sure foundation, we
lose our living order, and finally, we lose our hope.

Let the publication of this book be a time to become renewed in the
undoubted Christian religion. Let it be a time when we return to our
great statements of the faith. Let it become the occasion of every
Christian confessing with heart and mouth:

My only comfort, in life and in death, is that I am *not* my own, but belong—body and soul, in life and in death—to my faithful Savior Jesus Christ. He has fully paid for all my sins with His precious blood, and has set me free from the tyranny of the devil. He also watches over me in such a way that not a hair can fall from my head without the will of my Father in heaven: in fact, all things must work together for my salvation. Because I belong to Him, Christ, by His Holy Spirit, assures me of eternal life and makes me whole-heartedly willing and ready from now on to live for Him.[15]

It's really an either/or matter. Either we'll join the saints to hear God define all things, as at the burning bush, or we'll join those who would attempt to define God, imagining Him bound on a Procrustean bed, destroying themselves with every vain attack on Him.

Meet me at the bush.

---

[15] The peerless Heidelberg Catechism, answer #1.

12

Open Idolatry

Little children, guard yourselves from idols.

I JOHN 5:21

Joost F. Nixon

For several years now the Open theism paradigm was a matter discussed by "professional theologians and philosophers" in the byways and back alleys of technical theological journals.[1] Confined largely as it was to academic circles, where denials of historic doctrines are marks of cutting-edge scholarship, Open theism did little damage to the church at large. But in their magnanimity, the Openness fellows have decided to share their little secret with common folk. Now admittedly, this is a boon if these men are making a true correction to Christian theology gone astray for two millennia.[2] But if, as we suspect, this is stale heresy warmed over and garnished with postmodernism, then thank you very much, but pass the meat and potatoes.

The contributors to this volume assert that Openness theology is not only ugly and erroneous, but it is also evil. And here inevitably someone will cry *foul*. "Here we were having a peaceable *dialogue, wrestling* with difficult issues, *exploring* a new paradigm regarding the nature of God, and these churls start getting nasty." Appeals are made for us to "love one another in the midst of our disagreements," because this is just a "debate about the nature of the future."[3] And "compared to our common faith in the person of Jesus Christ and the importance of loving unity in him, this issue and other theological

---

[1] Clark Pinnock et al, *The Openness of God* (Downers Grove: InterVarsity Press, 1994), 9.

[2] Ibid., 59–60. See Peter Leithart's chapter in the present work for a refutation of this.

[3] Gregory A. Boyd, *God of the Possible* (Grand Rapids: Baker Book House, 2000), 19–20.

issues are peripheral."[4] But while agreeing that we ought to love one another, we certainly disagree about the importance of the debate. The debate is not merely about the nature of the future, but about *the very nature of God and the gospel.*[5] And when the stakes are so high, what precisely does love require? Love requires that unfashionable words like "anathema," "heresy," and "sin" be employed where appropriate. Admittedly, in our day where lack of toleration is the only thing really untolerable, we are at a decided rhetorical disadvantage when we resort to such plain speaking. But we trust the reader will understand that love, and not a nasty disposition, compels language that will surely be read as unloving by our insipid generation.

Other sections of this work have been devoted to demonstrating that open theism doctrine is ugly and unbiblical. But there are also *moral* implications in advancing false doctrine, especially doctrine as pernicious as Open theism, that beg to be expounded. Thomas Ascol and Steve Schlissel have addressed the pastoral and cultural ramifications of open theism doctrine in their contributions to this work. And I hope to add to their witness by focusing on a single but, I think, very significant point: Open theism breaches the third commandment by imputing to the living God characteristics the Bible uses to identify idols.

IDOLS OF THE HEART

Though open theism has soteriological ramifications that are truly scary,[6] its main assault is against the very person of God. Recognizing that attributes of transcendence like God's immutability and omniscience are two centuries out of *vogue,* advocates of Open theism have whipped out their theological scissors to fix the apparent problem. Tragically, in their attempts to make God relevant, they have robbed Him of His majesty. And in robbing God of His majesty they have left man bankrupt and without hope. This is the net effect whenever anyone depreciates God. Idols, whether crafted in foundries of iron or the

---

[4] Ibid., 20.

[5] Besides its errant doctrine of God, Openness theology has ramifications on biblical soteriology and anthropology—for starters. See Clark Pinnock's interview with *Modern Reformation,* November/December 1998.

[6] See John MacArthur's contribution to this volume.

ivory towers of academia, always have a devastating effect on those who worship them. In the words of the psalmist, "Those who make them will become like them, everyone who trusts in them"[7] (Ps. 115:8). And what are idols, that idolaters will become like them? As we shall examine more fully later, they are vain, worthless, and insignificant. It is no wonder, then, that God prohibits idolatry in the second commandment:

> You shall not make for yourself an idol, or any likeness of what is in heaven above or on earth beneath or in the water under the earth. You shall not worship or serve them; for I, the LORD your God, am a jealous God, visiting the iniquity of the fathers on the children, on the third and fourth generation of those who hate Me, but showing lovingkindness to thousands, to those who love me and keep my commandments. (Exod. 20:4–6)

Idolatry has massive cultural ramifications. We learn to sin like our fathers, and it usually takes multiple generations to *unlearn* it—once we discover our error. While we're doing so, covenantal sanctions and judgments are operating against us. The advocates of Open theism are not unknown fellows, and their influence in evangelicalism should not be underestimated. If their theology wins the day, generations of Christians will fall into idolatry.

The second commandment primarily addresses idols of wood, stone, and metal. But children of Western culture are far too sophisticated to bow down to glorified kupie dolls. And as a subset of Western culture, professional theologians are no exception—after all, what would they say to their tenure committee? No—for moderns a much safer, more respectable form of idolatry is the mental variety.[8] But just because modern idolaters do not erect Asherah poles in their backyards does not mean that they are exempt from God's censure. God informs Ezekiel:

---

[7] All Scripture quotations in this chapter are from the New American Standard Bible (La Habra: The Lockman Foundation, 1960, 1962, 1963, 1968, 1971, 1972, 1973, 1975, 1977).

[8] Unfortunately, Open theism proponents are not the only ones prone to this sin. Most Christians are in constant need to correct and refine their view of God. See "Why We Must Think Rightly About God" in A.W. Tozer's *The Knowledge of the Holy* (Lincoln: Back to the Bible Broadcast, 1961). But orthodox Christians commit this sin intermittently, whereas Openness theologians do so consciously.

Son of man, these men[9] *have set up idols in their hearts,* and have put right before their faces the stumbling block of their iniquity. Should I be consulted by them at all? (Ezek. 14:3)[10]

Idols of the heart can take a number of different forms. But for our purposes, we want to zero in on the type of heart idolatry that worships a *false* god under the name of the *true* God, Yahweh. This kind of idolatry flies in the face of the third commandment by attributing to the true God the vanity of idols. It is an attack on the reputation of the living God.[11] And this is the idolatry that Openness theologians commit.

WHAT'S IN A NAME?

Of all the ten *words* given in fire and smoke on Mount Sinai, perhaps the least understood is the third. Few verses have been so rich, and yet understood so superficially by Christians:

You shall not take the name of [Yahweh] your God in vain, for [Yahweh] will not leave him unpunished who takes His name in vain. (Exod. 20:7)[12]

The context is particularly important here. The ten commandments were given on Sinai and the people "did not see any form on the day the LORD spoke to [them] at Horeb out of the midst of the fire" (Deut. 4:15). The second commandment addresses this, forbidding men to represent God by any form or image. Instead, God—who is

---

[9] The elders of Israel who had come to consult Yahweh through Ezekiel, after setting up idols of the heart.

[10] Emphasis mine.

[11] "The evidence points to the fact that taking the Lord's name (i.e., his reputation) 'in vain' will surely cover profanity, as it is understood today, or swearing falsely in the Lord's name. But it will also include using the Lord's name lightly, unthinkingly, or by rote." "*shāw*'", by Victor P. Hamilton, in *Theological Wordbook of the Old Testament*, vol. 2, R. Laird Harris et al, eds. (Chicago: Moody Press, 1980), 908.

[12] Since the Achaemenid period, the covenant name of God, "Yahweh," has been rendered (and pronounced) "Lord" (Adonai) out of reverence for His name. I think this in itself is a misapplication of the third commandment. The commandment does not prohibit *use* of the tetragrammaton, so much as the abuse of it. As a result, I usually render the divine name in brackets throughout this chapter. See J.A. Motyer, "Name," in *The New Bible Dictionary*, 2nd Ed., J.D. Douglas et al, ed. (Wheaton: InterVarsity Press, 1992), 813.

spirit—is represented by something nonmaterial, viz., His *name*.[13] And thus we have the *third* commandment, which ensures that the *lawful* representation of God (His name/reputation) is not to be degraded.

What's in a name? Plenty—especially to the biblical writers. God's name is a metonym for His person.[14] It is a word-symbol that denotes the person of God. In Messiah's High Priestly prayer, He prays, "I have manifested Thy *name* unto the men which thou gavest me..." (Jn. 17:6). Jesus did not mean that He had a fancy for pronouncing God's name all the time. Rather He meant that He was demonstrating in the flesh the person and character of God while walking the earth.[15] Another example is Psalm 20:1, which reads, "[Yahweh] hear thee in the day of trouble; the *name* of the God of Jacob defend thee." Here again, God Himself is the One being invoked for protection, *as represented by His name*. But metonyms and symbols are not unfamiliar to us, which is why we get angry when someone burns the flag or spits on a picture of our mother.

But God's name is more than just a metonym of His person. God's name reveals aspects of His character, and therefore an assault on God's character is an assault on His name. The LORD intended to reveal previously unknown aspects of His character through His name, Yahweh:

> God spoke further to Moses and said to him, "I am the LORD; and I appeared to Abraham, Isaac, and Jacob, as God Almighty [El Shaddai], but by my name, LORD [Yahweh], I did not make myself known to them. (Exod. 6:2–3)

A superficial look at this text might first suggest that the name

[13] "God's name takes the role of the cultic symbols such as the ark or a cult statue having 'a constant and *almost* material presence...at the shrine.'" B.F. Huffmon, "Name," in *The Dictionary of Deities and Demons in the Bible*, 2nd edition, Karel van der Toorn, et al, ed. (Grand Rapids: William B. Eerdman's Publishing Company, 1999), 612.

[14] Metonymy is "the use of the name of one thing for that of another associated with or suggested by it (e.g., 'the White House has decided' for 'the President has decided')." *Webster's New Universal Unabridged Dictionary* (New York: Simon & Schuster, 1983), 1134.

[15] "Jesus recalls that He has revealed God to the disciples. The 'name' stands for the whole person (see Jn. 1:12). To manifest the name of God then is to reveal the essential nature of God to men." Leon Morris, *The Gospel According to John*, in NICNT, F.F. Bruce, ed. (Grand Rapids: Wm. B. Eerdmans Publishing Company, 1971), 723.

"Yahweh" was not known until Moses' day. Yet the name appears in Scripture *prior* to Moses' encounter with God at the burning bush (as early as Genesis 2:4), and men began to call upon it in the days of Enosh (Gen. 4:26). So though the name was employed prior to Exodus 6, God had not yet revealed the meaning He intended to convey by it. J.A. Motyer offers the following interpretive translation of Exodus 6:2–3:

> And God spoke to Moses, and said to him: I am Yahweh. And I showed myself to Abraham, to Isaac, and to Jacob in the character of El Shaddai, but in the character expressed by my name Yahweh I did not make myself known to them. . . ."[16]

The name Yahweh, then, was to convey—in a way that a physical image could not—the character of God. As it stood at the beginning of Exodus, the name was like an empty canvas. But from the events of the Exodus on, God would be filling the canvas with a picture of His character, demonstrating to the people what it meant to be *Yahweh*. In fact, when Moses cried out to God to reveal His glory (Exod. 33:18–19), God answered by *proclaiming His name*, along with a divine exposition of it:

> And [Yahweh] passed by in front of him and proclaimed, "[Yahweh], [Yahweh Elohim], compassionate and gracious, slow to anger, and abounding in lovingkindness and truth; who keeps lovingkindess for thousands, who forgives iniquity, transgression, and sin; yet he will by no means leave the guilty unpunished, visiting the iniquity of fathers on children and on the grandchildren to the third and fourth generations." (Exod. 34:6–7)

God's name is replete with significance. He is the God of glory, Who shows mercy and lovingkindness to His covenant people, and exercises justice (Exod. 34:6–7). He is a warrior Who destroys His enemies (Exod. 15:3–7). He is a redeemer Who decisively rescues His people from captivity (Exod. 20:2). And this is just dipping our toes into Exodus. God progressively reveals more about His nature throughout the Old Testament and into the New, so that the perfections of God are manifest. These perfections, as understood by the

---

[16] J.A. Motyer, *The Revelation of the Divine Name* (Leicester: Theological Students Fellowship, 1959), 12–13. See also Charles R. Gianotti, "The Meaning of the Divine Name YHWH," in *Bibliotheca Sacra*, vol. 142, Jan. 1985, 38–39.

historically orthodox for thousands of years, stand in stark contrast to the worthlessness and impotence of idols. This vision of God that the Bible gives us balances the immanence and transcendence of God in a way that idolatrous views of God cannot. In contrast to the notions of Deists, God *is* involved in His creation. He is omnipresent and through providence cares for all His hands have made. He is a Person, and thus He is relational, and not, as Pinnock caricatures, "an unblinking cosmic stare."[17] But in contrast to pantheism and process theology, God is also transcendent above and distinct from His creation (Rom. 1:23). It is this element—this transcendent element to God's perfections—that grosses modern egalitarians out.

MAKING GOD OVER

> All the inhabitants of earth are accounted as nothing, but He does according to His will in the host of heaven and among the inhabitants of the earth; and no one can ward off His hand or say to Him, "What hast Thou Done?" (Dan. 4:35)

Moderns read this verse, and verses like it, with curled lip and darkened brow. After their initial alarm at the divine hubris, they would be quick to sign God up for some sensitivity training. After all, who does God think He is, anyway? Surely God doesn't want to imply He is somehow *better* than us? Does He? Huh? And what's with God's authoritarian leadership paradigm? That's very *eighties*, you know. Doesn't God know that group decisions are vastly superior to this fascist top-down model?

Admittedly, Openness theists have a point. Taking Him at face value, God is neither heeding the recent management literature, nor being particularly sensitive to twenty-first century cultural norms.[18] The transcendent God of the Bible is terminally unhip. No *wonder* our tent revivals are so poorly attended. But never fear! Though the Openness fellows are somewhat embarrassed by God's retro leadership-style, being the loving, condescending fellows that they are, they're

---

[17] Inside cover blurb to Sanders, *The God Who Risks* (Downers Grove: InterVarsity Press, 1998).

[18] Clark Pinnock tells us that "I also do theology contextually, recognizing that *theology will reflect the culture in which it emerges*" (my emphasis). Clark Pinnock, "A Pilgrim on the Way," in *Christianity Today*, February 9, 1998. Open theism reflects nothing if not postmodern cultural prejudices.

212   BOUND ONLY ONCE

willing to help Him out of the jam with a little Clintonesque image consulting. A little clipping of the omnipotence here, a spin on those pesky foreordination passages there, and He's well on His way to becoming a more relevant, likeable deity. But no makeover is complete without updating the duds. The robes of divine majesty must be exchanged for the bell bottoms of mutability. There—that's better. Now God looks a lot more (*contented sigh*)...like *us*.

The problem with the Openness makeover is exactly this—their god looks too much like us, and too much like the picture the Bible paints of idols. God's name—His holy character—have been re-worked in such a way as to divest Him of His deity. But because God is not represented by molten images but by His name; because He is a spirit and His attributes cannot be seen with the naked eye, it is vitally important that He is represented with words accurately so His glory is upheld among the people and they do not sink into idolatry of the mind. And this brings us back to the third commandment:

> You shall not take the name of [Yahweh] your God in vain, for [Yahweh] will not leave him unpunished who takes His name in vain. (Exod. 20:7)

In the third commandment, Yahweh specifically prohibits *vanity* being attributed to His person. The Hebrew word, *shāw'*, means "emptiness, nothingness, vanity" whether referring to speech or conduct.[19] The same word is employed for a Hebrew vowel (*shewa*) that is so short and insignificant as sometimes to be unpronounceable. Thus, the word "designates anything that is unsubstantial, unreal, worthless, either materially or morally. Hence, it is a word for idols."[20] As we examine its usage in Scripture, we see that sometimes the word denotes *men and idols who are unworthy of trust*. An example is found in Jeremiah 18:15:

> For My people have forgotten Me,
> They burn incense to worthless [vain] gods
> And they have stumbled from their ways,
> From the ancient paths,
> To walk in bypaths,
> Not on a highway. (Jer. 18:15)

---

[19] *A Hebrew and English Lexicon of the Old Testament*, Brown, Driver, Briggs, Gesenius, eds. (Oxford: Clarendon Press, 1978), 996.
[20] Hamilton, *Wordbook*, 908.

Rather than walk in the ancient paths, the children of Israel have forgotten God and pursued impotent idols[21]—inanimate blocks of wood that cannot help those who pray to them (cf. Ps. 115:1–8). What a contrast they are to the living God, whose arm is not so short that it cannot save! Another occurrence is found in Psalm 60:10–11:

> Hast not Thou Thyself, O God, rejected us?
> And wilt Thou not go forth with our armies, O God?
> O give us help against the adversary,
> For deliverance by man is in vain.
> Through God we shall do valiantly,
> And it is He who will tread down our adversaries.

"Vanity" is a word used to describe men and idols who are worthless and impotent. They cannot save. But the concept is wholly inappropriate to use regarding the living God. And while Open theists never employ the actual word "vain" to describe God, they do employ the *concept* by limiting God's ability to accomplish His purposes.

Open theists would affirm that sometimes God's will is thwarted.[22] Or rather, God can accomplish His will, but in some instances only *if other free agents cooperate.*[23] This applies to prayer. Sanders writes, "Our failure to practice impetratory prayer means that *certain things that God wishes to do for us may not be possible*[24] because we do not ask. In the words of Peter Baelz, 'Our asking in faith may make it possible for God to do something which *he could not have done without our asking.'"*[25] God's beneficent intentions are constricted by man's prayer? Men *empowering* God? Mercy! Perhaps Sanders would rewrite Psalm 127:1 to read:

---

[21] Perhaps the irony of the situation will not escape the reader. The Openness theologians reject, at the minimum, the ancient paths of the last 2000 years of Christian theology and exegesis, to follow after a god they openly admit cannot accomplish at least some of His purposes. And they call this god "Yahweh." Some things never change.

[22] "[God's plans] are not ironclad decrees that fix the course of events and preclude all possible variations. For God to will something, therefore, does not make its occurrence inevitable. Factors can arise that hinder or prevent its realization." Richard Rice, "Biblical Support for a New Perspective," in *The Openness of God* (Downers Grove: InterVarsity Press, 1994), 26.

[23] "[Jesus accepting the suffering God assigned to Him] supports the conclusion that the fulfillment of God's plans for humanity generally requires the cooperation of human agents." Ibid., 44.

[24] The incredulity is mine.

[25] Sanders, *Risks*, 273. I've added the italics.

Unless the laborers cooperate,
The Lord builds the house in vain.

Sanders also applies his theology to the incarnation, "God places his trust in [Mary and Joseph] giving his consent to the risks involved. The incarnation does not come about through sheer overwhelming power but through the vulnerability of *being genuinely dependent on some Jewish peasants.*"[26] It is astonishing to me that instead of men placing their trust in God to fulfill His promises, we have God placing His trust in men! Moreover, it is ironic that the *psalmist* is wise enough to know that deliverance from man is vain (Ps. 60:11), but according to the Open theists, *God is not.* And if God's assistance is dependent upon the assistance of millions of free agents with bad attitudes—assistance the Scriptures tell us is vain or unreliable—then what does that tell us about God? It tells us His omnipotent arm has been amputated below the elbow. Or perhaps a more tenable explanation is that Open theists are engaging in idolatry and attributing to God behavior that He Himself rebukes as accursed:

> Thus says [Yahweh]:
> Cursed is the man who trusts in mankind
> And makes flesh his strength
> And whose heart turns away from [Yahweh]. (Jer. 17:5)

Here *Yahweh* is the proper locus of faith and dependence, and man even at his best is a bad bet. The open theism assertion that God is unable to accomplish elements of His plan demeans God's majesty and puts the Most High on the same level as a bronze Buddha.

But Open theists do not only question God's ability to work *"all things* after the counsel of His will" (Eph. 1:11),[27] they also call into question God's omniscience as it regards the future. As others[28] have so amply pointed out, God's very *Godness* is connected with His

---

[26] Sanders, *Risks*, 93. My emphasis.

[27] Again, the emphasis is mine. Search in vain for a cogent Open theism interpretation of this verse. You won't find one in Boyd (2000), Pinnock et al (1994), or Sanders (1998).

[28] See Jonathan Edwards, *The Freedom of the Will*, ed. by Paul Ramsey, in: *The Works of Jonathan Edwards*, vol. 1 (New Haven: Yale, 1957), 239–269; John Piper, "Why the God of Glory is at Stake in the 'Foreknowledge' Debate," in *Modern Reformation*, Sept./Oct. 1999, 39–43; and Stephen N. Williams, "What God Doesn't Know," in CT's sister publication *Books and Culture*, Nov./Dec. 1999.

foreknowledge. In fact, God identifies an inability to tell the future to be a mark of idols:

> "Present your case," [Yahweh] says.
> "Bring forward your strong arguments,"
> The King of Jacob says.
> Let them bring forth and declare to us what is going to take place;
> As for the former events, declare what they were,
> That we may consider them and know their outcome;
> Or announce to us what is coming.
> Declare the things that are going to come afterward,
> That we may know that you are gods. (Is. 41:21–23a)

God considered the failure of idols to predict future events to be damning evidence that they were frauds. An ability to predict the future (indeed, to decree it), is part of the *Godness* of God. In another context where He is comparing His incomparable glory with the vanity of idols, Yahweh says:

> I am [Yahweh], that is My Name;
> I will not give my glory to another,
> Nor my praise to graven images.
> Behold, the former things have come to pass,
> Now I declare new things;
> Before they spring forth I proclaim them to you. (Is. 42:8–9)

God wants no confusion between real deity and impotent idols. His glory, as represented by His name, will not be given to idols. In contrast to them, Yahweh does something they cannot—He "declares new things before they spring forth." But notice, now, how Open theists "give His glory to another." They have taken His holy name and assigned it to a deity who does not know, and thus cannot declare, the future. For example, events as significant as the fall were "totally unexpected";[29] and even the cross was unplanned.[30] Sanders knows he is making a radical statement "The notion that the cross was not planned will seem scandalous to some readers."[31] In this much,

---

[29] Sanders, *Risks*, 46.

[30] Ibid., 101,

[31] Ibid. He then makes an unconvincing effort to explain away Psalm 22:16; Ephesians 1:4, 1 Peter 1:20, and Revelation 13:8 and 17:8.

Sanders scores full marks; such an assertion *is* scandalous. And it is scandalous because it is a direct assault on the deity of Christ.

On the night He was betrayed, Jesus told His disciples that "From now on I am telling You before it comes to pass, so that when it does occur, you may believe that I am" (Jn. 13:19). John Piper explains the import of this statement, "With the words *'I am'* Jesus lays claim on deity in words that God uses of himself in texts like Isaiah 43:10 ('You are my witnesses, declares the LORD, "And My servant whom I have chosen, so that you may know and believe Me and understand that *I am*"'). And the warrant for believing that he is divine, he says, is that he is telling the disciples what is going to befall him before it comes to pass."[32]

The gospels are so explicit in demonstrating that Christ foreknew what was to befall Him that Sanders has to go to extraordinary lengths to explain that really He *didn't* know. One example is his excruciating treatment of Judas' betrayal. Judas is not really betraying Jesus, but rather arranging a private meeting between Jesus and the High Priest so they could "resolve their differences and bring about needed reforms."[33] It's curious that such a friendly chat would occur at the pointy end of a sword (Jn. 18:3)—but let's not be hindered by *trifles*. Sanders concludes that "it is clear that Judas is not betraying Jesus and that Jesus is not issuing any prediction of such activity."[34] Clear? Clear as mud.

Let's return to our point. Foreknowledge of future events is a mark of deity, and the absence of that ability an attribute of vain idols. Omnipotence is a perfection of God, and impotency a characteristic of idols. Open theists deny Yahweh the former qualities,[35] and attribute to Him the latter, thus worshipping a false god under the name of the true. This, I have been asserting, is exactly what is prohibited by the third commandment.

---

[32] Piper, "God of Glory," 41. See his fuller discussion of the foreknowledge of Christ concerning His passion.

[33] Sanders, *Risks*, 99.

[34] Ibid.

[35] Proponents of Open theism might quibble that they really *do* believe God is omnipotent (really guys! *Honest!*). But their explanation that God willingly allows His holy will to be thwarted by creatures is, practically speaking, a denial of omnipotence.

JEALOUS FOR HIS NAME

All sins are not created equal. There *are* such things as degrees of culpability and judgment. Jesus tells us, for instance, that Chorazin and Bethsaida will have it worse on the day of judgment than Sodom, for the Sodomites would have repented had they seen the miracles Christ performed (Mt. 11:21).

Some transgressions, because of their personal nature, affect fewer people than do other, more public sins, and we can reason they will receive a proportionally lesser judgment. And while *all* sins are ultimately committed against God, some sins are more personally directed against Him than others. These too, because of the exalted status of their Object, will incur a greater judgment. And of course some sins fall into both categories. They are public assaults on the person of God that have enormous societal consequences. Idolatry, which has always been a snare, is one of these sins. And idolatry that misrepresents the very nature of Yahweh to His people is perhaps the most subtle and devastating form of public sin. Such sin is that of Jeroboam, who redefined Yahweh and whose "sin caused Israel to sin."[36]

God takes such sin very seriously and promises to reward the transgressor accordingly. Considering all that it conveys, Yahweh is jealous for His name and will not allow it to be profaned, or treated as common (cf. Ezek. 20:9, 14, 22, 44). God will Himself assert His distinctness and transcendence—without depreciating His immanence—against those who blur the lines. This is seen in the last clause of Exodus 20:7, "for [Yahweh] will not leave Him unpunished who takes His name in vain." If God's word is true, I think we can expect to see God judge this heresy with a firm hand. We hope, for mercy's sake, that He does so soon.

---

[36] The references to Jeroboam, and this phrase employed to describe him, occur too many times to list. Let the reader look at Kings and Chronicles to see the infamy of the man and the cultural effects of his sin.

Epilogue

Douglas J. Wilson

The historic Christian faith had a great deal of inertia behind it when it arrived on the shores of America. While various forms of fruitiness soon surrounded the faith here, and while confessional erosion certainly did occur, and while revivalism and subjectivism have been greatly damaging to the church, the historic Christian faith here was, to use Chesterton's phrase, reeling but erect.

The forces of the Enlightenment and modernity routed the standing armies of the faith in Europe, accomplishing what we currently see there, which is a nearly total hegemony on the part of unbelief. In this country, the forces of modernity captured all the key cultural centers, and metaphorically speaking forced the faithful up into the hill country. And from such an unlikely place, over the last century or so, believers have mustered a rag-tag, valiant, fundamentalist, vibrant resistance that has functioned as a fairly effective guerilla movement— hard to track, and all over the landscape. From Faith Community Chapels to Knee Deep in Glory worship centers, Christians, a lot of them, still believed that God was God, Christ was Christ, the cross was salvation, and the Bible was truth—yesterday, today, and forever. But because of our embarrassing deficiencies, and the widespread anti-intellectualism in our ranks, we were forced into fighting armored tank divisions with some sticks we found lying around. But at least we fought.

This is no longer the case. The older mainstream denominations are now moribund, and the numerical center has shifted in favor of the evangelicals, who are far more energetic and active. Since the Second World War, modern evangelicalism has gradually become the dominant form of religious expression in America. This may be hotly

denied—what about the New Age!?—but we should face facts. Every
seventh radio station in this country is a Christian station, there are
parts of the country where you can't swing a cat without hitting a
Christian megachurch, and we have our own enormous network of
Jesus junk gift centers. Just imagine what would happen if the com-
munists or Muslims had what we have.

But with these numbers, and the money, and the influence, and the
academic respectability, has come a hankering to get in on all that hot
Enlightenment action. There are the evangelicals for you—several
centuries late and a dollar over. We are discovering that modern evangelicalism has carefully followed the example set by the liberals a generation ago and by Jeshurun long ago—it has waxed fat and kicked.

And the central threat today is presented to us in the Openness of
God movement. The threat is twofold. The first is the obvious problem of accepting and believing the heresy. If all the tenets of this "new
model" theology were taken out of articles, journals and books, and
assembled together in a statement of faith, we ought to consider it to
be on a par with the doctrinal commitments of the Jehovah's Witnesses or the Mormons. This is not a disagreement over which Christians are able to differ in good conscience. This divide is not comparable to the differences that separate Baptists from Presbyterians. The
Openness of God position is not any recognizable form of the Christian faith at all. Those who embrace this teaching therefore are, at the
very least, in the early stages of apostasy. Whether they fall from the
faith entirely is a question that will only be answered after they reject
one or two faithful warnings.

The second threat is even more insidious. This comes from orthodox believers who have trained themselves over time in a refusal to
make careful distinctions. They are orthodox *personally*, and do not
themselves *agree* that God does not know the future, but at the same
time they think that the Openness evangelicals should be accepted as
evangelicals. In short, they understand the doctrinal difference on
paper, and could tell you about it, but do not comprehend the mag-
nitude of the doctrinal difference. They have no idea what is at stake.

But the Bible requires Christian leaders to know such issues, re-
quiring in effect that Christian shepherds know what a wolf looks
like. A man can be orthodox and yet be disqualified for ministry. A
man can like the sheep without being qualified to fight the wolves.

In this conflict, we face false teachers, whose mouths must be stopped (Tit. 1:11). This cannot be done by those who do not think it needs to be done. Such noncombative elders are not excluded from the Church, but they certainly are disqualified from ministry. They are being unfaithful to the charge that was given to all elders—to guard or shepherd the flock over which they were made overseers. This is a central concern in the New Testament.

> Take heed therefore unto yourselves, and to all the flock, over the which the Holy Ghost hath made you overseers, to feed the church of God, which he hath purchased with his own blood. For I know this, that after my departing shall grievous wolves enter in among you, not sparing the flock. Also of your own selves shall men arise, speaking perverse things, to draw away disciples after them. Therefore watch, and remember, that by the space of three years I ceased not to warn every one night and day with tears. (Acts 20:28–31)

Because we have been reluctant to preach the whole counsel of God, we have come to the point where we cannot effectively oppose those who deny the whole counsel of God. Because we have not fed the church of God, we have lost our ability to fight those who speak perverse things, and who draw away disciples after them.

> Preach the word; be instant in season, out of season; reprove, rebuke, exhort with all longsuffering and doctrine. For the time will come when they will not endure sound doctrine; but after their own lusts shall they heap to themselves teachers, having itching ears; and they shall turn away their ears from the truth, and shall be turned unto fables. (2 Tim. 4:2–4)

We would love nothing more than to teach the truth and forget about error. We do not want to attack lies because we have perverse love for attacking lies. The central reason a biblical minister hates a lie is because it threatens the truth, which is precious to him. A man who watches complacently while rapists drag his wife off does not love his wife, whether or not he promises to visit her in the hospital. In situations like this, the *only* thing that love knows how to do is fight. Far too many Christian leaders treat the truth of the gospel the same way the Levite treated his concubine in the book of Judges. "Hope it works out for you. Come on, get up—we have to go."

Beloved, when I gave all diligence to write unto you of the common salvation, it was needful for me to write unto you, and exhort you that ye
should earnestly contend for the faith which was once delivered unto
the saints. For there are certain men crept in unawares, who were before of old ordained to this condemnation, ungodly men, turning the
grace of our God into lasciviousness, and denying the only Lord God,
and our Lord Jesus Christ. I will therefore put you in remembrance,
though ye once knew this, how that the Lord, having saved the people
out of the land of Egypt, afterward destroyed them that believed not.
(Jude 3–5)

As this volume has shown, if this "new model" theology is not heresy, then there is no such thing as heresy. If it does not deserve to have
these severe condemnations of Scripture applied to it, then the contributors to this volume need to get a useful job, like driving a truck or
something.

Index of Scripture